A History of
The Free Churches

A History of

The Free Churches

PAUL SANGSTER

HEINEMANN : LONDON

William Heinemann Ltd
10 Upper Grosvenor Street, London W1X 9PA

LONDON MELBOURNE TORONTO
JOHANNESBURG AUCKLAND

First published 1983
Copyright © Paul Sangster 1983

SBN: 434 67134 7

Printed in England by
Mackays of Chatham Ltd

Contents

Acknowledgements

I would like to thank Dr. J. D. Walsh, M.A., the Rev. Charles Taylor, M.A., B.D., Miss M. I. Telford, B. A., the Rev. Peter Jennings, M.A., and the Rev. C. Leonard Tudor for help with references and illustrations, Mrs. Rita Catley and Mrs. Marjorie Closs for typing the manuscript, and Mr. Morris Walker for help with photographs.

The illustrations have come from a variety of sources acknowledged elsewhere, but I wish to record my gratitude for most generous help from the Staff of the National Portrait Gallery, and especially from Miss Valerie Vaughan. The Department of Prints and Drawings of the British Museum, the Department of Incunabula, the Bodleian Library, the Principal of Regent's Park College, Oxford, the Minister and Trustees of Wesley's Chapel, City Road, Lambeth Palace Library, and the Clerk of Stationery have been equally helpful.

Paul Sangster

Illustrations

vii

Introduction

THESE PAGES ARE CONCERNED with the Free Churches in England only. The term 'Free Church' is taken here to mean any Protestant Church not controlled by the State, but the definition has been stretched to include at least some reference to pseudo-churches and to establishments that totally reject the name of Church.

The fact that the Free Churches are Protestant implies that they started after the Reformation, and this is strictly true. However, the ideal of a Free Church existed centuries before that name was used, and that is why the study begins with Wyclif. If he was not the first to protest at the abuses of the Church of his day, Wyclif was the first in England to challenge its authority and form an order free of any authority except God's and its founder's. In a sense Lollards were the first Free Church.

Wyclif challenged the very basis on which the Catholic Church was built – the pope as the supreme earthly representative of God, priests as intermediaries between God and man. The same challenge was later at the heart of the Reformation. Protestants claimed that all God's instructions were clearly written down in a book, and the Bible is therefore the supreme authority. Protestants therefore bound themselves into churches but needed no intermediaries. They accepted ministers as their leaders, but not priests, for priesthood is the privilege of all believers.

Some of these Protestants went further. If the Bible was their

sole authority, what right had any earthly man to claim spiritual
authority over them? Not the King himself could dictate to their
souls. They demanded freedom of thought, of worship, of conscience. They demanded, in fact, to be Free Churchmen. Thus
began the 'separated' churches, the 'independent' churches, those
founded by Robert Browne, later to be called the Congregationalist
Church. Out of Congregationalism, by secession over one particular doctrine, grew the Baptist Church. From Scotland, even
more independent in religious matters than its Southern neighbour, came Presbyterianism. These three Free Churches are the
earliest, and among the most important, of the Free Churches,
and their heroic ages were their beginnings.

Another Free Church was formed later by even more radical
religious thought. One man found his peace with God only
through personal pietism. He esteemed and accepted the
Scriptures as God's word, but found them of secondary importance, for God speaks directly to his people. No ministers are
necessary, no church services, though a meeting place could be
useful for here those of like mind could gather and listen together
for the promptings of God. So thought George Fox, and so began
the work of those usually called Quakers.

It has been said that the Reformation was strictly the beginning
of the Free Church Movement, and this remains true. It is worth,
for the sake of clarity, explaining the terms used. The Church of
England was a compromise between the earlier Catholic tradition
and the growing influence of the reformers Luther and Calvin,
with ultimate earthly power transferred from the pope to the
monarch of England. If 'Protestant' means protesting at the
former abuses of the Church, 'Puritan' has a similar origin.
Puritans were the logical successors to the Protestants who wished
to 'purify' the Church of England from what they considered the
remaining vestiges of 'popery'. For some this meant abolition of
the priestly vestments, for others change in the administration
of Holy Communion, for yet others radical change in Church
government. Because of the varieties in applying the principle of
purification, the Puritans tended to divide. A number of them, in
pursuit of a Church untainted by the secular State, rejected the
State Church. These men are the spiritual fathers of the Free
Churches. When their zeal for purifying brought them into conflict
with any real or imagined form of worldliness they acquired their

reputation for being killjoys, gloomy critics of the innocent amusement of others. The charge had a certain amount of justice, but the heart of puritanism is a desire to serve God purely and to set one's face against any intrusion of the world between the soul and its creator.

These pages trace the history of the Free Churches, glimpsed distantly by pre-Reformation prophets, and then slowly emerging from among the Protestant extremists during the reigns of Henry VIII, Queen Mary and Queen Elizabeth. The Free Churchmen (and women, and children) were continually persecuted, some were martyred and many fled abroad. Only during the brief period of Cromwell's protectorate was there toleration for almost all of them. It was also at this period, however, that strange Protestant sects multiplied and intolerantly warred against each other. Some were at least as bigoted as their enemies who had tried to destroy them. The return of the Stuarts in the form of Charles II and James II meant renewal of persecution not so much from the kings as from Parliament, who enacted law after law to destroy the Free Churches.

By this time the Free Churchmen, worshipping in the secrecy that persecution demanded, were in clearly defined groups, and these were forming into infant Churches. The Toleration Act of 1689 gave tremendous impetus to Nonconformists (another term for Free Churchmen, as Dissenters was yet another) to found more and more chapels. Under William and Mary they flourished, and even under Anne, who hated them, they survived well enough so long as the Whigs were in power.

During the first quarter of the eighteenth century all branches of the Church had become stagnant. Formalism crept into the most radical of sects. A great religious revival then swept across England, much more in Protestantism than in Catholicism. This was the Evangelical Revival. Chief among the leaders of this revival was John Wesley, who accidentally founded a new Free Church, Methodism.

All the Free Churches increased vastly in numbers, importance and in missionary zeal. The Revival began about 1730 and was one of the greatest influences on the religion and therefore life of nineteenth-century England, on the Church of England as well as on all branches of Nonconformity. This happened in spite of powerful forces lodged against religion during that age. There

were the apparent contradictions in the Bible pointed out by
scientists, the rise of socialism, the hideous condition of the poor,
itself the fruit of the industrial revolution. Notwithstanding all
these things, Nonconformity continued to flourish until the end
of the nineteenth century, by which time most discriminatory laws
against Free Churchmen had been repealed.

The twentieth century brought great problems. Two world
wars helped create a drastic decline in the number of adherents of
the traditional Free Churches. Materialism and material ideologies
infected all. In the present century, as in the nineteenth, there was
a proliferation of new Free Churches, some of them barely
Churches, some not even strictly Christian. It has ever been the
folly of Protestanism to splinter, to divide, to spawn more and
more groups. One section of the community wishes to be more
devout than its neighbour or senses more light in the divine
mystery; it separates, and a new Church is born. Currently, the
hiving is into house-groups out of existing Churches. The new
separates claim their way to be in imitation of the primitive
Church and a saving of the vast expense of church buildings.
Those opposed to such splinter groups suggest that rootless
communities without pastors will be prey to false prophets and
spiritual vanity.

The ecumenical movement was one in which the Free Churches
were inevitably involved, and it divided them. Some were anxious
to return to a 'main-stream' Church, and talked of a divided
Church as unpleasing to God, wasteful of resources and a bad
advertisement to non-Christians. They stressed how much more
could be done by a united Church. Other Free Churchmen
commented on the rich and varied forms in which God had been
worshipped through the ages. Was, perhaps, this variety God's
wish? Such men preferred harmonious relationships between
Churches to ecclesiastical unity.

Some Free Churches, under ecumenical direction but also
well aware that to fail to join others would mean extinction, have
resolved their differences with other branches and become one.
More recently, huge numbers of immigrants have come into
England, some bringing their own religions with them. It is this
influx that has forced attention by the whole country on a new
attitude towards foreign missions in particular and proselytising
in general. How do we react to members of other faiths? Are all

faiths equal? Is it our duty to convert the heathen (an abandoned word) to Christianity? At what point is toleration a refusal to obey Christ's command "Go ye therefore, and teach all nations . . ."?

The Free Churches had and still have a tremendous interest in foreign missions and home missions. They have watched with the rest of Christendom the gradual secularization of society, the devastation of two world wars and the possibility of global annihilation, social revolution, the loosening of morals and family ties, and the growth of materialism as a way of life. Where do the Free Churches go now? Underground, as new persecutions strike? Back to the main folds which they left centuries ago? Into oblivion, their tasks fulfilled or unfulfilled? Or have they still work to do? Is their end in their beginning, an intensity of the spiritual life, a passion for the ways of God?

Paul Sangster
Hunmanby Hall School

CHAPTER I

Wyclif, the Pioneer

WYCLIF WAS OBVIOUSLY NOT a Free Churchman, for he died in 1384, nearly two centuries before the Free Churches began. Nevertheless, he anticipated the Reformation, and it was out of the Reformation that the Free Churches grew. Further, many of his ideas became part of the Free Church tradition. It is on these grounds that Wyclif the pioneer demands brief attention.

We do not know the date of his birth, though he certainly came from Yorkshire. He was a pre-eminent scholar at Oxford, a member of Merton College in 1356 and of Balliol from 1360, and had lodgings in The Queen's College, though he was never a member of that foundation. He had a great following among the scholars, as outstanding lecturers did in the mediaeval universities. He was influenced in his thought by Augustine. Most of his life was spent in Oxford, and he did not rise to international notoriety until the last few years of his life. His income was largely derived from two successive ecclesiastical appointments outside Oxford, the second being rector of Lutterworth from 1374. This was the normal custom of the day, though it is a little strange in Wyclif, who protested so loudly at clerical abuses, including pluralism and non-residence. In fact, by force of circumstances, he became totally resident in Lutterworth during his last years, but he seems to have been very rarely in his other benefice, Westbury-on-Trym, near Bristol. In addition to these incumbencies, Wyclif had wider duties for a time when he was employed in the service of the crown about 1370, and was a spectator of the Parliament of 1371. It was this office – which meant some travelling abroad – that introduced Wyclif to the powerful John of Gaunt, son of Edward III and effective ruler of England for some years. John of Gaunt's championship of Wyclif was to protect the reformer from his enemies.

Wyclif published lectures which he had delivered in Oxford between 1374 and 1376. They were in the form of two treatises, on divine power and human power. While men of that age could lecture to learned groups of scholars with relative impunity, to publish was to reach a world-wide audience, and the works – always in Latin – were scrutinized for signs of heresy. Wyclif wrote that all ownership belongs to God, and God gives the use of it on condition that the holder gives faithful service in his use of that ownership. A sinful man has no right to the use. Indeed, if he demonstrates abuse in his ownership, then the property should be taken from him. Wyclif was quite explicit that these conditions applied equally to civil or ecclesiastical ownership, but what his audience noticed especially was that Wyclif categorically said that if ecclesiastical powers abused their stewardship, then the secular power had not merely the right but the duty to take it away. In an age when the secular powers – such as John of Gaunt – were resentful of the vast estates owned by the Church, many of them mismanaged, and the Church was watching every predatory move that the secular powers made, Wyclif's theory was explosive. It divided the two great powers. Nor was this all that Wyclif said. He said that a pope and cardinals could be wrong, that neither was essential for the government of the Church. He also said that a worldly pope was a heretic and should be deposed from his office.

These theories were as popular with some as they were a scandal to others. John of Gaunt, who had long coveted Church lands and welcomed a reason for depriving ecclesiastics of their property, was enthusiastic. Secular interests in general approved; for instance, London merchants saw advantage in it. The Popes of that period were unpopular, corrupt, worldly and, from an English point of view, foreigners. The Pope, inevitably, was outraged, and began writing 'bulls' (formal letters of protest which could lead to excommunication) against Wyclif. Oxford University authorities, instructed by the Pope to quell this dangerous man, took no serious notice; they resented interference from outsiders. Meanwhile, Wyclif sent a tract to the first English Parliament of Edward III's reign saying that in particular cases England could detain money due to the Pope.

In 1378 and 1379 Wyclif published more tracts, each more radical than the last. It was as if, having risked criticism of the Church and feeling the rush of support for his views from others, Wyclif then proceeded to launch a full-blooded attack, almost tearing the Church's foundations. One tract stressed the authority of the Scriptures above all earthly authorities. Another queried the whole structure of the Church and yet another objected to the earthly power of the papacy. The true Church, he said, was made up only of the elect, and was invisible. If the Church was chosen by God it followed that salvation could not be the gift of an earthly Church, or arranged through the mediation of priests. It could be given by God alone and was in his foreknowledge. Equally, earthly men had no right to admit members into the Church or exclude the unworthy. Salvation depended not on a connection with a visible Church but on God's election.

These were some of Wyclif's major points. There was also scathing criticism of some ecclesiastics. Unworthy monks and friars, the latter Wyclif's particular hate, worldly priests and prelates, were all condemned. Priests had no honour as an accompaniment of their office: honour came of a pure and dedicated character. Wyclif denied that the religious life had any scriptural foundation. There was criticism also for many Church practices. Indulgences were totally condemned, and this criticism was shared by many. Wyclif had yet more targets to attack. He rejected masses for the dead, though he still accepted that there was a purgatory – a waiting-time after death before entry to the presence of God. Wyclif repudiated the cults of relics and saints and pilgrimages. Apart from the bogus nature of many relics and the doubtful existence of some saints, all were unnecessary intermediaries between man and God. If priests were of doubtful relevance, how much less relevant, argued Wyclif, were dead saints or their bones. Consistent with his belief that there was no absolute division between priest and layman, Wyclif said that in certain circumstances a layman might officiate in the eucharist. He accepted the seven sacraments, but considered that confirmation was unnecessary. In general Wyclif said that form and rite in worship were minor concerns; it was sincerity and intelligence in worship that should be primary.

It was in matters of doctrine that Wyclif caused most offence. His rejection of transubstantiation, though he accepted the real presence of Christ in the bread and wine, was heresy. John of Gaunt, who prided himself on his orthodoxy, quickly dissociated himself from Wyclif's view. Pressure was put on the University authorities to silence their upstart scholar, but his following was still great and teachers as well as students were anxious to protect him. The Chancellor, Robert Aygge (d.1410), befriended Wyclif as long as he dared, but later was compelled to beg pardon on his knees of the Archbishop of Canterbury, William Courtenay (c.1342–1396), for supporting the heretic. Finally, and by a narrow majority, the Oxford theologians condemned his writings when Wyclif flatly refused to recant. He promptly appealed to the King. John of Gaunt, regent during the King's minority, told Wyclif to leave well alone. No formal answer was ever received. Nevertheless, Wyclif prudently left Oxford.

It was unfortunate that 1381 was coincidentally both the year of the Peasants' Revolt and the publication of Wyclif's most heretical tract. His enemies were anxious to see a connection between the two, though there was none in fact. Hereafter, all Wyclif did was viewed with suspicion both by ecclesiastics and civil authorities.

Lutterworth was Wyclif's home for the rest of his life. Here, with one scholar as assistant, he sent out a stream of tracts and also organized a work of immense importance. This was the translation of the Bible into English. He believed, and he had said in his tracts, that the Bible was the supreme authority, that bishops and priests should be familiar with them (in that age many clerics were totally ignorant of the Scriptures) and that even simple, unlettered men could understand them and profit from them. What was needed, therefore, was a translation from the scholars' Latin version into the English of the common man. Papal and ecclesiastical authority were nothing compared to the authority of the Bible. Wyclif opened this door for all. It is probable that Wyclif and Nicholas of Hereford (c.1390) did the first translation, a very literal one from Latin. John Purvey (c.1353–c.1428), Wyclif's secretary, companion and disciple, revised this translation so effectively that the result of his work was virtually a new translation in more idiomatic English, and this was the work which enabled the Scriptures to be spread beyond the world of scholars.

The translation alone, however, was not enough. There was a great need for men to preach, to take the Scriptures to the humble, effectively to ignore the Church and preach and teach as Christ had done. To answer this need, Wyclif organized, or inspired – we do not know to what extent the arrangements were his – a travelling ministry. These men were called Lollards – a term of abuse derived from the Old Dutch and meaning 'a mumbler'. Variously called 'poor priests', 'poor priests that preach', or 'itinerant preachers', they preached wherever they could get a hearing – in fields, on roads, on village greens or in churchyards. They were sent out with a long russet robe and forbidden to carry a staff or purse or wear sandals. They were to eat what was given them and sleep where they could. They were equipped with parts of the translation of the Bible, especially the Gospels and some of the Epistles. Tracts, sermon outlines and some paraphrases of the Scriptures were written to assist them. All preaching and teaching was to be in English. Initially some of the Lollards were gentry and university graduates; later all appeared to be of humble birth. They were first, as one would expect, strong in Oxford, but were all but exterminated there. They appear later to have flourished in London, East Anglia, the Chilterns and the North. Persecution was inevitable. While some men of substance sheltered and helped the Lollards, the power of the Church ensured that these were few. The bishops hated Lollards, for they were outside their power. Indeed, if every man was at liberty to preach and teach, the Church itself would become redundant. Lollards were therefore branded heretics on behalf of their founder Wyclif. A law was passed against heretics in 1401, and a law specifically against Lollards was passed in 1406. Between 1407 and 1409 the Archbishop of Canterbury led a campaign against them. Some Lollards were burnt. During the reign of Henry V (1413–1422) more measures were passed against them, though there was something of a revival in the reign of Henry VII (1485–1509).

We know few of the Lollards by name. John Purvey, already noted, we know more about than most. He was much persecuted. Imprisoned in 1390, he probably remained there until 1401 when he was tried for heresy and forced to recant. His crime was to publish a tract, in the spirit of Wyclif, condemning the corruptions of the Church. For a while he became part of the establishment as a parish priest, but finding it not to his taste or conscience, left his parish and preached in the fields again. He was imprisoned again in 1421 and fades out of our knowledge until his death seven years later.

The most famous Lollard was Sir John Oldcastle (c.1378–1417), famous in his own right, perhaps more famous as the original of the totally different comic character of Shakespeare, Falstaff. The real man was a brave warrior, the focal point of a rising against the Church, and a close friend of Henry V when the King was Prince of Wales. Oldcastle had great courage. When tried for heresy and urged to seek absolution, he replied as Wyclif would have done, that he would seek absolution from none but God. At another point he lost his temper with the interrogators and told them that the Pope was the head of Anti-Christ, the prelates were his members and the friars were his tail. He then turned to the bystanders who were watching his trial and told them not to listen to his judges, for if they did it would lead them to hell. He was, predictably, declared a heretic, but escaped from the Tower and for four years his loyal supporters hid him. In 1417 he was captured after a ferocious defence and hanged.

Wyclif himself died in peace on the last day of 1384. His bones were undisturbed for forty years until in 1428 they were exhumed and burnt. It was a piece of childish stupidity, the sort of super-stitious act that Wyclif had condemned. His views, however, never died out. They survived in England, secret for the most part, until men were brave enough to repeat them and risk the stake.

Wyclif was a colossus. Three things he said were important above all others. The first was that the Bible was the final authority; the second that private judgment in matters theological is a right of free men; the third that the true Church consists not of stone and mortar, nor even in professional ecclesiastics, but in the sum of those who belong to God and are known only to him. These three stresses were to be a vital part of Protestantism and later of Free Church belief. When Wyclif wrote to Rome in 1383, refusing to attend a papal court to answer for his heresies, he said: "I assume that as Chief Vicar of Christ upon earth the Bishop of Rome is of all mortal men most bound to the law of Christ's gospel, for among the disciples of Christ a majority is not reckoned by simply counting heads in the fashion of this world, but according to the imitation of Christ on either side. Now Christ during his life upon earth was of all men the poorest, casting from him all worldly authority. I deduce from these premises, as a simple counsel of my own, that the Pope should surrender all temporal authority to the civil power, and advise his clergy to do the same." Wyclif was a prophet as well as a reformer.

CHAPTER II

Small Beginnings – the First Martyrs

THE FREE CHURCHES GREW out of Protestantism. The chief pioneer of Protestantism was Martin Luther (1483–1546), a German monk whose anguished spiritual experience convinced him of the truth of Romans 1.17: "the just shall live by faith". Faith alone, he believed, brought justification. Though good works are the fruit of faith, it is the faith that is the heart of the matter. Luther became famous through his attack on indulgences – the remission of punishment due for sin by absolution in exchange for money or favours. The Pope, he said, had no power to release souls from purgatory. Many shared the view. What made Luther different was that, following the logic of the Scriptures and reason, his criticisms multiplied until he undermined the whole structure of the Church. He said that the Scriptures alone were authoritative, that popes and church councils were fallible. He rejected the superiority of clergy over laity, the clerical claim of exclusive rights in interpreting the Scriptures, and the Pope's exclusive right in summoning and ratifying the acts of church councils. Next, Luther attacked the denial of communion wine to laymen and the doctrine of transubstantiation. He found no justification in the Scripture for seven sacraments – only for two, Baptism and Holy Communion.

The distinctive features of Protestantism as taught by Luther have remained constant through the centuries – justification by faith alone, the priesthood of all believers, the final authority of

God resting in the Scriptures, and the right and duty of every Christian to interpret them.

In 1520 Luther launched his five tracts and in 1521, at the Diet of Worms, he was summoned to answer grave charges of heresy. Apparently alone against the might of the Church, and his almost certain fate to be burnt at the stake, he would not shift an inch in his opinion. "Here I stand," he said; "I cannot do otherwise." He was excommunicated, captured by friends for his own protection, and spent a year translating the New Testament into German. In 1522 he took over the leadership of his own movement, which was in danger of anarchy, and for another twenty-two years Protestantism flourished and spread under his organizing genius.

Henry VIII (1491–1547) acceded to the English throne in 1509 and the same year married Catherine of Aragon, the widow of his dead brother, Arthur. Henry was a strict Catholic and wrote a book against Luther. For this service the Pope rewarded him with the title 'Defender of the Faith', though Luther was unimpressed and said, "It is of little consequence if I despise and bite some earthly king, considering that he did not hesitate to blaspheme against the King in heaven and commit sacrilege with his poisonous lies." Ironically, little more than ten years later, Henry was excommunicated and technically a Protestant.

There was no Luther in England, and the few who were infected by Luther's doctrines were exterminated. Thomas Bilney (d.1531), a gentle and harmless man, had said in a sermon, "Pray you alone to God, and to no saints." He was arrested, imprisoned in the Tower, tried, recanted at the last moment, and was released after a year. He grew bolder, repeated his offence, and was burnt for it as a heretic. It is true that many Englishmen felt that the monasteries, places of vast wealth, had long outlived their usefulness and that a number of them were corrupt. It is also true that Henry's extravagance at Court and his wars in France had been heavy drains on the wealth of the country. Neither of these reasons, however, would have been sufficient causes of the Reformation. The root cause was Henry's failure to solve the problem of succession. Who was to rule England when he was gone? The horrors of the Wars of the Roses were recent enough for all to dread a return to battles for the crown between warring barons. A male heir was essential, but of the Queen's six children, only a girl had survived. Henry wondered if he had sinned in marrying his deceased brother's wife. Later, when Anne Boleyn bewitched him, her pregnancy gave him another reason for a speedy divorce. It was his anxiety to obtain a divorce and the Pope's refusal to grant it that was the primary cause, if not of the Reformation in England, at least of the Henrician Reformation. As Macaulay put it, "A good catholic, he preferred to be his own Pope." The work was largely accomplished in 1534 when the Church was nationalized and a series of acts proclaimed Henry 'supreme head, next under Christ,' of the Church of England. The new head, as his first reform, plundered church property. The English had long resented their money going to Rome as well as the interminable delays in the settlement of ecclesiastical matters. With an upsurge of nationalism to add to their natural insularity, the English also began to hate foreigners. For most, the reformation was popular. There were 563 religious houses, 7,000 male religious, 2,000 nuns and 35,000 laymen employed by the monasteries. All were dissolved. The monastic report began, "Foreasmuch as manifest sin, vicious, carnal and abominable living is daily used among the little and small abbeys . . .", a clear indication of what was to come. In 1535, when the doom of the monasteries was decided, Queen Catherine died and Henry danced in yellow silk 'for mourning'. His dynastic problems, he felt sure, were over. Meanwhile, the brave few who defied the King – John Fisher, Sir Thomas More, and a handful of Carthusians – were executed.

The Church in practice changed little. The Mass was the same as it had always been. The doctrine of the eucharist was unchanged. 'Cranmer's' Bible was placed in every church in 1538, but the King condemned other translations and ordered that women and the lower orders were not to read the Bible at all. The King saw no inconsistency in repudiating papal infallibility and asserting his own. Nor did he hesitate to burn those who strayed from catholic doctrine. William Tyndale (c.1494–1536), who translated the Bible into English, was burnt as a heretic in Holland, but ten Anabaptists (a Protestant sect from the Continent) were burnt in England in 1535, and in 1540, Robert Barnes (1495–1540), who accepted Luther's views and had been in trouble with ecclesiastical authority on several occasions, was burnt as a heretic. When he was brought before Wolsey on an earlier occasion the Cardinal had begged him to recant. "I thank your grace," he had said, "for your good will. I will stick to the holy scripture and to God's book, according to the simple talent that God hath lent me." The same year Richard Mekins, a boy of fifteen, was burnt at Smithfield. He had spoken against the Sacrament and had said that Robert Barnes had died holy. The most remarkable martyr, however, was Anne Askew (1521–1546). Highly educated, she had made herself unpopular by worsting priests in debate. She was tried for heresy in 1545 but eventually freed. Tried again in 1546 she was hideously tortured on the rack but refused to recant. Asked again to recant at the stake, she steadfastly refused, and died with immense courage. None of these was a Free Church-man, though all were Protestants. Anne Askew, interestingly, had Free Church descendants. One of them, Margaret Fell, married George Fox.

Henry died in 1547, having ruled England for nearly thirty-eight years. He was succeeded by Edward VI (1537–1553). As Edward was only a boy, the regency was controlled first by his uncle, Edward Seymour, Duke of Somerset, and then by John Dudley, Duke of Northumberland. The boy himself was a con-vinced Protestant as were his regents, and it was during his short reign that Protestantism was encouraged from the throne. The Book of Common Prayer was introduced. Edward, as he lay dying, bequeathed the crown to the Protestant claimant, Lady Jane Grey, but it was his half-sister, the Catholic Mary (1516–1558), who became Queen. Mary's brief and bloody reign made England terrified of Catholics. She was well-educated and deeply devout, but a bigot. 'Bloody' Mary has always been a devil for Protestant writers. She was no devil – indeed, she sought sanctity – but the list of her executions shows why she should be thought so. Henry VII burnt 10 heretics in 24 years, Henry VIII 81 in 38, Edward VI 2 in 6, Elizabeth I 5 in 44; and Mary 283 in less than 4 years. Catholics were persecuted for centuries because of Mary's ruthless cruelty. John Foxe's book, which told the story of these martyrdoms, fed the Protestant cause for generations to come. Mary's bigotry may be judged by her reaction to a letter from Cranmer in prison. She asked Archbishop Pole "whether she was permitted to read, or even accept, a letter written by a heretic; so wise and holy was this woman in matters concerning the Catholic faith" – or so stupid.

While Mary reigned, those who had fled abroad from her

persecutions were imbibing Protestant opinions from the followers of Luther and Calvin. They were also acquiring some very radical views. John Knox (c.1505–1572), for instance, who was later to establish Presbyterianism in Scotland, was busily writing a book suggesting that subjects had not only the right but the duty to resist wicked rulers. Possession of such books, ordered Mary, meant instant death by martial law without trial.

The first Marian martyr to die was John Rogers (c.1500–1555), a Lutheran. Among the hundreds who followed were Latimer (c.1485–1555) and Ridley (c.1500–1555) and Cranmer (1485–1556). Latimer spoke for all in his last famous words: "Be of good comfort, Master Ridley; we shall this day light such a candle, by God's grace, in England as I trust shall never be put out."

Mary's unhappy life ended in 1558, and Elizabeth I (1533–1603), her half-sister, whom Mary had imprisoned in the Tower and plotted to destroy, began her long reign. Self-preservation was a high priority for Elizabeth. Her childhood had been spent in constant danger; she had been declared a bastard; two Queens of England had ended their lives by execution, as had the last Protestant claimant to the throne. Elizabeth had much of her father in her – enormous strength, considerable learning, an ability to choose and use people, and above all, a knack of getting her own way. She chose William Cecil as her Secretary of State, and he served her with distinction for her whole life.

Elizabeth had no serious choice in her religious settlement. She had never embraced Catholicism seriously, despite Mary's constant pressure on her. Her instinct was for the sort of settlement her father had contrived – a modified Catholicism with herself as Pope. Mary's reign, however, had made Catholicism anathema to most English. Further, the accession of Elizabeth had brought radical Protestants flocking back from the Continent, their minds filled with the new teachings. Elizabeth had no love for either extremes – the Calvinist John Knox on the one hand, whose Presbyterianism would mean the destruction of the Anglican Settlement, or papal supremacy at the other extreme, which would take the country back to Rome. England had suffered enough from religious loyalties which made the heresy of one reign the orthodoxy of the next. What was needed, she judged, was a permanent settlement, a compromise between the two extremes which would be acceptable to most. She passed Acts of Supremacy and Uniformity in 1559.

A compromise always offends. To Catholics she was a heretic, to extreme Protestants a papist. John Wesley, with untypical injustice, thought her as just and merciful as Nero, and as good a Christian as Mahomet. Certainly there is no evidence that she was deeply religious; there is no evidence either that she was anything else. Her half-sister might well have warned her of the dangers of devoutness – the distinction between devoutness and bigotry is a subtle one.

The clergy and the laity were given the Lord's Prayer, the Ten Commandments, the Apostles' Creed, the Epistle and the Gospel in English: the rest was to be in Latin. There was to be no preaching, for it was preaching that led to dispute and dissension, and to religious divisions. The 39 Articles, after all, contained all that was necessary. They were carefully written so that the doctrine of transubstantiation was neither asserted nor denied. For centuries to come enemies of the Church of England would claim that the 39 Articles could cover almost any beliefs. What truth there was in the charge was intended; Elizabeth's concern was for national unity, and religion had been the great national divider.

At Elizabeth's succession, there were seventeen Marian bishops in office, only one of whom signed the oath of Supremacy. A reluctant Matthew Parker (1504–1575) became Archbishop. He had hidden during Mary's reign, but under Elizabeth he attempted the almost impossible task of steering a middle course between the two extremes. In fact, at least as far as the clergy were concerned, relatively few found it necessary to resign from their offices. Only 200 clergy left the Church. For a while the laws of the Church were not enforced rigorously. Catholics and extreme Protestants were largely left in peace. Only when defiance of the Church laws bordered on sedition was extreme action taken. For instance, when Mary Queen of Scots fled her country after her involvement in her husband's murder and adulterous relationship with Bothwell and became, as Elizabeth's prisoner in England, a focus for Catholic plots, and again in 1569 when there was a Catholic rising by some English earls Catholicism became equated with treason. The first to die for their faith were Dutch Anabaptists in 1575; the Catholics Cuthbert Mayne and Edmund Campion were executed in 1577 and 1581 respectively.

Elizabeth wrote to her successor, James I: "Let me warn you that there is risen, both in your realm and mine, a sect of perilous consequence, such as would have no kings but a presbytery, and take our place while they enjoy our privilege, with a shade of God's word, which none is judged to follow right without by their censure they be so deemed. Yea, look we well unto them. When they have made in our people's hearts a doubt of our religion, and that we err if they say so, what perilous issue this may make I rather think than mind to write . . ." It was late in her reign when Elizabeth wrote this, and she was referring to the early Presbyterians, those who believed that the Bible knows nothing of bishops but only of Churches governed by elders (or presbyters) elected, not by bishops, but by the congregation. Presbyterians were later to become one of the major free churches; in Scotland, under the power and organization of John Knox, they became the national Church. At this point they were part of the Protestant opposition to Elizabeth's church settlement. They were, in fact, Puritans.

The term 'puritan' implied dissatisfaction with the settlement in as much as it was not 'pure' enough – it did not conform at all points with the pattern laid down in the Scriptures. The Church of England was what Elizabeth intended it to be, a half-way house between Rome (Catholicism) and Geneva (the chief city of Continental Protestantism). It was in Geneva that John Calvin (1509–1564) founded a theocratic republic. He followed Luther's thought but went beyond him in his theological doctrines of predestination and salvation for the elect. Since God knows all, he can foretell the future. Man has therefore no free will; all is pre-ordained. It follows that some are destined for heaven and some for hell. God has already chosen his elect, and these will dwell with him in heaven. Those who are not elect will perish. This is the heart of 'Calvinism'. Most Puritans were Calvinists. The doctrine contrary to Calvinism is Arminianism, named after Jacobus Arminius (1560–1609) and his successors. Arminianism taught predestination also, but a predestination based on divine foreknowledge of the use men would make of the means of grace offered to them. Christ, said the Arminians, died for all, though only believers benefit from his death. For Arminians as for Calvinists, man can do no good himself – all is of divine grace. The essential difference is that for Calvinists their final end is predetermined; Arminians have free will.

The work of Wyclif ensured that the roots of Protestantism and of Puritanism were already in England. Nevertheless, it was the returning exiles after the Marian persecutions that gave great impetus to the cause. During the reign of Edward VI, distinguished Protestants had been invited to each University, and this influence also had waited until it was no longer a crime to be a Protestant. What Elizabeth offered was not enough. The exiles had seen a state – albeit a small one – governed by God. They objected to much in the Church of England, and they based their objections on the Scriptures. They had grave doubts about the vestments worn by priests – they judged them an offensive Catholic survival. They differed in their attitude to the Scriptures. Anglicans – a useful term to distinguish the main body of the Church of England from the Puritans – said the Bible was authoritative in matters of doctrine and conduct, but the Puritans said it was authoritative in all things, in church government and worship and discipline as well as doctrine. The Puritans longed for a return to the primitive Church of the New Testament, a Church stripped of wealth, gorgeous robes, titles, earthly power, and practices unknown to the Scriptures. Mixed with their rejection of the unscriptural was a hatred of any hint of Catholicism – the fires of Smithfield were a recent, nightmarish memory.

It is unfortunate that the very word 'Puritan' suggests a pleasure-hating hypocrite. Malvolio in *Twelfth Night* is thought typical. In fact he was most untypical. Throughout history there have been upsurges of religious fervour. It has been so from the beginning. Whenever it happens it is initiated by one or more God-intoxicated men who inspire a following and for a while form a deeply religious community, or the men simply proclaim the mind of God to an unheeding world. The leaders and their followers are despised by more worldly people – hence the names given in mockery which have remained when the sneers have gone – Lollards, Quakers, Methodists, Shakers. The Old Testament prophets and William Booth, George Fox, John Wesley, Savonarola, St. Francis, all were the objects of ridicule in their day. All rejected lip-service to God as an insult; all demanded a purer life, a greater devotion to God. In some measure the Puritans were such a movement, but they were different because they were not the followers of one man, nor were they at this time even a coherent movement. They had been influenced by Calvin, by Luther, by other Continental Reformers, by Protestant forbears in England. With no leader to weld them into a group they were searching for an identity. Contempt, nevertheless, is the normal reaction to those who are different, and especially to those who set themselves higher standards of behaviour than their neighbours. This the Puritans received in full measure.

It would be an error to pretend that they had no vices. All humans have. They also had a tendency to particular errors. Spiritual vanity is a sin reserved for the very good, and the Puritans, or most of them, were very good indeed. Their reverence for the Scriptures sometimes led them into another error – worship of the Bible. So anxious were the Puritans to live by the Word of God that they almost identified the Bible with God himself. They could also be pedantic to the point of lunacy in their discussion of the Scriptures – arguing text against text, proving the minutiae of Christian conduct for the sixteenth century from apocalyptic works written some two thousand years earlier. It was in their attitude to the social habits of their neighbours that they caused most offence, in their distaste for anything that even hinted of ungodliness. They were not content to find lewd plays, lascivious poetry, indecent dress sinful. For some of them, all plays, all poetry that was not religious, all bright or expensive clothes were equally sinful. The Puritans in general, and the later Presbyterians in particular – and especially was this true in Scotland – got dangerously close to suggesting that all fleshly appetite is of the devil, dangerously close to dividing man in half and saying that his spiritual part is of God, the rest devilish.

It is in Chapter III that the specific beliefs and practices of the Puritans will receive fuller consideration, for by that time they were a powerful party with clearly defined viewpoints. In Elizabeth's reign they were only just beginning, and they were unpopular in proportion to the strength of their Puritanism. Elizabeth hated them, as she hated all who disagreed with her and who might upset the unity of the nation. The Anglicans also hated them, for they themselves lived by human reason, which the Puritans rejected. Anglicans had many facets to their lives and many interests; Puritans had one interest only, God, and nothing else mattered. It is easy to see why many considered the Puritans fanatics, though in fact few of them could justly be called so.

In 1562 Archbishop Parker had revised the Articles and reduced them from 42 to 39, and in 1565 he began to insist on conformity with the publication of his 'Advertisements', which spelt out in detail the due order of services, including prescribed vestments. Rather than conform, 37 out of the 110 clergy in London refused and were ejected. This act inevitably made fellow feeling among the Puritans, bound them together in some measure, and prompted them to begin warfare against the establishment, both from pulpit and from pamphlet. If their first complaint against the Church was over compulsion to wear 'Romish' vestments, their second was against the Book of Common Prayer. It did not, in their judgment, conform with the practice of the early Church in many ways. For instance, there is little reference to 'prophesying' as opposed to 'speaking with tongues', the former pressed by St. Paul on his correspondents in I Corinthians 14. 'Prophesying' meant the free preaching of God's Word. True, a sermon appeared as a possible ingredient of a service, but few ministers had licences to preach, and these were expected to say what ecclesiastical authority told them to say. Puritans resented this. Preaching, for them, was the heart of their ministry. They were often very literal-minded. St. Mark 11:25 says, "And when ye stand praying . . .", but the Book of Common Prayer asked the people to kneel. Almost every point in the Prayer Book could be confuted by Scripture, and pamphleteers on both sides, Anglicans and Puritans, fought bitter battles, sometimes over matters of import and sometimes over points which to us seem trivial. One can only understand the bitterness of their disputes when one remembers that a very literal heaven or hell would be the result of conformity to the truth or error.

The Puritans, banished from the establishment, had no intention of remaining silent. They met, as so many had done during the days of Mary, at home or abroad, in secret 'separated' churches. Some meetings were held in private houses, some in the open air, some in ships. Nothing would prevent them from doing the will of God as they received it. These men and women were the founders of the Free Churches. They ordained their own ministers, and were governed by duly elected elders and deacons on the Scriptural pattern. Wisely, authority ignored them as long as it could.

One group met at Plumbers Hall in London. They ingeniously met as if for a wedding, so that if officers arrived, they immediately assumed another innocuous purpose. Finally, this subterfuge failed. In 1567 the fifteen chiefly responsible were summoned to appear before Edmund Grindal (1519–1583), then Bishop of London and later to be Archbishop of Canterbury. Grindal was a Puritan sympathizer. Their plea to him he found unaswerable. "So long," they said, "as we might have the Word – freely preached and the Sacraments administered without the preferring of idolatrous gear about it, we never assembled together in houses. But when it came to this, that all our preachers were displaced by your law, so that we could hear none of them in any Church by the space of seven or eight weeks, and were troubled and commanded by your courts from day to day for not coming to our parish churches, then we bethought us what were best to do. And now if from the Word of God, you can prove we are wrong, we will yield to you and do open penance at St. Paul's Cross; if not, we will stand to it by the grace of God." Though these men had been gaoled until their appearance before the Bishop, Grindal's remonstrance was gentle. Richard Fitz, the leader of the group, was later to die in prison of fever, as was his deacon.

It was in 1570 that Thomas Cartwright (1535–1603), a considerable figure among the early Puritans, was deprived of his Professorial Chair at Cambridge. Cartwright had left the University during Mary's reign but returned, a zealous Puritan, at Elizabeth's accession. A brilliant scholar, he was appointed to the Lady Margaret Chair of Divinity in 1569. His lectures contained criticisms of the constitution and hierarchy of the Church of England. The University divided on the issue. Cartwright's chief enemy was Whitgift (c.1530–1604), Vice-Chancellor of the University and a future Archbishop. Cartwright's defence, a typically Puritan one, was that he taught nothing that did not proceed from the text he was treating, though he admitted saying that the Church had departed from the primitive model. Cartwright's stand frightened the authorities. It was one thing for a group of nonentities to meet secretly for private worship, however illegal; it was quite another for a man of eminence to use a University Chair to attack the establishment. Cartwright was on record as denouncing vestments, pluralities and non-residence. He had doubts about many in 'Holy Orders', for 'the sole credentials of a teacher which he consented to recognize were the intellect and spirit which had been received direct from God.'

He thought that bishops should be elected only by the Church. Such views were intolerable to Whitgift: hence Cartwright's expulsion. He first went abroad, bravely saying, "It were an intolerable delicacy if he could not give up a little ease and commodity for that whereunto his life was due if it had been asked; or that he would grudge to dwell in another corner of the world for that cause for which he ought to be ready altogether to depart out of it." Cartwright spent two years in Geneva but returned two years later at the request of his friends.

A few months before his return in November 1572, two Puritan clergymen, Thomas Wilcox (c.1549–1608) and John Field (d.1572), had published 'An Admonition to Parliament', an extreme Puritan manifesto which objected to established worship and ecclesiastical government. In particular, it demanded a constitution for the Church without bishops. The authors were imprisoned; Field soon died and Wilcox was released eighteen months later only after insistent protests from many sources. Cartwright visited them in prison, supported them, and himself wrote and published 'A second Admonition to the Parliament'. The second pamphlet went further than the first. Effectively it was a plea for a Presbyterian system. Cartwright was arrested and both pamphlets suppressed. He spent much of the rest of his life abroad. England for him invariably meant imprisonment by Whitgift.

It was also in 1572 that the first Presbyterian Church of which we have certain knowledge was set up in Wandsworth. The minister was Nicholas Crane (c.1522–c.1588). He had been imprisoned in 1568 for performing a service in the London diocese out of the Geneva Prayer Book, and for speaking against the usages of the Church. He was released after a year through the help of Grindal on condition that he conformed. This he did not. On the contrary, he founded a Presbytery in Wandsworth, not over doctrinal matters – he had no quarrel with Church doctrine – but because of his abhorrence of vestments and Church practice. We know little more about the Church and less about Crane, who had died of jail fever in Newgate by 1588.

Puritanism was becoming a force in Parliament and it was there that its correlation with liberty became most apparent and most feared. Peter Wentworth (1530–1596), who served as an M.P. for twenty-two years, had fallen foul of the bishops when serving as a member of a Parliamentary Commission which had been examining the 39 Articles. Why, the Commission had been asked, were some of the 39 rejected, including the consecration of bishops? It was an astonishing omission. "Because they were so occupied in other matters," Wentworth had unwisely replied, "that they had no time to examine them how they agreed with the Word of God." The Archbishop said that matter could safely be left to the bench. Wentworth retorted, "Know, by the faith I bear to God, we will pass nothing before we understand what it is. For that were to make you Popes; make you Popes who list, for we will make you none." Elizabeth, furious, dissolved the Parliament. Early in 1575 Wentworth risked the Queen's anger again in a famous speech on behalf of the liberties of the House. One of his complaints was that in 1572 the Queen had refused permission for the House to discuss bills involving ecclesiastical or religious matters unless they were first approved by the clergy. That, said Wentworth, was denial of liberty. He had gone too far and the House knew it. He was sent to the Tower and forced to acknowledge his fault before he could obtain release. Again he was imprisoned in 1586–7 for pressing questions about Parliamentary liberty. It was in the Tower, yet again a prisoner, that he died. Elizabeth was no tyrant such as Henry VIII became, nor a bloodthirsty bigot like her half-sister Mary, but she had a will of iron and no one could thwart her with impunity. Wentworth paid the price of her displeasure.

Grindal, already noted, became Archbishop when it seemed politic for the Queen to lean towards the Puritans. Further, he was Cecil's nominee, himself a moderate Puritan. Elizabeth took her Secretary's advice and immediately regretted it. Grindal told her that preaching was "the only mean and instrument of the salvation of mankind." This was not Elizabeth's view. For her, all that was necessary had been provided in the Prayer Book – lessons from the Scriptures and homilies. As for more extensive preaching, three or four men licensed to preach in each county was more than sufficient. Grindal's disagreement was also ill-timed. He wrote it in 1576, the same year that Peter Wentworth told the Queen that he "chose to offend your earthly Majesty, rather than to offend the heavenly Majesty of God . . . Remember, Madam, that you are a mortal creature and although you are a mighty prince, yet that he who dwelleth in heaven is mightier."

Grindal was as sensitive as Wentworth on infringement of liberty. He told the Queen that he deprecated her interference in spiritual matters, and he flatly refused, though ordered to do so, to discourage preaching and suppress 'prophesying'. Elizabeth therefore took the extraordinary step of sequestrating her own Archbishop for six months – he retained the title, but all his duties were taken away. After the sketchiest of half-apologies, he was restored to his duties at the end of 1582, five years later. He was a learned, gentle, kindly man, his private virtues great, his public virtues hardly seen. Less than a year after his restoration, he was dead.

In 1580 or 1581 the forerunner of churches which would later be called 'Congregational' had been formed in Norwich. The founder was Robert Browne (c.1550–c.1633). A Cambridge graduate, he would have heard Cartwright's lectures before the latter was expelled. For a while he was chaplain to a nobleman and in that office he got into trouble for his extreme views. He was next a schoolmaster and then, for six months, was the incumbent of Benet Church in Cambridge. His brother obtained a bishop's licence for him to preach, but he destroyed it, his reason being that he would not pay for a preaching licence since he preached only "to satisfy his duty and conscience." Similarly, he returned the money sent to him for his labour at Benet Church and resigned from the office. With Richard Harrison, a Cambridge friend, who like Browne was a member of Corpus Christi College, he founded his Church in Norwich. The members made a Covenant. They joined themselves to the Lord. They elected leaders and promised them obedience. They adopted an order for receiving members and another for expelling the unworthy. They also promised to watch over each other and offer warnings, first privately and then if necessary, publicly. They also laid down a system of synods – a joining of the authority of a number of such churches. The first principle of Browne's model Church was that it should consist only of believers, and this distinguished it from the Church of the establishment, to which all automatically belonged. Browne explained his principle in pamphlets which he published later: "The Church planted or gathered is a company or number of Christians or believers, which, by a willing covenant made with their God, are under the government of God and Christ, and keep his laws in one holy communion: because Christ hath redeemed them unto holiness and happiness for ever, from which they were fallen by the sin of Adam." In this statement are seen the totality of their attitude to religion, the doctrine of the priesthood of all believers, and a representative system of government. These were some of the hall-marks of succeeding Congregational Churches. How original Browne was in his theories it is impossible to know. He could have been influenced by Anabaptists, for there were a large number of Dutchmen with these views in Norwich. Equally, he may have been drawn to Norwich initially because he had heard that the Dutch community there had views similar to his own. It is just as likely that all the thought was his own.

His Church in practice was certainly what Browne had been preaching in theory. He rejected episcopacy as a system, for it lacked biblical authority, and he claimed that his Norwich Church was founded according to the Scriptural pattern. The Church, however, did not survive long. The authorities heard of it and moved swiftly. Browne was arrested at Bury St. Edmunds, where he had gone to preach, and was imprisoned. Through the help of Cecil, who was a distant relation, Browne was released with the warning that he would not be helped again. Meanwhile, the Church at Norwich was contemplating flight abroad. Browne had written from prison to advise that they should not leave England until they had spread their views further. Imprisonment for some of their number soon followed, and at last all of them "were fully persuaded that the Lord did call them out of England." They left as a company in the autumn of 1581 and reached Middelburg in Holland. Thomas Cartwright was already there and appears to have offered a welcome to the latest fugitives. Browne rejected the offer and began a pamphlet warfare against Cartwright. He also quarrelled, privately and publicly, with Harrison and with members of his own Church until bitterness and rancour rent their society from top to bottom. While it is impossible to know the whole truth of this unhappy situation, the tenor of Browne's published correspondence shows a remarkable lack of Christian charity.

Nevertheless, it was during 1582 that Browne published his most important pamphlets. These were 'A Book which showeth the Life and Manners of all true Christians . . .' and 'A Treatise of Reformation without tarrying for any'. These two brief works contain Browne's views about the Church. They were published in Holland to be circulated in England, and they were very influential. They were also highly offensive to English authority and were banned. Among those who distributed the works of Browne and Harrison were John Copping (d.1583), who spent much of the years 1576 to 1583 in prison, and Elias Thacker (d.1583), about whom very little is known. Both accepted Browne's church principles and refused to conform to the rules of the established Church. They were arrested and charged with distributing banned literature. Copping was also accused of treason for denying that Queen Elizabeth was the head of the Church. Not only did they fail to show a sense of shame at their offences; they had the effrontery to preach their pernicious doctrines to other prisoners and, according to an unsympathetic account, caused such an uproar that an appeal was lodged to remove these dangerous prisoners to Norwich gaol. Both were finally charged with treason in denying the Queen's headship of the Church, and with circulating heretical works. The trials were brief. "The two men acknowledge Her Majesty chief ruler civilly . . . and no further". Both admitted unqualified admiration of Browne's books; they "commended all things in the said books to be good and godly." As far as the court was concerned this was tantamount to an admission of guilt and both were convicted. Thacker was immediately taken out and hanged, denied even his legal right of appeal to the Council or Queen. His last words addressed to his judge were, "My Lord, your face we fear not, and for your threats we care not, and to come to your read service we dare not." Copping was hanged the next day, and at the execution of each of them confiscated copies of the works of Browne and Harrison were publicly burned.

The indecent haste with which the trial concluded and the severity of the sentence is a measure of the seriousness with which the authorities were treating the rise of Separatism. There were clearly more than a handful of people who were looking to a new type of Church, both because they could not accept episcopacy, and because they protested also against the complete obliteration of the distinction between the Church and the world. If bishops were vast landowners and kept sumptuous households and hundreds of retainers; if a priest, notwithstanding flaws in his private life, was spiritually superior to all laymen, what did a Church

stand for? Browne had written, "If then, it be demanded who
shall call and consecrate ministers, excommunicate and put down
false teachers, let the word of God answer, which appointeth
the chiefest and most difficult matters to be judged by them
of chiefest authority and gifts . . ." And these chief people, said
Browne, should be chosen by those whose spiritual needs they
served. It was a doctrine which was totally unacceptable in that
age. Privilege was by rank, by preferment to rank by those of rank.
Democracy was a seditious thought.

When Thacker and Copping were hanged at Bury St.
Edmunds, Archbishop Grindal was dying, old and blind and in
disgrace. Browne himself would appear before Whitgift. Whitgift
was a distinguished Cambridge man, successively Master of
Pembroke and Trinity as well as a Lady Margaret Professor of
Divinity before he became Vice-Chancellor. A Calvinist in theology, he disliked the Puritans not for their doctrine but for their
opposition to episcopacy, which he devoted his reign to defending.
He was able, strong and vigorous. He was also a close friend of the
Queen with whom he totally agreed in her policy of unifying the
country by the middle way of the Anglican Church. He inherited
a private fortune and lived like a prince. His seven score horses
and his private army were duly noted by his enemies. He rigorously
enforced church discipline, seeing the stifling of Puritanism as
one of his chief ends. On his accession he drew up a series of
stringent articles which prohibited preaching, reading, and
catechizing in private houses. All ministers must subscribe to the
Royal Supremacy, the Book of Common Prayer and the 39
Articles. The following year he drew up a list of questions to aid
Courts in their examination of suspect ministers. This step was
opposed by Cecil, by the Queen's favourite, Leicester, and by
Parliament also. Cecil wrote of Whitgift's 'Interrogatories', "I
think the Inquisitors of Spain use not so many questions to
comprehend and to trap their prey . . . according to my simple
judgment this kind of proceeding is too much savouring of the
Romish inquisition; and is rather a device to seek for offenders
than to reform any." Whitgift forced it through despite them all.
Total press censorship was imposed. The censors were the
Archbishop of Canterbury and the Bishop of London. Criticism
of the Church was hereafter illegal. Macaulay called Whitgift "a
narrow-minded, mean, and tyrannical priest, who gained power

by servility and adulation, and employed it in persecuting . . ."
Whitgift's defence would have been the Queen's also, that
England needed unity above all things and all must conform to a
carefully reasoned, carefully administered middle way. It was,
however, a tragedy that a very powerful and devout section of the
Church was to be totally alienated from it. Whitgift's way ended in
the Civil War and the execution of the King.

Browne had quarrelled so fiercely in Holland that his departure
was a relief to many, though his powers of leadership are demonstrated by the fact that a small group went with him to Scotland
where he had another unhappy time. With monumental tactlessness he attacked John Knox and told the Presbytery at Edinburgh
that their "whole discipline was amiss," and was promptly imprisoned. Released, he toured Scotland before returning to
England and publishing a book which contained a passage remarkably like a famous line which Milton used in his sonnet 'On
the new forcers of Conscience under the Long Parliament'. Should
Parliament, wrote Browne, replace Episcopacy by Presbyterianism,
"then instead of one Pope we should have a thousand, and of
some lord Bishops in name a thousand, lordly tyrants indeed
which now do disdain the names."

England meant immediate imprisonment for Browne, interrogation, threats, release and imprisonment again. He was imprisoned a total of thirty-two times and in the end he was broken
in mind and body. When he was excommunicated, he at last
recanted and was received back into the Church, despised equally
by the Establishment and his former friends, the Separatists. It is
easy to pass judgment on his apostasy, but one should remember
that he had suffered for years and met persecution with courage.
His breaking-point, it seems, was the denial of all the Church's
blessings to him for ever and, according to the Church, even into
eternity. His writings show him mercurial, intense, almost un-
stable. It may be that he suddenly believed that his convictions
were wrong and seized the last chance to struggle back to conformity; it is more likely that he could not endure any more
suffering and recanted for the sake of peace. We shall never
know.

The rest of his life appears to be unhappy. He was made master
of a Church School in London and a few years later given a
Northamptonshire living, where he survived until he was eighty.

If the only account we have of his death is true, he died miserably. He had assaulted a constable who demanded unpaid rates, and was taken to prison on a cart. He died in Northampton gaol and was buried in an unmarked grave. The work he began went on. Browne stopped short of martyrdom. Some of his followers went all the way.

Henry Barrowe (c.1550–1593) and John Greenwood (c.1560–1593) were both Cambridge men, though Greenwood was there some ten years later than Barrowe. Barrowe had been a profligate in his youth but a sudden conversion changed him totally. He became deeply influenced by Browne's writings. Greenwood took orders after graduation and was for a time chaplain to a nobleman. The two men, their principles the same, joined with others to form a secret Separatist Church. They met early every Sunday and spent the whole day in collective worship and spiritual exercises. Such meetings were illegal. The authorities heard of them and hunted down the leaders. Greenwood, when he was arrested, was reading the Scriptures at the house of a friend. He was confined in the Clink prison. As soon as he heard of the arrest, Barrowe went to visit his friend, and the gaoler, on no authority but his own and in defiance of the law, immediately imprisoned Barrowe also. This was in 1586, and Barrowe at least never knew freedom again until their executions seven years later. They were not alone. Many men suffered like this. A 'Lamentable Petition' of 1588 addressed to the Queen told of 'cold and noisome' cells, of some bound hand and foot 'with bolts and fetters of iron', and of others cudgelled to death. Barrowe's 'Supplication' of 1592 addressed to the Lord Treasurer said: "These enemies of God detain in their hands within the prisons about London (not to speak of other gaols throughout the land) about three score and twelve persons, men, women, young and old, lying in cold, in hunger, in dungeons and in irons." The offence of all these prisoners was to wish to worship God in ways other than the establishment decreed. They were victims of Whitgift's purge. Their belief was that the Church of England, which did not distinguish between believers and unbelieving, was not the true Church of Christ. The true Church took its rules from Scripture. No earthly ruler, they claimed, had the right to make laws for the Church other than could be read in God's Word. "Christ," said Greenwood, "is only head of his Church, and his laws may no man alter." It was this last point which made the offence of the Separatists treasonable – they were denying the Queen's power as head of the Church.

Several of the prisoners, and especially Barrowe, continued to write pamphlets while in prison and smuggle them out for publication. These included two defences of their views on the Church; 'A Brief Summary of the Causes of our Separation' (1588) and 'A True Description of the Visible Congregation of the Saints' (1589). Barrowe and two other prisoners also wrote 'The Examination of Henry Barrowe, John Greenwood, and John Penry, before the High Commissions and Lords of the Council, Penned by the Prisoners themselves before their Deaths' (1593). The moving document rings with authenticity. It gives a remarkable insight into the workings of the Court of High Commission in Elizabeth's reign.

The Court spared no effort to obtain a recantation. There were five lengthy examinations in all, spread over a period of years. Cecil himself was sometimes present, Whitgift frequently. In addition to the interrogations, the fifty-two Separatist prisoners in London were made to receive deputations of clergy, some of them Puritans, to argue the evils of Separatism. The prisoners never faltered. Sometimes Barrowe and Greenwood were examined separately, in the hope that they would contradict each other. Even this did not work.

Barrowe records how, on one occasion, he lost his temper. He had been asked who the Archbishop, who was present, was. "The Lord gave me the spirit of boldness," wrote Barrowe, "so that I answered, 'He is a monster, a miserable compound. I know not what to make of him; he is neither ecclesiastical nor civil, even that second beast spoken of in Revelation'." Later, back in his cell, he regretted the outburst: "The Lord pardon my unworthiness and unsanctified heart and mouth, which can bring no glory to the Lord or benefit to his Church, but rather reproach to the one and affliction to the other." He vowed to "set a more careful watch" over his lips. It was a hard time for Puritans. The 'Mar-Prelate' tracts, satirical attacks on the Bishops, were circulating throughout England, and Whitgift was furiously pursuing the secret authors, publishers, and circulators. John Udall (c.1560–1592), suspected of complicity in producing the tracts, and sentenced to death by Whitgift, died in the Marshalsea prison from the ill-usage he had received there, and did so on the point of release, his freedom forced on Whitgift by public outrage. Cartwright was in the Fleet prison. Countless others, their names unknown, rotted and died in the foetid prison air.

Precisely what the crimes of Barrowe and Greenwood were in law it is difficult to determine. They were conflictingly found guilty of writing books 'with malicious intent', or 'defamation of God's Majesty' or 'stirring up of insurrection or rebellion' or possibly all three. All three charges are patently absurd. They were guilty of opposing Elizabeth's religious settlement and following the Puritan doctrines to their logical conclusion. Both were sentenced to death. The following day they were told to prepare to die, their irons were taken off, and they were led out to the cart which was to take them to execution. At that moment a reprieve arrived and they were taken back to their cells. It was March 24, 1593. On March 31 they were again taken to execution very early in the morning and nooses put around their necks on the gallows. They were allowed to say a few words and, that concluded, waited for death. A messenger arrived from the Queen with a second reprieve. Back in prison Barrowe wrote on their joint behalves to a noblewoman, a distant relation, asking her to intercede with the Queen and tell her of their "entire faith unto God, unstained loyalty to her Majesty, innocency and good conscience towards all men." This appeal might have succeeded, but the Bishops were currently forcing an unpopular Bill specifically against 'Barrowists and Brownists' through the House of Commons. To reprieve two of their leaders would have looked like weakness. On April 6 Barrowe and Greenwood were taken for the last time to execution. The only account we have of their deaths, probably accurate, was reported to the Queen when she asked how they died: "A very Godly end, and prayed for your Majesty and the State". It is unlikely that we will ever know why there were two reprieves. It could have been an effort to terrify the victims into a recantation: it could have been a genuine effort to save their lives, thwarted by Whitgift.

Nor are we ever likely to know who wrote the 'Mar-Prelate' tracts, though we know who died because of them. John Penry (1559–1593) was a Welshman, Cambridge- and Oxford-educated, and a Puritan. He may have taken orders but if he did he repudiated them early. He preached in the open air and especially in his native Wales. That experience gave rise to a moderate pamphlet, 'The Aequity', 1587, addressed to the Queen and Parliament, pleading that "some order may be taken for the preaching of the Gospel among the people", especially in Wales. The pamphlet contained suggestions for lay preachers, and asked for a Welsh translation of the Old Testament. There was also criticism of non-residence and pluralism. Penry was arrested for violating the censorship law and was interrogated. His heresy, it appeared, was to deny that clergy who never preached were true ministers of Christ. "I thank God," said Penry, "that I ever knew such a heresy, as I will, by the grace of God, sooner leave my life than leave it." Whitgift was present at the interrogation and no doubt judged that criticisms which every Puritan in the country shared and many Anglicans too, would hardly make a case for heresy. Penry was released after a month.

The 'Martin Mar-Prelate' tracts (Martin from Luther's Christian name, and 'Mar-Prelate' meaning 'Spoil-Bishop') were seven in number and appeared between November 1588 and September 1589. They were wittily written and contained reference to every known failing of the bishops, and the chief targets were Whitgift, Aylmer of London and Cooper of Winchester. The purpose of the tracts, however, was serious. "I am called Martin Mar-Prelate. There be many that greatly dislike of my doings. I have my wants, I know . . . but my course I know to be ordinary and lawful. I saw the cause of Christ's government, and of the Bishops' anti-Christian dealing, to be hidden. The most part of men could not be gotten to read anything written in the defence of the one and against the other. I bethought me therefore of a way whereby men might be drawn to do both, perceiving the humours of man in these times . . . to be given to Mirth . . . for jesting is lawful by circumstances even in the greatest matters. The circumstances of time, place and persons urged me thereunto. I never profaned the word in any jest. Other mirth I used as a covert wherein I would bring the truth to light. The Lord being the author both of mirth and gravity, is it not lawful in itself for the truth to use either of these ways when the circumstances do make it lawful?" Whitgift's wealth and ostentation, Aylmer's games of bowls on Sundays and alleged misappropriation of Church funds, Cooper's marital misfortunes, all were faithfully recorded to the delight of their enemies and the fury of the bishops. Aylmer, when a poor priest, had published an attack on the princely earnings of the bishops. "Come down, you bishops," he had written, "from your thousands and content you with your hundreds, let your diet be priestlike and not princelike." Mar-Prelate asked him, "I pray you, Bishop John, dissolve this our question to your brother Martin: if this prophesy of yours come to pass in your days, who shall be Bishop of London?" Part of a sermon of the Bishop of Worcester which he preached in Gloucester is quoted verbatim – or so Mar-Prelate says. With one farcical exaggeration it has an air of authenticity; one has heard similar sermons. The Bishop, Mar-Prelate said, "Came at length to the very pith of the whole sermon, contained in the distinction of the name of John, which he then showing all his learning at once, full learnedly handled after this manner. 'John, John, the grace of God, the grace of God, the grace of God; gracious John, not graceless John, but gracious John. John, holy John, holy John, not John full of holes, but holy John.'"

Mar-Prelate offers the bishops a bargain. If they will encourage preaching and appoint only godly preachers, if they will publish a book of Cartwright's and stop persecuting clergy for refusing to wear Popish garments or leaving out Popish passages from the Prayer Book, then he, Martin, would promise "never to make any more of your knavery known unto the world." Whitgift's spies were everywhere, tracing the pamphlets to their source. If he could find the press he could find the authors. The press was moved secretly from place to place, taken by night across England when Whitgift got close. The damage being done to the Church the bishops judged to be great. The highest ecclesiastics in the land were being held up to ridicule and contempt, and the establishment with them. The catalogue in Mar-Prelate of persecution of Puritans brought sympathy for that cause. As for the personal attacks on the bishops, while some of the charges were falsehoods, their enemies could not know that, and other charges were much too close to truth for comfort.

The printing-press was finally seized near Manchester. Penry had been in Scotland, where Whitgift's warrant and a personal request of Elizabeth to James for Penry's arrest followed him. No attempt, however, was made to arrest him there. It was when he returned to London – naïvely, it is said, intending to appeal to the Queen for permission to preach in Wales – that Whitgift finally caught him. He had been attending a Separatist Church in Southwark led by Francis Johnson and John Greenwood, the latter briefly out of prison at this time. His movements were watched, he was arrested, escaped, made no serious effort to get far away, and was arrested again.

Penry was suspected of being the author of the 'Mar-Prelate' tracts. He was almost certainly not the author. His own published works are in a totally different style. Another suspect was Barrowe, an even more improbable suggestion. Job Throckmorton (1545–1601), Puritan Member of Parliament, was certainly involved in the tracts, but to what extent we shall never know. He denied both being Martin and knowing who Martin was. He is a likelier author than Barrowe or Penry, but there is no strong evidence. It is sure that Penry owned the press on which the tracts were printed and sure that he was deeply involved in the distribution of them, but there was not a scrap of evidence that he was the author. While flouting the laws of censorship was a serious offence, not even Whitgift could make it a capital one. The Archbishop made careful searches, and in the end he found what he wanted. Among Penry's possessions were some unpublished jottings, notes to himself, which allegedly said that the Queen prevented her subjects from serving God according to his Word, and calling ministers of state and religion conspirators against God as well as persecutors of Christ's true followers. All Puritans held similar views to these, but that was an irrelevance. The notes were enough to prove Penry guilty of treason. He was hanged on 29 May 1593, just two months after Barrowe and Greenwood had died. The Sheriff had express orders that Penry was to utter no words from the scaffold. What he had most wanted to say he had written in his farewell letters. "If my blood were an ocean sea, and every drop thereof were a life unto me, I would give them all by the help of the Lord for the maintenance of the same my confession." Penry was no republican. He wanted only a reformed Church. "If my death," he wrote at the very end of his life, "can procure any quietness unto the Church of God, and unto the State of my Prince, and his kingdom wherein I was born, glad I am that I had a life to bestow in this service."

Penry, Barrowe and Greenwood were among the first martyrs of the Free Churches. The cause did not die with them: their martyrdoms strengthened it. In the year they died, 1593, Whitgift persuaded the Queen to pass a Conventicle Act. Hereafter, all who refused to attend the established Church or who persisted in attending unauthorized religious meetings should be banished. Catholics were fined, imprisoned or executed; extreme Puritans were banished. On the advice of Penry, shortly before his execution, most of the London Church of which he had been Pastor planned flight to Amsterdam. They got there towards the end of 1593 under the leadership of Francis Johnson (1562–1618) and his brother George (1564–1605). They began with some 300 communicants. Two years later they were joined by Henry Ainsworth (1571–c.1623), a distinguished scholar and 'Brownist' in principle. Almost from the start the Church was rent by internal disputes, most of them because of a feud George Johnson waged against his sister-in-law, for Francis Johnson had married a wealthy widow, Mrs. Thomasine Boyes, who still wore the clothes of her previous rank. George charged her before the whole Church with being as proud as the wife of the Bishop of London, with wearing four or five gold rings, and with affecting a hat that was 'too toppish'. He then published his account of the whole wretched dispute. Secessions followed secessions and it was years before there was peace. Their enemies might well have said that it was precisely what was to be expected – take away ecclesiastical authority, precedence, and a firm Church discipline, and in a very little time there will be anarchy. In fact anarchy resolved itself in due course, and from such unpromising beginnings came the work of Thomas Helwys (c.1550–1616), the foundation of the Baptist Church under John Smyth (c.1570–1612), and the faith of the Pilgrim Fathers, who took Christianity to America. These matters will be considered in Chapter III.

By the end of Elizabeth's reign the Puritans were a minority, but a powerful one. They were divided among themselves. Some wanted only liberty to be free of vestments and a few other 'Romish' practices. Others already considered that 'Separatism', total separation from the established Church, was the only possible way ahead. The latter were the fathers of the Free Churches. Browne was the originator, Barrowe, Greenwood and Penry the first martyrs. Whitgift's persecutions had given the cause maximum sympathy and publicity, and he had also ensured that if in England Separatists had to meet in secret, there was a larger world outside where the Free Churches could flourish.

CHAPTER III

Puritans and Early Stuarts

ELIZABETH OF ENGLAND HAD never named her successor. As she lay dying, too ill for speech, she indicated by dumb show that James Stuart (1566–1625), King of Scotland, a man she detested, should follow her on the English throne. A horseman thundered North with the news.

Elizabeth's had been a long and successful reign. It was difficult for the nation to imagine another ruler. Her people had grown to love and respect her. Quixotic, ceaselessly prevaricating, imperious and familiar by turns, she yet possessed the qualities that make for greatness in leaders, an iron will and the intelligence to satisfy it. She knew how to flatter, but when she said "I care not so much for being a Queen, as that I am Sovereign of such subjects", it was more than flattery. She passionately loved England; she passionately loved her subjects when they proved their love by doing what they were told. She needed no doctrine of the divine right of Kings; it never occurred to her to doubt that she was right, and she could look after herself. True, by the end of her reign there were financial problems caused by her reluctance to alienate Parliament by asking for subsidies and her greater reluctance to appear as a beggar before her people – but her successor could deal with those worries. With skill and patience she had made collaboration with the ruling classes a partnership that worked, though by the end of her reign it was clear that only a master tactician could keep Parliament in its place.

Elizabeth had inherited from the reign of Edward VI a compromise Church which was a combination of extremes, and by a policy of punishment by fine rather than savage persecution, she had simultaneously satisfied most of her subjects in matters religious and made a heavy profit from the remainder. There were few martyrs and little sense of injustice, except in Catholic minds.

What, the English wondered, would James be like? A change of monarch today would make little difference. A change then could make a world of difference, as old men could remember. The face of England had changed when Mary died and Elizabeth became Queen.

James had a sad, lonely childhood. He was brought up in the knowledge that his father had murdered his wife's secretary, Rizzio, a man alleged to be her lover, and that his mother, Mary, Queen of Scots, had formed an adulterous relationship with Bothwell, had arranged the murder of her husband, Darnley, and had then been forced to flee, banished from Scotland. She was executed for plotting against Queen Elizabeth's life while James was still a boy. An ungainly child with weak legs, protruding eyes and a tongue too large for his mouth, all his life he had a grotesque appearance. For all that he was a fine horseman, a brave soldier and – what should have mattered most – a very great scholar, one of the finest in Europe. In some measure his learning was one of his greatest demerits, for he was arrogant and pedantic and incapable of seeing any view other than his own.

Early in 1603 James travelled triumphantly South to take his throne. He showered honours and gifts on all who greeted him, he spent extravagantly in the access of sudden wealth, and he offered soft words to all who asked for help. Among those who sought it were a group of Puritan clergymen who claimed to represent a thousand of their brethren – hence the name of the 'Millenary Petition', which they gave to the King. "Most gracious and dread sovereign", it began, "We, the ministers of the gospel in this land . . . as the faithful servants of Christ and loyal subjects . . ." and it asked for reforms in the Church to be decided by "a conference among the learned". There were four sections in the petition. The first concerned the Church Service. The ministers asked to be relieved of their "common burden of human rites and ceremonies", namely the sign of the cross in baptism, wearing of the surplice, confirmation (which they considered unnecessary), the ring in marriage, the length of the service (often too long, they thought), the use of liturgical music (there was too much), bowing at the name of Jesus, the profanation of the Lord's Day, and reading the Apocrypha in the lessons. A second section asked for ministers of higher quality, "able and sufficient men and those to preach diligently and especially upon the Lord's Day," a third section pointed out the abuses of pluralism and non-residence, and a fourth asked for the reform of Church courts.

Those who presented the petition had reason to hope for the King's support. He had been brought up a Presbyterian and had said to the General Assembly of the Church at Edinburgh in 1590 that "he praised God that he was born in the time of the light of the Gospel, and in such a place as to be King of such a Church, the sincerest Kirk in the world . . . I charge you . . . to stand to your purity, and to exhort the people to do the same; and I, forsooth, as long as I brook my life, shall maintain the same." The petitioners could hardly know that their new King hated the Scottish Kirk. As he received it he offered them gentle words and the promise of a Conference which would resolve their problems, and the Hampton Court Conference duly took place the next year.

The Petition illustrates the great division in the Church of England, and the passion with which the views were held. While the last three points were matters of church abuses which most deplored, the prominence is given to the first point, and most of the 'common burden' seems from a modern viewpoint a list of trivia. Not so then. To the Puritans they were matters of deep significance – matters over which some of them would have gone to the stake.

The Puritans were now a strong body. They varied in details of doctrine and church organization, but they had emphases in common. The word 'puritan' was a word first used in contempt and throughout the seventeenth century it was used as a term of abuse for all radical protestants who differed from one's own opinions, just as 'communist' has been so used in the twentieth century. Bishop Curl defined a Puritan as "such an one as loves God with all his soul but hates his neighbour with all his heart." The Puritans claimed that the Church over the centuries had moved further and further from the biblical ideal: they wanted it restored to its original purity.

The first emphasis that all Puritans shared was a belief in the supreme authority of the Scriptures. The widespread circulation of the Bible effectively meant an alternative to priestly inter-mediaries – a man's own path to the knowledge of God through the pages of God's book. Trevelyan wrote: "A new religion arose . . . of which the pervading spirit was the direct relations of man with God, exemplified in human life. And while the imagination was kindled, the intellect was freed by this private study of the Bible. For its private study involved its private interpretation . . . Hence the hundred sects and thousand doctrines that astonished foreigners, and opened England's strange path to intellectual liberty." Puritans studied the Bible, discussed it, preached it, lived by it. It is no accident that many of the Free Churches began with the Bible-reading Puritans. For Puritans, the Bible was not only a handbook for doctrine and conduct – the Anglicans believed that too – but also was the authority on church government, worship, discipline and indeed, all matters. Texts could be adduced for every situation of life.

It was also through reading the Bible that Puritans began to doubt many things – the system of church government they lived under, the un-Christlike behaviour of some of their bishops, power-seeking and wealthy prelates. Should not a church be a collection of those who loved Christ and freely met to learn from him and live like him? Virtually all of the distinctive beliefs of the Puritans stemmed from their study of Scripture. From the same source came their objections to the contemporary 'rites and ceremonies'. Where was the scriptural authority for the surplice, for the ring in marriage, for confirmation?

Preaching was the second emphasis of the Puritans. Queen Elizabeth vetoed all preaching several times during her reign and the first two Stuarts dictated the contents of sermons. Most Puritans objected to set forms both of homilies (preaching) and liturgies (prayers). In 1640 clergymen were compelled to preach the doctrine of the Divine Right of Kings one Sunday in each quarter. The Puritans thought preaching their most vital function. It spread the knowledge of God; it expounded the Scriptures; it taught the ways of God to man; it inculcated holiness. Authority (civil and ecclesiastical authority were one) feared preaching for it assumed a dangerous liberty which could lead to sedition. Successive monarchs and archbishops therefore discouraged it;

silent clergy were safer. Yet by the time of James' accession there was a deep hunger for a preaching ministry. The laity would take notes of the sermons to use them as a basis for family discussion later. Wyclif's tradition, so ruthlessly put down, rose again to elevate teaching and preaching as opposed to the ceremonial and sacramental aspects of religion. The Duke of Newcastle said: "There should be more praying and less preaching, for much preaching breeds faction, but much praying causes devotion." It was the fear of faction which led Elizabeth and her successors to set their faces against preaching. But the preachers would not be silenced; they found another way.

The way, and the third emphasis of the Puritans, was lecturing. There was both an insatiable appetite for preaching and a ready supply of preachers. These were ordained men of Oxford and Cambridge who had no benefice to which to go and therefore no employment. They were paid locally by voluntary contribution, and therefore there was little ecclesiastical control over them. A popular lecturer – and local groups preferred to choose their own preachers – could earn more than the ill-paid beneficed clergy. In this way, and normally without any consciousness of doing so, groups of Puritans were effectively following the example of Browne, Barrowe, Greenwood and Penry, and becoming congregational in practice and spirit. Independence of this sort was accidental but felt to be a threat to the Church.

The Church of England signally failed to deal with the problem. Had they paid their own beneficed clergy more, had they allowed them to preach more often and encouraged the ablest, they could – at least for a while – have minimized the embarrassment that lectureships caused. Instead, they took the worst possible course by persecuting the lecturers and ejecting them from their lectureships, the inevitable result of which was to force some of their ablest clergy into dissent.

The fourth stress of the Puritans was observance of the Lord's Day after their own particular pattern. Their reading of the Scriptures taught them that God rested on the seventh day; it followed that his creatures should do the same. 'Holy-days' which in mediaeval times had become numerous, were unscriptural. The Sabbath must shine in its pristine glory. There was to be no work on the Sabbath. After Church attendance, Christians should devote the rest of the day to godly pursuits such as reading the

Bible, discussing it, preaching, praying, or similar devotional duties. Any other pursuit was satanic. Sabbatarianism effectively dated in England from 1595 with the publication of Nicholas Bownde's 'The Doctrine of the Sabbath', though Calvin's 'Institutes' had long prepared the way. The Sabbath, said Calvin, was a day when "believers were to cease from their own works, and allow God to work in them, . . . a stated day on which they should assemble to hear the law and perform religious rites . . . meditating on his works, and be thereby trained to piety."

All this sounds reasonable enough, but it was anathema to the King and to the other wing of the Church. Servants, they said, were servants seven days a week, and it was fitting that all should join in the traditional relaxations (dances, bull-baiting, bear-baiting, bowls in the country, the play-house, dicing, cards or the ale-house in the town) once church attendance had been fulfilled. Both James I and Charles I successively pressed this view by royal proclamation in 'The King's Book of Sports', 1618 and 1633.

It is easy to sentimentalize the old English maypole dances, which Puritans hated. They were in fact derived from a pagan fertility rite, and nine months after it, the latest crop of bastards was counted. Well might the Puritan, William Prynne, ask with reference to the King's book, "What could Beelzebub, had he been the Archbishop, have done more than in publishing the book against Sunday?" Forced to read the King's proclamation from the pulpit, one London minister did so, then read the ten commandments and told his congregation: "you have heard now the commandments of God and man. Obey which you please."

The fifth stress of the Puritans was their religion of the home. For them, family prayers became as important as public worship. Thomas Taylor said: "Let every master of a family see to what he is called, namely, to make his house a little church, to instruct every one of his family in the fear of God, to contain every one of them under holy discipline, to pray with them and for them . . ." Nor did the family mean only parents and children. Servants and apprentices were all part of the family of God which met daily for worship in the home.

The last stress of the Puritans was to make their religion permeate every aspect of their lives. They lived frugally and dressed simply, for they discarded the ephemeral pleasures of the world and looked only to heaven for happiness. They therefore became distinctive even in their dress. It was practically their austerity and their condemnation of any pleasure which was not God-centred that gave them the reputation of being gloomy kill-joys. In fact that reputation was caricature. There were cranks and hypocrites among them but the vast majority were pious people who tried to live a Christian life exactly as the Bible instructed them. Nor had they forgotten that the Reformation stood for the 'priesthood of all believers'. There should be no intermediaries between a man and his God. 'Saints' in its New Testament sense meant simply servants of Christ. They were Christ's servants. At home as in Church, they were his saints.

Such were the emphases of the Puritans, and it was the representatives of their clergy, devout members of the Church of England, who petitioned their new King.

There were already groups of men and women, noted in Chapter II, most of them meeting secretly, who had given up allegiance to the national Church and had united in self-governing churches in the spirit of Robert Browne. They are sometimes referred to as Congregationalists before Congregationalism, but labels can be misleading. The general terms 'Separatists' and 'Independents' were used of those who seceded from the Church and this is label enough, for there were no organized Free Church bodies, only groups anxious to worship God as they thought the Bible instructed them. Puritans, they had rejected the national Church and for a variety of reasons. Some thought episcopacy unscriptural; others simply hated the way the bishops carried out their duties. Of these, some leaned to a Presbyterian system of church government with elders instead of bishops, but to call them Presbyterians would be to confuse them with Scottish Presbyterians. Others thought that each individual church should govern itself and leaned to congregationalism. They were Puritans but Puritans whose futures would be less affected by James' decisions, for they were spiritually outside his jurisdiction already. There could have been only a few hundred Separatists in England at this time.

The great majority of Puritans, however, wanted to remain in the Church. The Hampton Court Conference, which James summoned in 1604, was to settle the future of religion in England as the petition had requested. If a compromise could be reached, and the tender consciences of the Puritans satisfied, the Church could remain one.

On the first day of the conference only the bishops and the Council of State were present. It was an occasion James enjoyed. Servility from ecclesiastics was new to him; he had been called 'God's silly (i.e. simple) vassal' in Scotland. He had decided that there were three elements in English religion; the religion "publicly allowed and by the law maintained" and "another sort of religion (the Roman Catholics), besides a private sect lurking within the bowels of this nation." The sect consisted of "Puritans and Novelists, who do not so far differ from us in points of religion as in their confused form of polity and parity, being ever discontented with the present government and impatient to suffer any superiority, which maketh their sect unable to be suffered in any well governed commonwealth." It was on that first day that James made it quite clear he would do nothing to help the Puritans, for he said he saw "yet no cause so much to alter and change anything as to confirm what he found well settled already." He also made clear his views on the Scottish Kirk: "Scots Presbytery agrees with monarchy as well as God and the devil", and blessed episcopacy with his famous dictum: "No Bishop, no King". As the Conference ended, he told the Puritan Dr. Reynolds that if the aggrieved ministers did not conform, he would "harry them out of the land". The next day the King boasted, "We have kept such a revel with the Puritans here these two days as we never heard the like."

Three hundred beneficed clergymen felt compelled to resign their livings, and the Church could ill afford to lose them. Men of integrity, anxious to serve the Church, were forced out by James' blundering insensitivity. Of those who remained, more than a few were among the feeblest. James' act was inept, for it made martyrs of the ejected ministers who, in defiance of the law, preached and published to sympathetic hearers. The King appeared a tyrant, the Bishops his malignant creatures, the Courts, vehicles of injustice. It was not James' only serious tactical error, but it was one with great consequences, for the total alienation of the Puritans was a step towards civil war and the execution of a king.

Only a month after the Hampton Court Conference, Archbishop Whitgift died, to be succeeded by Richard Bancroft (1544–1610). Episcopacy, he believed, was of divine origin. At the Conference his bitterness against Puritans was so extreme that even James was shocked. He was a fitting tool for the persecutions that followed. Not only beneficed clergymen suffered. Lecturers suspected of Puritan sympathies were ejected, many to flee abroad and worship as Separatists in the Low Countries or America. Separatists were ruthlessly tracked down. The wisest fled abroad; those who remained were imprisoned.

There was much sympathy for those who suffered for conscience's sake, much anger against the King. James cared nothing for unpopularity. His passionate belief in the divine right of kings, on which he had written a book, protected him from self-doubt as it protected him from considering that anyone but himself could be right. He was a repulsive man. Uncouth in manner, totally lacking in dignity, cruel, extravagant, arrogant and dictatorial, he grew more unpleasant as he grew older. He disgusted even sycophantic courtiers by publicly slobbering over his male favourites, one of whom (Robert Carr, Earl of Somerset) was to be disgraced by being found guilty of murder, and the other (George Villiers, Duke of Buckingham) to be impeached by Parliament and later assassinated by a madman. If he did not endear himself to his courtiers still less did he endear himself to the common people, for he hated the unwashed multitude, and avoided them as much as he could.

Nor were his private failings an irrelevance in an age when kings ruled personally. A scandal to Puritans, a source of resentment to the ruling classes, they were failings that affected public life. His arrogance made a relationship with Parliament almost impossible. Parliament had been growing restive during the last years of Elizabeth's reign. It had enjoyed a taste of power and was thirsting for more. Was the true seat of authority King or Parliament? Parliament was beginning to consider itself more than a body to receive the King's instructions and tentatively make suggestions. It involved itself in public policy, finance, and in religion. It was conscious that power went with financial control and that the King, deeply in debt, could only get money through them unless he resorted to illegal means. James was furious. Had he not written, "The state of monarchy is the supremest thing upon earth; for kings are not only God's lieutenants upon earth and sit upon God's throne, but even by God himself they are called gods"? Parliament was told it had "merely a private and local wisdom": the greater concerns were his alone. For much of his reign James ruled without Parliament.

His foreign policy was a curious one. He believed himself, by

God appointed, the saviour of Europe. The Church of England he viewed as a half-way house between Geneva and Rome. As peacemaker, he would heal Europe of all its troubles. Hence his tolerance towards Catholics, an untypical piece of generosity which was the more surprising after Guy Fawkes attempted to blow him and Parliament into eternity in 1605. Hence also his philo-Spanish policy, which was as unpopular in England as his attempted tolerance of Catholicism.

One great debt England owed his reign was the publication of the King James Bible in 1611. Many versions have been written in succeeding years, yet it is difficult to believe that the authorized edition can ever be bettered. Its magnificent, seventeenth-century prose might well have persuaded contemporary readers that it was personally dictated by God.

By his bigoted hatred of Puritans, James was directly responsible not only for an increase in the number of Separatists, but also, through his persecution of the already existing Separatists, for the foundation of the Baptist Church.

John Smyth (c.1570–1612) was a Cambridge graduate. Little is known about his early life. He was probably a preacher suspended from preaching in Lincoln. His early publications prove that he was not a Separatist when his ministry began. Nevertheless, he later had connections with two Separatist groups which met in Gainsborough and Scrooby Manor, Lincolnshire, "as the Lord's free people . . . in the fellowship of the Gospel, to walk in all his ways . . . whatsoever it should cost them, the Lord assisting them." William Brewster (c.1560–1644) was of the company, apparently their leader. Brewster had once served at Queen Elizabeth's court, but had been dismissed when the Queen found it expedient to clear herself of blame in signing the death warrant of Mary, Queen of Scots. Later he was to be joint leader of the 'Pilgrim Fathers' when they sailed to America. Another was John Robinson (c.1576–1625), a suspended preacher who was later to be a distinguished pastor of a church in Leyden. His writings defended and advocated a congregational type of church government. Also of the company were Thomas Helwys (c.1550–1616) and John Murton (c.1578–1621), of whom more will be said later.

In 1607, warned of imminent persecution, the group resolved to flee. Their first attempt, to sail from Boston, ended in robbery and imprisonment, their second, a more secret flight from the Humber, ended in disaster, when only the women and children were taken by a captain nervous of his boat running aground. The men were left helplessly in England for more privation. By the end of 1608, in twos and threes, the men had rejoined their families in Amsterdam, where religion was a man's private concern, and there was freedom of the press. A pamphlet of 1607 shows John Smyth had 'Brownist' principles of church government, but his views changed rapidly in Amsterdam.

Smyth practised as a physician, for exiles need livelihood, but he refused fees from the poor and was as generous to others as he was mean to himself. It is probable that, once abroad, the leadership of the group effectively passed from Brewster to Smyth. Smyth's tortured conscience was their spiritual guide, he was more scholar than Brewster, and in the free air of Amsterdam they could follow their passion, which was religion. It is highly probable that Smyth's group first worshipped with the earlier immigrants led by Johnson and Ainsworth, mentioned in Chapter II. It is certain that before long, Smyth disagreed with that church and he and his group formed their own, 'the second English Church at Amsterdam,' with Smyth as pastor. Pamphlets published by Smyth proved him still a 'Brownist' in his theory of church government. His 'Differences of the Churches of the Separation', written to explain his secession from the first English church of Amsterdam, illustrates how little the differences were, how literal-minded these students of the Bible had become, how tender their consciences.

Anabaptists had existed on the continent in several distinct groups from the sixteenth century. They had in common a belief in baptism for believers. All were Calvinists in theology, but each group had other distinctive beliefs. One such group, the Mennonites, called after their founder, Menno Simons (1496–1561) believed in a connexional type of church organization, the local responsibility of each congregation, non-resistance, the rejection of Christian participation in the magistracy and consequent refusal of church membership to magistrates, and that Jesus did not derive his flesh from the Virgin Mary, but came from a celestial body. A church of Mennonites worshipped near the exiles in Amsterdam.

At this point it was only the baptism for believers that compelled

Smyth's attention. He studied the Scriptures. He became convinced of the logic of the belief. In the spring of 1609 he published 'The Character of the Beast', in which he argued that 'infants ought not to be baptized, because 1. there is neither precept nor example in the New Testament of any infants that were baptized by John or Christ's disciples, and 2. Christ commanded to make disciples by teaching them and then to baptize them.' But who, after the gap of centuries, was to baptize these new converts? An unsympathetic contemporary account by John Robinson explains: "After much straining of courtesy who should begin, Mr Smyth baptized first himself and next Mr Helwys, and so the rest making their particular confessions." So began the first English General Baptist Church – in 1609 in Amsterdam.

John Smyth's almost morbid conscience could not rest here. He began to be tortured by fears that his self-baptism was not valid, that the Mennonites had more of the truth than he. After only a few more months, Smyth considered himself in error and persuaded some forty or fifty of his congregation of eighty to seek membership of the Mennonite Church. The Mennonites in fact delayed so long in accepting them that Smyth was dead before he could be received.

Thomas Helwys, a member of a distinguished Nottinghamshire family, and Smyth's close companion since they fled together, was a layman and a lawyer trained at Gray's Inn. He had been compelled when they left England, to leave behind his wife and seven children, all under twelve. His wife was imprisoned in York Castle for three months after his departure. Helwys deeply loved John Smyth. They had suffered and triumphed together, and Helwys had followed his leader every step of his tortuous spiritual way. He could not, however, follow him to the Mennonites. He judged their doctrine of Christology unsound, he could not accept exclusion of magistrates, for it "is contrary to the liberty of the Gospel, which is free for all men at all times and in all places" and "they are ministers of God to take vengeance on them that do evil", and he could find no evidence that Mennonite baptism was more valid than their own. The two men were utterly divided, both hurt by the break, both implacable in their views. In 1611 Helwys published three pamphlets in defence of his position. The first was a Baptist Confession, the second a rejection of Calvinism, the third to show where he differed from the Mennonites. The same year he decided that it was his duty to return to England to appeal to the King to stop persecuting his subjects for their religious beliefs, to face persecution himself and if necessary to die for his cause.

It was in 1612, the year Helwys left Amsterdam, that John Smyth died. Controversy died first in him and he wrote with sorrow of his censures on other churches, "I utterly revoke (them). All penitent and faithful Christians," he said, "are brethren in the communion of the outward Church." He wrote it most of all for his estranged friend, who a few months earlier had reached London and founded the first General Baptist Church on English soil at Spitalfields. Helwys brought with him copies of his plea for toleration, 'The Mystery of Iniquity' printed in Amsterdam, and the copy for King James, inscribed in his own hand, is still extant in the Bodleian Library, Oxford. "Hear O King, and despise not the counsel of the poor, and let their complaints come before thee. The King is a mortal man, and not God, therefore hath no power over the immortal souls of his subjects, to make laws and ordinances for them, and to set spiritual lords over them. If the King have authority to make spiritual lords and laws, then he is an immortal God and not a mortal man. O King, be not seduced by deceivers to sin so against God whom thou oughtest to obey, nor against thy poor subjects who ought and will obey thee in all things with body, life and goods, or else let their lives be taken from the earth. Spitalfields, near London. Thomas Helwys." To give an address was as brave as it was foolish.

It was not long after James received this proof of Helwys's colossal courage, that Helwys and some of his followers were imprisoned in Newgate. It was a matter of policy that such men should rot and die in prison, neither charged nor tried. The King, as Fuller's *Church History of Britain*, 1655, explained, "politicly preferred that heretics hereafter . . . should silently and privately waste themselves away in prison rather than to grace them and amuse others with the solemnity of a public execution." Helwys had written in his book, "Let them be heretics, Turks, Jews, or whatsover, it appertains not to the earthly power to punish them in the least measure." Yet he died in prison and we do not know the precise date, only that he was dead by 1616.

The work went on. John Murton succeeded Helwys as the

leader of the little church in London. Often in prison, he wrote pamphlets echoing the works of Helwys. 'Objectives Answered', 1615, was a plea that no man should be persecuted for his religion. In 'Truth's Champion', 1617, he supported the Arminian view of redemption against the Calvinist view, and when the King was forced to summon a new Parliament, after a gap of seven years, he sent him from prison "A most humble supplication of many of the King's Majesty's loyal subjects . . . who were persecuted only for differing in religion." He tells of the sufferings of those in prison: "Our miseries are long and lingering imprisonments for many years in diverse counties of England in which many have died and left behind them widows, and many small children: taking away our goods, and others the like, of which we can make good probation; not from any disloyalty to your majesty, nor hurt to any mortal man, our adversaries themselves being judges; but only because we dare not assent unto, and practise in the worship of God, such things as we have not faith in, because it is sin against the Most High." Such pleas were ignored by the King. He was used to them. Another Baptist, Leonard Busher, probably a member of the Helwys group, had published 'Religious Peace' in 1614, and insisted in it that it was "lawful for every person . . . yea, Jews and papists, to write, dispute, confer and reason, print and publish any matter touching religion . . ." John Milton had been born in 1608, and it was long before he would demand freedom for the press, longer before it was granted, longer still before there was a serious measure of religious liberty. Nevertheless, the early Baptists flourished under the persecution, and soon there were churches in Lincoln and Coventry, Salisbury and Tiverton, and then a second one in London.

Among almost all the early Separatists, as their enemies noted with derision, was a tendency to internal dispute. It seemed as if the removal of major ecclesiastical authority meant each man was his own authority. Certainly the unhappy disputes in Francis Johnson's Church, and the secessions which John Smyth felt compelled to make were striking instances. At least one branch of the Lincolnshire exiles proved as striking an exception. This was the group led by William Brewster and John Robinson, and their origins had been in Scrooby rather than Gainsborough.

In Amsterdam they quickly wearied of the dissensions in Francis

Johnson's church, nor could they follow John Smyth in his doubts and difficulties away from the teachings of Robert Browne. In 1609 they moved to Leyden where Robinson was publicly ordained Pastor and Brewster was made Teacher. The church lived in perfect happiness. Edward Winslow, who sailed on the *Mayflower* with Brewster, said of his years in Holland: "I persuade myself never people on earth lived more lovingly together and parted more sweetly than we the Church at Leyden did."

The greatest contribution that King James made to religion was in America. His laws compelled many of the finest men of his age to seek abroad the toleration they were denied at home. It effectively meant that a deep sense of religion and a love of toleration were the first principles that the new world were to receive from the old. For the most part, the new world therefore escaped much of the bigotry that was an inevitable part of religion in Europe. John Robinson, a liberal and enlightened Christian, pressed this point as he sadly said farewell to his friends – he had so longed to go with them. "I charge you that you follow me no farther than you have seen me follow the Lord Jesus Christ . . . the Lord has more truth yet to break forth out of his holy Word . . . I beseech you, remember, it is an Article of your Church Covenant, that you be ready to receive whatever truth shall be made known to you from the written Word of God . . ."

In England, George Abbot (1562–1633) succeeded Bancroft as Archbishop in 1611. He received the office in exchange for service in Scotland. He was himself by origin a staunch Protestant, but this made him more ruthless against Catholics, and no less savage towards Separatists. He quarrelled intermittently with the King, especially over the 'Book of Sports' which he thought obnoxious, and his usefulness was marred in 1621 when he accidentally killed a gamekeeper with a crossbow. He never recovered from remorse at the accident, though James thought his self-reproach absurd. Nevertheless, a serious result was that William Laud, the next Archbishop and a lifelong enemy of Abbot, began to exert his influence against the Separatists long before his primacy began.

It was in Abbot's term of office, however, that Bartholomew Legate (c.1575–1612) and Edward Wightman (d.1612) died at the stake, and Edmond Peacham (c.1554–1616) was condemned to death but died in prison.

The 'Seekers' was a minor sect of the seventeenth century, an offshoot of the Anabaptists. The members had considered the church of their day in the light of scripture, and they concluded that Anti-Christ had the real power in the church. A true church no longer existed. God in his own good time would ordain new apostles and new prophets and would found a new Church. Meanwhile Christ's patient followers were to wait. They were not to attempt to hasten the process. Bartholomew Legate was one of their preachers. His doctrines were originally similar to those of the Mennonites, but he first rejected that sect's belief in the celestial origin of Christ's body, and later he taught that Christ was "a mere man, as were Peter, Paul, or I; only . . . born free from sin." His heresies were well known and ignored by the authorities until 1611, when he was arrested with his brother Thomas and flung into Newgate prison. Thomas died there. The King, proud of his theological learning, naïvely imagined that Legate's views could be confuted by argument, and took a deep interest in the case. Legate predictably refused to accept the jurisdiction of the Court which tried him. In March 1612 he was burned at Smithfield as a heretic, the hideous punishment having the usual effect of providing sympathy for the victim, and anger for the oppressors. It was in part because of the reaction to the deaths of Legate and Wightman that James changed his policy from death by fire to death by imprisonment. Legate's views were clearly unorthodox, yet he harmed no man and died preaching the Gospel as he interpreted it. Fuller, the contemporary historian, called him a man "of a bold spirit, confident courage, fluent tongue, excellently skilled in Scriptures . . . his conversation (for ought I can learn to the contrary) very unblamable." Wightman was the last man burned for heresy in England. Another Anabaptist by early persuasion, his heresies became startling. The Puritans thought his views best ignored – for in him fanaticism verged on insanity – or answered by reason, but he forced the issue by presenting a petition to James who promptly had him arrested. Among his judges was William Laud. During cross-examination he horrified his judges by first denying the Trinity, and finally declaring himself the Holy Spirit. His end was horrible. As the flames scorched him at the stake he cried out that he would recant and a great crowd risked their lives in rescuing him. When his judges demanded a formal recantation he refused it, and the second time was taken to the stake where, according to a contemporary account, "he died blaspheming". Poor mad Wightman did not deserve this cruelty.

Still less did Edmond Peacham deserve his fate. Because of his Puritan views, he was taken before the Court of High Commission in 1614 and deprived of his Orders. This was a commonplace. What made his case exceptional was the discovery, after his dismissal, of sermon notes which charged the King's ministers with misconduct, the ecclesiastical courts with tyranny and the King with extravagance. They also prophesied the King's sudden death and a popular rebellion as the probable result of the misrule of the government. The sermon had never been preached – the notes were private thoughts. Nevertheless James was furious at the references to him, and wanted him charged with treason. Repeatedly Peacham was tortured in front of his judges, examined before and during and after the torture, but he said nothing. In the end the old man was condemned to death, though he died in prison.

The interrelationships of the early Separatists are remarkable. Henry Jacob (1563–1624) was a graduate of Oxford, one of the Puritan clergy, and a leader among those who presented the Millenary Petition to King James. Whitgift and Bancroft called him "a very insolent person, of much more boldness than either learning or judgement," and he was later imprisoned by the Bishop of London. After release Jacob fled to Holland. He became a member of John Robinson's church in Leyden between 1610 and 1616 after a brief time as pastor of a church in Middelberg. In 1616, he returned to England and set up a Separatist Church on clear congregational principles in Southwark. After a day of fasting and prayer "each of the brethren made open confession of his faith in our Lord Jesus Christ; and then, standing together, they joined hands and solemnly covenanted with each other in the presence of Almighty God, to walk together in all God's ways and ordinances, according as He had revealed, or should further make known to them. Mr. Jacob was then chosen pastor by the suffrage of the brotherhood, and others were appointed to the office of deacons with fasting and prayer and imposition of hands." This pattern of church foundation and government became the norm for Separatist foundations in the congregationalist pattern. The covenant as opposed to a creed was distinctive. Like John Smyth's spiritual path before him, Jacob's was neither easy nor straight, but until 1645 he remained Pastor of his Church, daily risking prosecution.

The largest group of Puritans at this period were those favouring Presbyterianism. They long hoped to stay within the fold of the Church of England. Separatism was not their wish. Initially, as Chapter III suggested, they desired only the removal of what they believed to be Catholic accretions – rites and vestments, for instance. Increasingly, however, and as a result of their studies of Scripture, as well as careful notice of the pattern of church government in Geneva, they began to demand the abolition of episcopacy and the substitution of the four orders of pastor, teacher, elder and deacon. There were church courts provided. The Presbyterians were distinct from most other Puritan groups, and one with the Anglicans, in accepting the conception of a national Church as opposed to a group of God-selected believers. They were also, as opposed to the general Baptists, Calvinists.

James had ceased to reign long before he died. Prematurely old, ill, drunken, afraid of death, he left most of the work of state to others. His eldest son, Henry, a man with Puritan sympathies, had died of typhoid in 1612, and Charles became his heir. It was Charles and the Duke of Buckingham, especially the latter, who ruled England, largely in defiance of Parliament, until the death of James in 1625 and Buckingham's assassination in 1628. James' legacy to his son was a vast debt and a totally alienated Parliament.

Charles I (1600–1649) had great gifts. Reacting against his father, he early acquired the attributes of a cultured gentleman – courtesy and dignity, learning without pedantry, wit without venom. He also had an artist's eye and a deep and genuine piety. He had strength, too. When his French wife of fifteen brought a household of 440 attendants as well as dogs and apes, he endured them for a very little and then, deaf to her screams, sent almost all of them packing. Unfortunately, he also had great flaws. He was stubborn and inflexible and totally untrustworthy. The doctrine of divine right he inherited from his father, and this no doubt seemed to him excuse enough for breaking his word. Plato's ideal of a benevolent dictator as king was Charles' ideal, with the added advantage of divine approval. Unlike James, Charles honestly tried to live up to the ideal of a divinely appointed King and his pure private life and personal piety set an excellent example. Like

James, however, he could never see any point of view but his own. Unable to get the money he needed from a parsimonious Parliament, he used his royal prerogative to flout the law and gain money by a variety of means. The most resented was 'ship money'. This tax, originally on ports only, became increasingly resisted as it spread inland and became a means of getting money without Parliamentary approval. Nothing Charles did so infuriated his subjects as attacks on their property. Men who refused loans to the King were imprisoned. Buckingham was impeached in 1626 as a sign of the anger of Parliament against the King. Lords and Commons joined to send Charles a 'Petition of Right', a list of their specific grievances. By 1628 he was forced to accept it. In 1629 the Speaker of the Commons was held in his chair by Puritans who would not allow him to rise and dissolve the House until they had read and voted on three resolutions, two about taxation and the third about Arminianism. When this Parliament was finally dissolved, Charles ruled without one for eleven years.

One of the men involved in the 'Petition of Right' later came to the aid of the King and became one of his two main advisers. This was Thomas Wentworth, Earl of Strafford (1593–1641). The other adviser was William Laud (1573–1645), Archbishop from 1633.

James, as part of his divine right theory, saw himself as the Christian Prince in sole charge of his Church. Charles viewed his Church as of divine origin, but, possibly because he lacked the weighty theological lore his father carried, and possibly because he was a more genuine Christian and therefore more humble, never claimed this title, but saw his Archbishop effectively as the head of the Church. Hence Laud's proportionate importance.

Laud was a man of vast energy and ruthless determination. He wished to purify the Church, to unify it, to give it order and decency. He was always a staunch Protestant, though in this age of bigotry almost all he did was called 'popery' by his enemies. Abbot was a Calvinist, a throw-back to a former age; Laud was a fanatical reformer. On the scaffold he explained what he had tried to do: "No one thing hath made conscientious men more wavering in their own minds or more apt and easy to be drawn aside from the sincerity of the religion professed by the Church of England than the want of uniform and decent order in too many churches of the Kingdom. It is true the inward worship of the heart is the great service of God, and no service is acceptable without it; but the external worship of God in his Church is the great witness to the world that our heart stands right in that service of God. And a great weakness is not to see the strength which ceremonies – things weak enough in themselves, God knows – add even to religion itself."

Paradoxically, though he hated and persecuted them all his life, there was something of the Puritan in Laud. He had the fanaticism which some of them had, the singlemindedness, the hatred of clerical abuses, drunkenness, long hair and ostentatious dress. It was Laud who reformed Oxford, rewrote and enforced the statutes, closed alehouses, made the students conform to the rules, and expelled unworthy Fellows of Colleges. It was Laud who plucked from their livings unworthy clergy of all persuasions, though his chief victims were the Puritans and the Separatists. And in his private life Laud was a very good man. In 1645 his enemies seized his diary and published it. They accidentally did him a great service, for it revealed a man of inward sanctity. Few men have souls that are far sweeter than their public image, but Laud was such a man.

Laud dreaded enthusiasm, loved order, was obsessed with ritual. The punctilious observation of the rubric, the Eastern position of the altar, wearing the surplice, the use of the prayer book, these were his obsessions. Those who would not conform he pursued with venom and punished with cruelty. Those who attacked episcopacy, and Laud believed that bishops ruled by divine right, were therefore blasphemers as well as traitors. Those who worshipped God in their own homes in group religious meetings (and under Abbot, devout Anglicans as well as Puritans had done it) were almost as guilty as the Separatists, for Laud believed such people would slide imperceptibly into Separatism – and it was true.

There is little excuse for the means by which Laud pursued his policies. The Star Chamber had begun in the fifteenth century but the Court of High Commission began to function as a regular court only in the 1580s. Under Laud, both Courts were used interchangeably to hang those whose religious views or observances were thought doubtful by the Archbishop. Even in the seventeeth century the Court of High Commission seemed a disgraceful travesty of justice. Citations before it had to be paid for by the defendant so that, guilty or not guilty, those who appeared before it were heavily fined by the act of appearing. It operated by no known rules. It did what it wished without reference to any law or person. Some were not punished after appearing before it, but no one was ever declared not guilty. Penry had justly called it, in the reign of Elizabeth, "this bloody and tyrannous inquisition."

There were repercussions of Laud's policies beyond England. His attempt to force the Prayer Book on Scotland led to the rising of the Scottish Presbyterians, and possibly to the eventual establishment of Presbyterian as the national religion. His persecution of Puritans and Separatists, the two becoming one as they fled, led to a mass exodus by many of the finest Christians in England. Between 1620 and 1640 some 20,000 fled to the American colonies and there established God-centred communities. Most founded Calvinist church-states. Roger Williams, later a Baptist, fled in 1630, and in 1636 founded the Rhode Island Colony.

It was in England, however, that Laud's policies should sow the most bitter harvest, for in an age when the secular and the religious were inextricably bound, the attack on any form of religious liberty was as offensive as the attack on property, and the two led to the death of Strafford and Laud and finally the King himself.

Those who spoke out were savagely treated. Dr Alexander Leighton (1568–1649), a Puritan Scotsman, was arraigned in the Star Chamber in 1630. He had published "An Appeal to Parliament: Zion's Plea against Prelacy" in 1628. Not only did it attack episcopacy and called bishops "ravens and magpies", but it called the Queen "the daughter of Heth", a rather obscure insult, a reference to her Catholic faith and an implication that she was not one of God's people. The words were construed into being blasphemy and treason. He was first imprisoned in "a loathsome and ruinous doghole full of rats and mice." His punishment was as cruel as Laud could make it. In 1630 he was imprisoned in the Fleet for life, fined £10,000 (which he did not have; it meant the confiscation of all he possessed; the sum related to the enormity of his crime), and sentenced also to be publicly mutilated. He was whipped, pilloried in the snow, one ear cut off, one nostril slit, one cheek branded SS (stirrer up of sedition) and dragged out a fortnight later, "his sores not yet healed", to have the other half of his head mutilated and be whipped again. When Laud heard the sentence, he "off with his cap, and holding up his hands gave thanks to God, who had given him the victory over his enemies."

A much more obscure figure, John Heyden, of Devonshire, preached after being ordered to stop. He, on Laud's instructions, went to Bridewell to be whipped, given hard labour and "was confined in a cold, dark dungeon during the whole winter, being chained to a post in the middle of a room, with irons on his hands and feet, having no other food but bread and water, and a pad of straw to lie on." So suffered many.

The most famous of Laud's victims was William Prynne (1600–1669), Puritan and Presbyterian pamphleteer and formidable opponent of the bishops whom he consistently accused of being papists. An Oxford graduate, he had brought himself to the attention of authority by publishing 'The Unloveliness of Love Locks' in 1628 in which he condemned long hair on men as idolatrous, lascivious and unnatural, but it was 'Histrio Mastix, the Player's Scourge' that caused serious offence. He denounced all actors, male and female, as well as "effeminate mixed dancing, dicing . . . lascivious pictures and lascivious effeminate music and excessive laughter." Actresses were "notorious whores". Boys dressed as girls in plays "were instigated to self pollution and to that unnatural sodomitical uncleanness to which the reprobate gentiles were given over". The stage, in fact, was a sink of corruption. It drew scholars from their study, girls from their needles, was a sinful expense of money, and it was all for the "fomentation of lechery". The offence was that both Charles and the Queen delighted in masques, and the Queen herself often took part. In 1633 he was put in the Tower, and in 1634 he was fined £5,000, imprisoned for life, degraded from his academic and legal degrees, pilloried, one of his ears cut off at Westminster, the other at Cheapside, and both cheeks branded with the letters SL (seditious libeller). His offending books were burnt under his nose. In 1637 when, indefatigably and bravely still publishing the truth as he saw it, the remaining stumps of his ears were cropped so close that the mutilation "put him in so much pain that after it, it was a long time before his head could be got out of the pillory." Feted by the populace, he was imprisoned first in Caernarvon Castle under a monoglot Welshman and later transferred to

Mount Orgueil Castle in Jersey. Nothing but death would ever silence Prynne and amazingly, considering his barbaric treatment, he survived to turn on his persecutor.

In the same years, 1633 and 1637, two others, John Bastwick (1593–1654) and Henry Burton (1578–1648) were also tried. Bastwick was a Cambridge graduate and also a doctor of medicine. He had Presbyterian principles, hated the bishops, and attacked episcopacy in his book, 'A Litany of John Bastwick'. Among other grosser expressions, he called the bishops "the tail of the beast". He was fined £5,000, degraded from his professions and sentenced to lose his ears as well as life imprisonment. Treated, like Prynne and Burton, as a martyr by London crowds, he was sent first to Launceston, then to St. Mary's Castle in the Scilly Isles. Burton, another Cambridge graduate, a Congregationalist at heart, had served at court, but fell out of favour when he denounced Laud to the King. His offence was the publication of works denouncing the bishops. His fate was the same as Bastwick's and his prisons, first Lancaster, then Guernsey. Burton rejoiced in his punishment in the pillory: "I never had such a pulpit before." It was said that a crowd of 100,000 Londoners gathered to bid him farewell and at every town he passed through, his arrival prompted demonstrations of sympathy and presentations of money to his wife.

These horrible punishments were one of Laud's most serious blunders. When he heard that crowds had turned the public ignominy of the pillory into a scene of sympathy for the victims, he said all three should have been gagged.

Another victim of Laud, and one of the most curious and quarrelsome men in an age which seemed full of them, was John Lilburne (c.1614–1657). He was not a University man but fell early under Bastwick's influence and appeared before the Star Chamber on a charge of printing and circulating unlicensed books, including one of Prynne's. He refused to take an oath before the court, and in 1638 was sentenced to be fined £500, pilloried, whipped and imprisoned. He denounced the bishops from the pillory, threw copies of some of Bastwick's tracts to the crowd, and in the end was gagged. Lilburne is remembered as a radical politician rather than a man of religious conviction but in the seventeenth century there was no division between the secular and the sacred such as exists today. Religion and politics were one, and Lilburne was a Separatist by conviction. During the Civil War he rose to prominence as a soldier, and greater prominence as one of the 'Levellers', a movement which will be considered in Chapter IV.

Henry Jacob has already been mentioned as the pastor of a Separatist church of the congregational pattern in Southwark. There was a Baptist Secession from his Church in 1638. The Seceders thought that believers only should be baptized by immersion, but that the administrator of the baptism did not need to have been baptized himself. This avoided John Smyth's problem. Further, because they were Calvinist in theology, this group called themselves 'Particular' Baptists, for only the elect could be of their number. This is the beginning of a second Baptist group, distinguished by their Calvinism as opposed to the Arminianism of the other body.

About this year Henry Jessey (1601–1663) joined the Southwark Church, and took over the pastorate when Henry Jacob adopted Baptist views and was immersed in 1645. The Southwark Church was constantly harried, and in 1640 several of its members imprisoned in the Tower.

Only a few names of the persecuted are known to us. Records are scanty. We know of those who published works or who appeared before the Courts or became eminent for other reasons. The names of the vast majority of God-loving men and women who suffered because they insisted on worshipping their Lord in ways other than those laid down by the State are known only to God. It is an astonishing thing, the courage of ordinary people, who could have had an easy life but chose rather to face harassment, fines, prison, mutilation or even death rather than do what their consciences denied. They had, it is true, been nurtured on Foxe's *Book of Martyrs* but it was to an earlier authority that they clung. "Who", asked the book they knew best, "shall separate us from the love of Christ? Shall tribulation, or distress, or persecution or famine, or nakedness, or peril, or sword?" Not even Laud could do that.

The King blundered from crisis to crisis. Popular unrest grew. Parliament, although not in office, became as implacable as the King. Laud's attempt, at the King's command, to enforce the prayer book on Scotland had disastrous consequences. The people rose in revolt and an army marched South to confront the King.

Charles' army, half-hearted, unwilling to fight in so doubtful a cause, was never engaged. Humiliating terms were agreed and the Scots, well-pleased, returned to their homes. In 1640, desperate for money, Charles convened Parliament again to find he could do nothing with a hostile body brilliantly led by John Pym (1585–1643). He dissolved it in despair. Popular riots were put down by savage punishments.

Again the Scots invaded England, and no serious effort was made to stop them. Charles was compelled to call the second Parliament of that year and in November 1640, the 'Long' Parliament assembled. On 11 December, 15,000 'citizens and inhabitants of London' presented to it the 'Root and Branch' Petition, which effectively demanded the total abolition of the existing form of government. Seven hundred clergy of the Church of England signed another petition demanding reform of the government. If the petitioners did not prove to have the majority of the Commons with them – and they did not – it still proved an awful warning, would the King but have listened. Yet another warning was the reappearance of Prynne and Burton, Bastwick and Leighton, the last now seventy-two. The marks of their sufferings horrified even those accustomed to brutality. Mobs prowled the London streets. Churches were damaged. Communion rails were smashed.

There was no crumb of comfort for the King. By the end of the year, both Strafford and Laud were in the Tower. Both were to die and both were judicial murders. Strafford had served his King and country with loyalty and distinction. He was hated because he was the King's chief minister, and all the loathing the disenchanted subjects felt for their King they heaped on his representative. In fact Strafford's conviction turned on the almost certainly deliberate misinterpretation of his words. He admitted that he had said to the King, "You have an army in Ireland you may employ here to reduce this Kingdom." In the context the words "this Kingdom" could only have referred to the rebellious Scotland. His enemies chose to believe that by "this Kingdom" he meant England. The King did all he could to save Strafford. He had written to him, "Upon the word of a King you shall not suffer," but he signed the death warrant in 1641 and the memory tortured his conscience for the rest of his life.

Charles could not, would not, compromise. It was not in his nature. It was his principle and he was to die for it, that God had created him King, and no man could deprive him of that supreme authority. Restlessly he negotiated for money and troops with Scotland, Ireland, France, Spain, and even with the Pope. Every move, secretly though it was negotiated, made war inevitable and his defeat also, for hampered by financial restraints and without a navy, which had declared for Parliament, Charles was on the weaker side.

With the Long Parliament in charge of England and Laud in the Tower, Separatists grew bolder. Those who had met in secret now met openly. From Holland and Germany and even from America those exiled by persecution came home in anticipation of religious freedom in their own land. Sects proliferated. Lay preachers set up conventicles. In 1641 Bishop Hall acidly wrote that in London alone there were "no fewer than four score congregations of several sectaries, instructed by guides fit for them, cobblers, tailors, felt-makers and such-like trash." The same year the Commons abolished episcopacy; the Lords rejected the move. The Star Chamber was dissolved; 'ship money' was declared void.

It was about this time that the term 'Separatist' fell into disuse. It had always been merely a negative term implying separation from the established Church. Since the establishment was now barely established and since much radical thought favoured a Church independent of the State, the term 'Independents' was used for them. These were the former Brownists, later to become Congregationalists.

Opposed to Independents were the Presbyterians, with a for-midably large representation in Parliament. Many of these were survivors of the old Puritans whose repudiation of the establish-ment rested largely in their hatred of the bishops. They were not Presbyterians in the Scottish sense. They had little hope at this point of creating a state religion on the Presbyterian pattern. They desired rather a substitution of Presbyters for Bishops, which they considered more Scriptural, and with the substitution a more simple church constitution, a more balanced power structure between ministry and laity, and the removal of the Catholic Survivals which they saw in the Anglican Church – a Geneva gown to replace the surplice, for instance. The Presbyterians, theologically, were strict Calvinists.

In addition to the Independents and Presbyterians, there were a growing number of 'sectaries', the word Bishop Hall sneeringly used above. The term was rarely used by the congregations themselves. These varied tremendously in doctrine, church government and practice. Some seem more political than religious, some adopted or more commonly were given particular names. These will be considered in more detail in Chapter V, for they flourished during the interregnum. Those accounted sectaries which have already been noted include the General Baptists, the Particular Baptists, the Anabaptists and their offshoots (the Seekers, for example), and the Levellers. It was during the Civil War that George Fox (1624–1691), the founder of the Quakers, who had for long sought his way to God through the ministries of all the existing Churches, finally found his peace.

In 1642 the Commons delivered to the King the 'Grand Remonstrance', a lengthy and detailed list of all their complaints against him together with their suggested remedies. The section on religion had caused the most trouble when the committee prepared it. It finally proposed a general synod of divines to consider the future of the English Church, including some from Europe, though it also proposed one matter on which all were agreed, a curb on the powers of bishops. It is typical of the inconsistency of these confused times that only a few years later, in order to gain the Scots to their cause, Parliament proposed a 'Solemn League and Covenant' with Scotland to abolish episcopacy in England and accept Presbyterianism.

There was never any hope of Charles repudiating his religion, however much, to save his throne, he appeared to consider it to the Scots or to Parliament. His private view to the Queen was his real intention: "I will neither quit episcopacy nor the sword which God hath given into my hands." It was indeed at the Queen's goading that on this occasion he rejected the remonstrance and tried to arrest the five most offending members of the Commons on grounds of treason. The Commons outwitted the King; their members were hidden in safety. London had daily been growing more dangerous. The King fled. On 22 August 1642, he raised his banner at Nottingham and the Civil War began. Meanwhile the strongly Puritan city of London fortified itself against its monarch, and the five offending members of Parliament prepared their followers for an English republic.

CHAPTER IV

Religious Toleration under the Commonwealth

OLIVER CROMWELL (1599–1658) WAS born in Huntingdon of strong Protestant stock. A lasting influence on him was his schoolmaster Thomas Beard (d.1632), a Puritan divine. Oliver was sent to the most currently puritan of Cambridge Colleges, Sidney Sussex, though he was only there a year because of his father's death. He married in 1620, became a member of parliament in 1628, and by 1638 had completed his religious conversion. He had passed through a stage of deep melancholy and described himself as "the chief of sinners". Embracing the full beliefs that his Calvinist mentors had taught him, he now accepted himself as one of the elect, chosen of God, a man under God's direct command on earth and promised heaven beyond. His election was always in Cromwell's mind, and in all things he saw God's providence. Thomas Beard had written *The Theatre of God's Judgments*, 1597, in which all history was revealed as the judgment of God on the wicked. Cromwell, as he made history, examined his conscience in the light of that judgment.

Until 1640, when he was returned to Parliament, this time for Cambridge, not Huntingdon, Cromwell made his mark on local matters as he fought against fen drainage and 'ship money', and assisted an ejected Puritan Lecturer to a benefice in the establishment. There was much for him to do in the 'Long' Parliament – help abolish the Star Chamber and the Court of

High Commission, impeach Strafford, imprison Laud, exclude bishops from the House of Lords, agree to triennial Parliaments and declare the existing Parliament indissoluble. A leading 'root-and-branch' man, Cromwell spoke also against the Prayer Book, and instigated a move to set up lectureships in every parish where there was a non-preaching minister.

As Charles I raised his banner in Nottingham in 1642, Cromwell was busy raising a troop of horse in Huntingdon. He picked men with scrupulous care "who upon a matter of conscience engaged in this quarrel". Discipline was strict; godliness was the first test. Traditionally, officers were chosen only from the higher ranks of society. Cromwell shocked conservative opinion by choosing men who served God, however base-born. He recruited every sincere Christian without distinction of party – Independents (followers of Browne's ideal, men later to be called Congregationalists), Presbyterians, Baptists, Episcopalians and a host of minor sects) – and he produced a remarkable army. Chillingworth said of the King's army, "their discourse and behaviour do speak Christians, but I can find little of God or godliness in our men," and Clarendon called it "a dissolute, undisciplined, wicked, beaten army, whose horse their friends feared, being terrible only in plunder and resolute only in running away." Clarendon called the Common-wealth army "an army whose sobriety and manner, whose courage and success made it famous and terrible all over the world". "Truly," said Cromwell, when the war was over, "I think he that prays best will fight best," and his trust in God's providence was illustrated by his assurance, "It matters not who is our commander-in-chief if God be so". As a soldier and commander, Cromwell was a genius. He effectively proved that thoroughly trained amateurs, provided they were sufficiently motivated by a passionate belief in their cause, could beat professionals.

As Cromwell fought for freedom, bitterness and rancour were present in Parliament. The Presbyterian majority were per-secuting the rest. Cromwell wrote to Speaker Lenthall after the successful siege of Bristol in 1645: "Presbyterians, Independents, all had here the same spirit of faith and prayer . . . They agree here, know no names of difference; pity it is it should be otherwise anywhere. All that believe have the real unity, which is most glorious because inward and spiritual . . . As for being united in forms, commonly called uniformity, every Christian will for peace sake study and do as far as conscience will permit; and from brethren, in things of the mind, we look for no compulsion but that of light and reason."

'Light and reason' were, however, vague guides. Some of the minor groups in this period had strange beliefs – often mixtures of the political and religious. The 'Levellers' were never large in numbers, and only influential at one brief point in history. They were ably and vociferously led by John Wildman (c.1621–1693) and John Lilburne, the pamphleteer and agitator, whose early brushes with authority were noted in Chapter III. Cromwell's first speech in Parliament was to defend Lilburne from his enemies, an almost impossible task as Lilburne's quarrelsome nature gave him a positive genius for making enemies. A distinguished soldier, in the Civil War he had fought for Parliament but was captured at Edgehill. Only the threats of reprisals prevented him from being shot. The term 'Leveller' was a name coined by the enemies of the movement who said that its aim was to level men's estates. In fact the Levellers, when the time grew ripe, were to put their ideas into a written plan. The plan included sovereign power being transferred to the House of Commons, the Commons to be elected by a wide suffrage of all except servants and paupers. There should be a redistribution of seats and annual or biennial parliaments. There should also be complete equality before the law and complete freedom of religion. Lilburne based his case on a total misunderstanding of supposed Anglo-Saxon liberties which had been taken away by 'Norman Colonels'. Some of the Levellers were devout men, like William Walwyn (c.1649), who preached brotherly love. Others, like John Wildman, were professional plotters.

The 'Fifth Monarchy Men' were an apocalyptic movement, whose concern was the end of the world and the second coming of Christ. Such groups have flourished in all ages, rarely with more than a handful of followers. From obscure texts they find prophecies and await their fulfilment. In the case of the Fifth Monarchy Men, they awaited fulfilment of Daniel 2:44: "And in the days of these Kings shall the God of heaven set up a kingdom which shall never be destroyed." There had been four great empires, the Assyrian, Persian, Macedonian and Roman. A fifth and last would arise when Christ would come again and reign with his saints for a thousand years. There were abortive and thoroughly silly risings by this small band of fanatics in 1657 and 1661, the latter mentioned in Chapter V.

'Diggers', sometimes treated as a branch of Levellers, was the name given to a group of about twenty men who, in 1649, began to cultivate a piece of common land in Surrey, grow vegetables, and give the results of their labours to the poor. The group were communistic in theory, some 250 years before Communism as a political theory became fully formulated. They were attacked by mobs and harassed by authority. Among their beliefs were the social equality of all, and the common owning of property. The religious part of their beliefs included a belief in God's intervention in human affairs and his approval of their aims as his will. Their chief prophet was Gerrard Winstanley (1648–1652). These men were not fanatics; they were devout political radicals, centuries ahead of their time.

'Muggletonians' were a sect founded about 1651 by Ludowicke Muggleton (1609–1698) and his cousin John Reeve (1608–1658). Muggleton, a bombastic man, was frequently in trouble, once pilloried and at least twice imprisoned. Reeve was a gentle, pious man who liked the Quakers; Muggleton detested them. Muggleton's extravagant tracts proclaimed the two men to be the witnesses of the Book of Revelation. He promulgated the convenient doctrine that the unforgivable sin was to disbelieve them. This curious sect, always small, survived until 1868.

'Ranters' were antinomians and pantheists – antinomians in believing that Christians are by grace set free from the need of observing any moral law, and pantheists in believing that all creation, animate and inanimate, is part of God. Their leaders were Joseph Salmon and Jacob Bauthumley. Both were markedly individualistic, and their more outrageous conduct, however blasphemous or immoral, they excused by their theories. St. Paul had met antinomians in New Testament times and had denounced them. It was unfortunate that Ranters were confused with Quakers. Their similarities were slight. Like Quakers, Ranters had no ministers. Further, while Quakers admitted the Bible only as a secondary authority and Ranters gave it no authority whatever, a mob could hardly be expected to understand this world of difference. Fox denounced the Ranters, as Baxter did, and some of them were persuaded to abandon their dangerous notions and become Quakers.

The Westminster Assembly of Divines, appointed by Parliament, began its work on 1 July 1643. Its duties were to revise the 39 Articles, establish a Presbyterian form of church government, organize ecclesiastical discipline and ordination of ministers, and to produce a directory of worship, a Confession of Faith, and larger and shorter catechisms. There were 149 members. Of the 119 ministers, the great majority were Presbyterians, a few Episcopalians and 5 Independents. The Independents, led by Thomas Goodwin (1600–1680), exerted an influence out of all proportion to their numbers. Before the Assembly met, they had published their own views in a pamphlet, 'Apologetical Narration'. The Scriptures alone, they said, should be their guide, not the thoughts of men. Church government should therefore be on the pattern of the primitive Church. Every company of believers, they said, who met to hear the Scriptures and celebrate the two Gospel sacraments, was a true Church. All were equal. They also set out their views on toleration. All Churches and all individuals should be free in their worship from political or ecclesiastical interference.

As long as Parliament had a great Presbyterian majority there was to be no toleration for any other Church. The situation changed only as the influence of the Army made itself felt, and vacancies in Parliament were filled by young officers from Cromwell's 'model' army. It was a tragedy that for the Presbyterian party, liberty from bishops and their ecclesiastical rule meant liberty only for Presbyterians and their rule. Presbyterian power was strengthened in 1646 when Parliament, anxious to gain Scottish support against the King, accepted the 'Solemn League and Covenant', and so officially accepted Presbyterianism in England. For a year or two, while the Army became more radical and more tolerant, Parliament and the Assembly grew more intolerant.

Their treatment of Roger Williams (c.1604–1683) was typical. Williams, an Oxford-educated Welshman, had fled to Salem, Massachusetts, and there preached religious toleration. His ideas included the entire separation of Church from State, the protection of all forms of religious faith, the repeal of all laws compelling worship and the abolition of tithes. These views made him so unpopular in Salem that at one point he had to flee to the forests and live for months with the Indians. He found toleration in the Providence area and, by this time a Baptist, returned to England in 1643 to get a charter for his colony. He received it, published a pamphlet on religious toleration, and hurried back to America. The Assembly publicly burned his pamphlet. Nor was Williams their only victim. Several Independents were ejected from their livings or lectureships and John Milton was hounded for his tract on divorce. John Goodwin (c.1594–1665) suffered for his Arminian views; Hanserd Knollys (c.1599–1691) for his Baptist ones.

The Army's plea for toleration has Cromwell's hand in it: "Are we to be dealt with as enemies because we come not to your way? Is all religion wrapped up in that or any form? Does that name or thing give the difference between those that are members of Christ and those that are not? We think not so. We say faith, working by love, is the true character of the Christian, and God is our witness, in whomsoever we see any of Christ to be, these we reckon our duty to love, waiting for a more plentiful effusion of the spirit of God to make all Christians to be of one heart." A personal letter of Cromwell's reminded Parliament of the debt it owed the Army and what the Army required in return: "He that ventures his life for the liberty of his country, I wish he trust God for the liberty of his conscience, and you for the liberty he fights for."

The Army had become a Church militant in the most literal sense. Every kind of Christian was in it, united for one purpose, God's purpose in freeing England from the tyranny of that 'man of blood', Charles Stuart. They held solemn prayer-meetings, ministers and laymen of every kind preached, studied the Scriptures, examined their consciences, encouraged each other in a life of faith. Chaplains were chosen of every religious persuasion, prominent among them Richard Baxter (1615–1691) and Hugh Peter (1598–1660).

Baxter was one of the greatest men of his age. A Presbyterian, he was no bigot, and as he grew older his catholicity grew wider. He became a chaplain to the army after visiting the troops a few days after the battle of Naseby. He found deep religious earnestness among them but the widest differences in theology. Some of the views expressed, he thought, dangerous extravagance, especially those views which demanded total separation of Church and State. A rather austere man, he also disliked the rough humour of the soldiers – some joked even on religious matters.

He stayed as chaplain to try to argue the extremists out of their beliefs and bring a unity to the diverse views around him. Cromwell was not warm to the attempt, for he was a confirmed tolerationist and feared that Baxter's well-intentioned interference would only lead to divisions among troops who valued their religious liberty above all things. Baxter never forgave Cromwell for what he considered slighting treatment, and his admirable autobiography is unfair to the man who became Protector. Nevertheless, Baxter said of his leader, "The Lord Protector is noted as a man of catholic spirit, desirous of the unity and peace of all the servants of Christ." Baxter lived long, long enough to refuse a bishopric at the Restoration, to be ejected from the establishment, to write devotional books of lasting merit, to suffer under Judge Jeffreys, and to welcome the glorious Revolution.

Baxter's greatest contribution to the life of succeeding ages was his ecumenical thought. He anticipated it in his 'Saints' Everlasting Rest' of 1650: "Those whom one house could not hold, nor one Church hold them, no, nor one kingdom neither; yet one heaven and one God may hold ... Oh, how canst thou find it in thy heart, if thou bear the heart and face of a Christian, to be bitter or injurious against thy brethren, when thou dost but once think of that time and place where thou hopest in the nearest and sweetest familiarity to live and rejoice with them for ever!" He asserted that all who accepted the Apostles' Creed, the Lord's Prayer and the Ten Commandments as summaries of their religion were truly Christians, and he insisted that even those who did not believe in Christ but who lived virtuous lives might be saved by Christ's redeeming power. Near the end of his life he believed that in his theology he had managed to bridge the absolute division between Arminians and Calvinists. As he lay dying he was asked how he was. "Almost well," he said, and slipped into eternity.

Another Army chaplain and an astonishing contrast to Baxter was Hugh Peter (1598–1660). Cornish-born and Cambridge-educated, he had been a Puritan lecturer in London, an Independent minister in Rotterdam, and had then gone to America to succeed Roger Williams as pastor in Salem. He returned to London in 1641. He was a fierce soldier as well as a chaplain, and had the reputation of having his Bible in one hand and a pistol in the other. Genial, tolerant, with a coarse humour combined with religious zeal, he was much loved by the troops. Cromwell trusted him totally, and the two men were in close confidence until the Protector's death. On the evening before the King's execution Peter preached a fiery vindication of it. Like Cromwell, Peter encouraged toleration and cared little that some of the soldiers carried such strange doctrines in their heads. Also like Cromwell, it was only when some of these extremists threatened to damage the godly rule that was over them by internal dissension that he saw the limits of toleration. Otherwise, his tolerance was all-embracing. He was one of those who pressed with Cromwell for the return of the Jews to England. He was also one of the few close enough to Cromwell to know the pressures on him. "The Protector sleeps upon no easy pillow," he said. "If 'twas such a matter for King Charles to be Defender of the Faith, the Protector has a thousand faiths to protect."

At the restoration Peter could have fled. He chose rather to stay and be butchered for his part in the death of the King, which he believed, like Cromwell, to be a work of 'providence and necessity'. On October 16, 1660, he was hanged, drawn and quartered at Charing Cross. In prison he had been troubled, "fearing that he should not go through his sufferings with comfort and courage". To add to his torment the Sheriff held him close to the hanging, drawing and quartering of his friend John Cook. Peter said to him, "Sir, you have here slain one of the servants of God before mine eyes, and have made me to behold it, on purpose to terrify and discourage me; but God hath made it an ordinance to me for my strengthening and encouragement." He died bravely.

Parliament in 1647 was busy trying to establish Presbyterianism, insisting that army officers take the Covenant, and being as bigoted in their demands as ever Laud had been. The year before, Cromwell had become a civilian and therefore a member of the Commons. The army, angry at the attitude of Parliament, appointed 'Agitators' to represent their case. The Levellers influenced the army, and the situation became dangerous. Mutiny was a real threat. Cromwell was sent by Parliament to appease them, but his position was made impossible by Parliament's plan to disband the army without back pay or pension. It was at this point that the army, possibly with Cromwell's knowledge, seized the King. Whatever reluctance Cromwell may have felt in being forced to take a side in the confrontation between Parliament and Army, he must have known that nobody but he could prevent yet another bloody struggle, and this time between two parts of the side that had won the war. Worse, the Army itself was bitterly divided. Cromwell himself and the other highest officers drew up a plan called 'Heads of Proposals', which was a new constitution to include biennial parliaments, a redistributed franchise, a modified episcopal state church with toleration outside it, the ending of monopolies, reform of the law and tithes, but retention of the King and the House of Lords. This was a compromise which most of the Puritan party should be able to accept, but it was not radical enough for the Levellers, who got some army support, and especially from the Agitators, for a rival plan, 'An Agreement of the People'. Cromwell sympathized with many of the views of the rival plan, but knew it would be totally unaccept- able to Parliament. In November of 1647 the Army Council met at Putney, and there the rival plans were debated. Cromwell said all forms of constitution were "but a moral thing . . ., dross and dung in comparison of Christ." He called for a prayer-meeting; another meeting was decided on; the King escaped, and all decisions were deferred.

By the end of the year the Army was reunited, but the breach between the Army and Parliament bitter. The Presbyterians denounced toleration from their pulpits and demanded the restoration of the King. They passed draconian laws to punish heresy and blasphemy. Meanwhile, Henry Ireton (1611–1651), Cromwell's friend, companion-in-arms and son-in-law, de- manded the execution of the King. Cromwell, who was in Pontefract, returned to London convinced that Charles' life could be spared. He was persuaded that this was impossible and, once his mind was made up, ensured that the King's death should be carried out as swiftly as possible.

The execution shocked the world. In England not only were royalists horrified but republican groups were also disgusted at what they considered an act of barbarous tyranny. Charles, his broken promises and life-long flouting of the laws of the realm forgotten, was well on the way to being canonized. The Levellers rose in revolt. Five of them were shot, the leaders arrested, and Lilburne and others spent some time in the Tower. Lilburne poured out a stream of invective from his imprisonment, including a demand for the impeachment of Cromwell on a charge of treason. Had Cromwell been the dictator his enemies claimed, Lilburne would have been silenced for ever. In fact he was acquitted of all charges against him and devoted the rest of his life to plaguing Cromwell. Nevertheless, the brief power of the Levellers was at an end.

It was during this same year, 1649, that Cromwell put down the Irish Rising with a ferocity that has always tarnished his great reputation for humanity and tolerance. It is true that the inhabitants of Drogheda and Wexford had refused to surrender and therefore by the laws of war had no claim on mercy; true that there was what Cromwell considered a just vengeance in his heart and a sense of deep political danger from an Ireland in revolt; it is also true that these massacres were tiny ones compared to the wholesale slaughter of Protestants on the continent. Nevertheless, elsewhere Cromwell had always been generous to defeated foes and always kept his own troops under strict control. On these two terrible occasions there was no mercy and no orders to show restraint. Those few days seemed a denial of the nature of a good and great man who before and after these events, professional fighter though he was, had always tempered the justice he felt God demanded with the mercy he also demanded. One can only assume that, in the spirit of most men of his age though out of character for him, Cromwell was briefly possessed of a bigoted intolerance, and in the blood-lust of battle watched his troops slaughter men and women, priests and children, with approval. It is ironical that Cromwell's ruthless, totally successful and cheap campaign in Ireland was counted to his glory by English Protestants, his consistent kindness to Catholics in England an aberration.

The Scottish rising followed swiftly upon the Irish one, and Cromwell crushed it at Dunbar in 1650 and Worcester in 1651. The victories left the victor in a curious position – the most powerful man in England and in the Government with no power to rule or control policy. It was as if England waited for him to take the power. Bitter factions broke out in the Commons, and war-weariness, the vacuum left by the death of the King, religious disputes, all seemed to Cromwell to be God's promptings to him. He dissolved the Long Parliament which had sat for twelve and a half years and he selected a new one and resigned his powers into their hands. It failed as its predecessor had done and, late in 1653,

Cromwell was proclaimed Lord Protector, effectively king without that title, which he consistently refused. His God-given task he conceived to be the uniting of the nation.

Cromwell's religious settlement was a compromise that disappointed all extremists, as it was bound to do. The Church was to be neither Episcopalian nor Presbyterian nor Independent. None of these bodies – almost all the religious groups of England – was pleased at that. There was some discrepancy between Cromwell's personal view and his solution for England. He had a personal detestation of bishops, no love of bigoted Presbyterianism, a deep sympathy for Independency, and a wide toleration. His solution for England was, consistent with his conception of the rule of God, to leave God solely in charge of all branches of his Church. Cromwell was not 'defender of the faith' but 'Protector' of all faiths, and he did not believe that he or any man could be an intermediary between a soul and God.

Toleration was not popular. Each group only wanted toleration for itself, persecution for others. To the stiff Scottish Church, Cromwell had said a month before Dunbar, "I beseech you in the bowels of Christ, think it possible you may be mistaken." A preacher himself, though never ordained, he was defending lay preaching when he acidly asked the same body: "Are you troubled that Christ is preached?" On the same point of lay preaching he had told the Irish clergy that the terms 'clergy' and 'laity' were unknown to the primitive church: "It was your pride that begat this expression, and it is for filthy lucre's sake that you keep it up, that by making the people believe they are not so holy as yourselves, they might for their penny purchase some sanctity from you."

Again and again Cromwell made private exertions on behalf of those persecuted. John Biddle (1615–1662) was charged with Unitarianism, that he did "maintain . . . in a dispute that Jesus Christ was not the Almighty and Most High God." Biddle was a thoroughly good man and a considerable scholar, who was protected by a number of Baptist and Independent friends when the religious wolves of the period prowled round him. His theology certainly denied the divinity of Christ. James I would have had him burnt as a heretic; Cromwell banished him for his own safety to the Scilly Isles and gave him a pension so that he did not want. "What greater hypocrisy," asked Cromwell, "than for those who were oppressed by the Bishops to become the greatest oppressors themselves so soon as this yoke was removed?" He became increasingly irritated by those who refused to accept his tolerance. "Is there not yet upon the spirits of men a strange itch? Nothing can satisfy them, unless they can put their fingers upon their brethren's consciences to pinch them there."

For one religious group Cromwell found it hard to get tolerance. The Quakers were universally detested. George Fox (1624–1691) had sought help from all the religious leaders of his day but he received none. He found the preachers, the Church government, even the Bible itself barriers between himself and God. He struggled for years. In the end the solution was almost absurdly simple. "Now the Lord God opened to me by his invisible power, that every man was enlightened by the divine light of Christ and I saw it shine through all; and they that believed in it came out of condemnation to the light of life . . . I was sent to turn people from darkness to light." God speaks direct to each human soul. Predestination was a false idea. All men can recognize and respond to the voice and the love of God within him. The light needs no particular time nor place, no sacraments, no priests, not even the Bible. Fox was a religious genius, a prophet, totally original, mystical. He had moral passion and deep spiritual insight. He was also very human – violent, pedantic, scornful and defiant, yet also saintly. The negative side of his teaching was a protest against the formalism, not of Laud, but of Genevan influence. The idolatry of the Bible, the hair-splitting arguments in theology and doctrine and Church government were all anathema to him. Two of his peculiarities, neither matters of deep import, caused the most offence of all. He would take no oath, for his word was his bond and the Scriptures prohibited it; he would take off his hat for no man, not for the King himself, not for a magistrate, for in the sight of God all men were equal. Whatever his rationalization of these practices, the first could only look like an evasion of the law, the second a deliberate slight to authority as well as gross discourtesy. Fox talked of his followers as 'The children of Light,' then 'Truth's Friends' and finally 'The Society of Friends', though a magistrate in 1650 sneeringly called them 'Quakers', and that is the name by which most have always called them. Perhaps their most remarkable teaching, baffling to contemporaries, was a refusal to fight. They must not resist persecution. Passive resistance was permissible; but they must never fight.

The first meeting of the Quakers was in 1652. They were persecuted ferociously. They were usually convicted of contempt of court when they refused to take the oath. Hundreds were imprisoned. Many died there. The persecution was in part because of the different nature of their teaching; no ministers or sacraments, no formal creed, no churches in any normal sense, no oaths, no doffing of hats, no fighting. The persecution was also, however, because of the fanatical nature of some of Fox's followers. James Naylor (c.1617–1660) was such a man. He fought in the Parliamentarian Army and was converted by Fox. A fine preacher and a strikingly handsome man, his head was turned by the blasphemous adulation of female followers, who kissed his feet, threw garments before his horse's feet, shouted 'Hosanna!' and addressed him as 'the lamb of God'. To tolerate this was very foolish, but nothing more. He was seized, convicted of blasphemy, and sentenced to be flogged, pilloried, branded, his tongue bored, and imprisoned indefinitely. Cromwell was too late to save him from the first part of the hideous punishment, but he protested furiously. On whose authority had this injustice been done? he demanded. Cromwell also rescued Fox and his followers from imprisonment in Launceston in 1656 and employed Quakers in his own household. "Shall I," he asked protesters, "disown them because they will not put off their hats?" Whenever he could he tried to help them, but it was impossible to do much for the lunatic fringe of the movement who daubed themselves with dung and ran naked through the streets crying, "Woe to the bloody city!" There were usually more than a thousand Quakers in prison during the Protectorate.

Cromwell exercised control over the church by two bodies – 'The Committee of Triers' and the 'Lay Commissioners'. The Triers were a group of 33 divines and 10 laymen. Most were Independents; there were several Presbyterians and a few Baptists. Their duties were to seek out suitable candidates for benefices and lectureships. The lay commissioners were to eject "scandalous, ignorant and insufficient ministers and schoolmasters". This body was made up of 15 to 30 laymen in each county, their recommendations considered by 8 to 10 clerical assessors. Catholics were absolutely excluded but Episcopalians were acceptable if they did not use the Prayer Book. Calvinist theology was expected of all. Such a system sounds one that would founder because of the subjective judgment of the members of the two committees. In fact, at least according to Baxter, who was cool towards Cromwell's reign, it worked well. "The truth is, that though their authority was null, and though some few over-busy and over-rigid Independents among them were too severe against all that were Arminians, and too particular in enquiring after Evidences of Sanctification in those whom they examined, and somewhat too lax in their admission of unlearned and erroneous men, that favoured Antinomianism and Baptism; yet to give them their due, they did abundance of good to the Church: they saved many a congregation from ignorant, ungodly, drunken teachers . . . and that sort of ministers that either preached against a holy life, or preached as men that never were acquainted with it; all those that used the ministry but as a common trade to live by, and were never likely to convert a soul; all these they usually rejected; and in their stead admitted of any that were able serious preachers, and lived a godly life, of what tolerable opinion soever they were."

The astonishing fact is that between 6,000 and 7,000 Church of England priests were ejected from their livings. It would appear to be massive persecution, but not according to Baxter. "I must needs say, that in all the Counties where I was acquainted . . . 6 to 1 at least (if not many more) that were sequestered by the Committee, were by the oaths of witnesses proved insufficient, or scandalous, or both; especially guilty of drunkenness or swearing; and those that being able, godly preachers, were cast out for the war alone, as for their opinions' sake, were comparatively very few." If Baxter is right the state of the clergy of the day must have been deplorable.

Cromwell ruled the country by dividing it into eleven districts, a Major-General over each, to command the local militia as well as his own regiment. In addition, each commander was expected to keep a close watch over local government. Magistrates hated them and felt their own powers diminished. They were resented even more by the landed gentry, whose powers had always been great in fact if not in theory. The Major-Generals – and some of them were of lowly birth – infuriated local opinion when they interfered in such matters as local sports, and when they punished offenders for drunkenness, blasphemy, and Sabbath-breaking. However well-intentioned, the system made for bitterness, and was one of the chief reasons why the Restoration was so welcome. A law of 1650 even made adultery punishable by death, though juries, no doubt conscious of their own catalogue of sins, refused to find the accused guilty. Goodness by compulsion is difficult to maintain; the suppression of vice was one of the Puritans' least successful ambitions. They would have done better to note how Christ dealt with sinners in the Scriptures, when he asked the sinless to cast the first stone. Indeed, the reign of the Major-Generals made Cromwell's régime hateful to most Englishmen.

The Protector's greatest problems were, as one would expect, with the vociferous and bigoted godly. "When shall we have men," he asked, "of a universal spirit? Everyone desires to have liberty, but none will give it." He wanted a union of all godly men – "Scots, English, Jews, Gentiles, Presbyterians, Independents, Anabaptists and all." Sir Harry Vane said in 1656: "Since the fall of the Bishops and persecuting presbyteries, the same spirit is apt to rise in the next sort of clergy that can get the ear of the magistrate." Nevertheless, Cromwell appointed court chaplains from a variety of religious opinions, and some of them were distinguished men. Thomas Goodwin (1600–1680) was a graduate of Cambridge, received orders, and was then successively lecturer and incumbent of Trinity Church in Cambridge. He became an Independent, resigned his living, was pastor of an Independent Church in London, and had to flee from Laud's persecutions to Holland. He returned to London in 1640 and in 1649 was appointed a chaplain to the Council of State. The following year he was made President of Magdalen College, Oxford. A first-class scholar, he was also a pastor and one of a catholic spirit. He persuaded John Howe, though a Presbyterian, to attend his weekly meetings. It was Goodwin who got Cromwell's agreement to a synod of Independents at which they might discuss a confession of faith. A few days before the Synod met, however, Cromwell died.

John Owen (1616–1683) had accompanied Cromwell on his campaigns in Ireland and Scotland. He had been driven out of Oxford by Laud and had been hounded by him until the Archbishop's arrest. An Independent, he was a very able theologian. Like Thomas Goodwin, he was preferred to high office, that of Dean of Christ Church, Oxford, and Vice-Chancellor of the University. He grew a little apart from Cromwell when he pressed the Protector to make provision for uniformity of creed. This Cromwell rightly resisted; the attempt would only lead to dissension and rancour. Owen published a number of theological works and several tracts demanding religious liberty. His best remembered work is *Of the Work of the Holy Spirit in Prayer.* Lord Clarendon offered him high preferment if he would remain within the Church of England but, true to his conscience, he preferred ejection.

John Howe (1630–1705) was a close intimate of Cromwell's. A Presbyterian, he was contentedly looking after his pastorate in Devon, but Cromwell brought him to London as a chaplain. He became Fellow and Chaplain of Magdalen College, Oxford, until his ejection after the restoration. His most considerable work was *The Living Temple of God*, written in 1675 long after his ejection. Its theme was the destruction of the soul by earthly lusts and its regeneration by Christ. It is also a defence of orthodox Puritanism against Deism, the notion that God, having created the world, interfered no further. Deism is a rejection of the idea of God's providence beyond creation and the laws he laid down then. It was John Howe who, when asked by the Bishop of Exeter after the restoration how reordination could hurt him, replied, "It hurts my understanding, nothing can have two beginnings . . . I am sure I am a minister of Christ, I cannot begin again to be a minister."

Other distinguished men who might have suffered under the Stuarts flourished, though John Goodwin, already mentioned, was an Arminian, a rarity among the Puritans of this period, and would have been less objectionable than most. He had been ejected from his living by the Presbyterians in 1645, and had founded an Independent Church in London which had a large following. Cromwell's protection saved him from the further persecution his unpopular views would have brought upon him. He was therefore able to hold his pastorate until Cromwell's death and, under the Restoration, was ejected, and had to manage an eating-house as a means of livelihood.

Hanserd Knollys (c.1599–1691), also mentioned above, was a Baptist. He was the son of a Lincolnshire rector, had graduated at Cambridge, taken orders, and was appointed to a living. He had resigned because of scruples, became a Separatist, and was imprisoned under Laud's persecutions. He fled to America, was influenced by Roger Williams, became a Baptist, and returned to England in 1641. He preached in the Parliamentarian army and was allowed freedom from persecution from 1645 to 1660 despite hostility from the Presbyterians.

The greatest of the Independents after Cromwell himself was undoubtedly John Milton (1608–1674), arguably England's greatest poet after Shakespeare, and propagandist of the Commonwealth. He was Cromwell's Latin (Foreign) Secretary during the Protectorate. His reputation was already established as a great poet by 1640 when he began to publish pamphlets against episcopacy. In 1641 appeared his 'Reason of Church Government urged against Prelacy' in which he asserted that God had ordered one form of Church government, Presbyterianism, and man had set up another, Episcopacy. He changed his views later, however, to believe that "New presbyter is but old priest writ large". Even in his work of 1641 he appears to be moving towards Independency: "When every good Christian, thoroughly acquainted with all those glorious privileges of sanctification and adoption which render him more sacred than any dedicated altar or element, shall be restored to his right in the Church, and not excluded from such place of spiritual government as his Christian abilities and his approved good life in the eye and testimony of the Church shall prefer him to, this and nothing sooner will open his eyes to a wise and true valuation of himself ... Then would the congregation of the Lord soon recover the true likeness and visage of what she is indeed, a holy generation, a royal priesthood, a saintly communion, the household and city of God."

In 1644 Milton published his 'Areopagitica', perhaps his finest work in prose, a demand for freedom of the press. In February, 1649, a fortnight after the King's execution, appeared 'The Tenure of Kings and Magistrates': "proving that it is lawful, and hath been held so through all ages for any, who have the power, to call to account a tyrant or wicked King, and after due conviction to depose and put him to death." Few titles have been so informative. His republicanism found full explanation in his first and second 'Defence of the People of England'. No King ever had so able a propagandist as Cromwell had in Milton, for Milton wrote in absolute conviction and was a writer of genius. Milton was a close friend of Andrew Marvell, the other great poet of the

republican side, a man of great wit and charm. It is curious how
the image of Puritanism still suggests philistinism and a gloomy
hatred of pleasure. Cromwell loved music and poetry, patronized
Milton and Marvell, Waller, Wither and Dryden, as well as
painters and sculptors. He laughed uproariously when amused,
he indulged in horseplay. He could be wonderfully happy company. Milton was so fastidious in appearance that he had been
called 'the lady of Christ's' when at Cambridge. Cromwell, on
the other hand, astounded contemporaries by his humble dress.
Unlike the kings, who wore silk and ermine and gorgeous robes,
he usually wore "plain cloth suit, which seemed to have been
made by an ill country tailor".

Milton's greatest work was still to be written when Cromwell
died, but his service during the Commonwealth was very great.
He had supplied it with a defence argued by a first-class mind in
magnificent prose. He had also, in his championship of unlicensed
printing and religious liberty, left legacies for future generations.
One day there would be a free press: "Let truth and falsehood
grapple; who ever knew truth put to the worse in a free and open
encounter?" One day the battles of the Civil War, fought against
tyranny, would bring religious tolerance. In Milton's day,

> Yet much remains
> To conquer still; peace hath her victories
> No less renowned than war, new foes arise
> Threatening to bind our souls with secular claims:
> Help us to save free conscience from the paw
> Of hireling Wolves whose gospel is their maw.

Under Cromwell the young Free Churches had a toleration
they would not enjoy again for nearly 250 years. It is tragic irony
that through their own internecine warfare persecution still went
on, however much deplored by the Protector. It was his own deep
conviction of being elect of God that had guided him since his
conversion. All he did was an attempt to fulfil God's will on earth,
guided by providence. It was part of God's plan, so Cromwell
believed, that each group of worshippers could meet in the name
of God, bound by a covenant with him and each other to walk in his
ways and love one another because God first loved them. It was no
part of God's plan that his church on earth should be subject to
harsh laws which bound all to a rigid uniformity, punished those

who dared to differ by imprisonment or death, and interposed between man and God intermediaries of a special class, the most elevated of them men of great wealth and magnificence. Church democracy began in the free churches and it flourished during the Protectorate. It was enjoyed for a very brief period, but it was cherished as an ideal which one day might come again. In succeeding generations free churchmen remembered the days when they had freedom to worship as they chose and nursed the hope that it would return.

Cromwell was exhausted by the cares of state. "Our rest we expect elsewhere," he had said. He died on 3 September 1658, the anniversary of the victories of Dunbar and Worcester. His last prayer was, "Lord, though I am but a miserable and wretched creature, I am in covenant with thee through grace." He thought of his people; "Thou hast made me, though very unworthy, a mean instrument to do them some good, and thee service; and many of them have set too high a value upon me, continue and do good for them." He prayed also, with prophetic insight, for those who would despoil his grave: "Pardon such as desire to trample upon the dust of a poor worm, for they are thy people too." So Cromwell, "our chief of men" as Milton had called him, died when England most needed him. His son Richard succeeded him briefly, found the reins of government too heavy for his hands, and General Monck used the army that had built the Commonwealth to destroy it. Presbyterians and royalists formed a coalition to aid the restoration of Charles II. The Presbyterians were naïve; their trust in the declaration of Breda led to their own destruction. It seemed as if Puritanism had lost. In fact, Puritanism, and its expression in the Free Churches, is an ineradicable part of the English conscience. It would always survive. Equally, though monarchy was restored, the theory of the divine right of kings had gone for ever, and it had been established that in any struggle between King and Parliament, Parliament would win in the end.

CHAPTER V

The Stuarts Return, Toleration Departs

IN THE DECLARATION OF BREDA Charles II, waiting in exile, gave his solemn promise that "we do declare a liberty to tender consciences; and that no man shall be disquieted, or called in question, for differences of opinion in matters of religion which do not disturb the peace of the Kingdom; and that we shall be ready to consent to such an act of parliament, as, upon mature deliberation, shall be offered to us, for the full granting that indulgence."

If there was one thing the English should have learned from the reigns of the first two rulers of that dynasty, it was never to trust the word of a Stuart. In fact, although, as the chapter heading suggests, when the Stuarts returned toleration departed, it was no fault of the King's. Ironically, though Charles II held the doctrine of his divine right as surely as his father and grandfather, he was also a very tolerant man and devoted what liberty his pleasures allowed him to attempting to get toleration for churches other than the establishment, especially the Catholic community.

What Charles said at Breda he meant; the dishonouring of the promise was the work of Parliament, the most Anglican one for many years. It was more than this, however, for Parliament represented a majority opinion, which was weary of 'godly rule.' The godly rule had failed because the noble part of Puritanism had been hidden under some of its flaws. Hobbes listed some of the doctrines which led to the downfall of the Commonwealth: "that every private man is judge of good and evil actions", "that whatsoever a man does against his conscience is sin", "that faith and sanctity are not to be attained by study and reason but by supernatural inspiration." While every one of these doctrines is defensible, from the mouths of the not inconsiderable number of false prophets, they led to endless and bitter dissensions. More practically, the chief flaws of the Puritans, with all their greatness taken into account, were a conviction that justice is greater than mercy, and that the pleasures of the flesh are inherently evil. These were the flaws that made much of England rejoice when the godly rule was over.

It was for the same reason that many influential Englishmen were prepared to overlook the utter dissoluteness of their new King. His series of mistresses was acceptable to the court, costly as it was, and most men with no pretensions to virtue love a rake, possibly because by comparison their own modest virtues shine the brighter. For the rest Charles was witty, charming, forgiving, easy-going, lazy, clever and devious. He had the skill and the cunning to grapple with an exceedingly difficult series of parliaments and win – in the end by doing without them.

He began well by his generosity to his enemies, only insisting on the death of the regicides when many of his bloodthirsty advisers urged him to a wide revenge. Only to one man, Sir Harry Vane, not one of the regicides but an extreme republican, he declined mercy. "Certainly he is too dangerous to live," he said to Clarendon. By the standards of the day it was not an unreasonable decision, though it was also true that Charles had promised to spare his life.

The King had not owed his restoration to the Anglicans, and he always wished to repay his debt to others. True, his temperament was utterly alien to Puritan thought and he said to Lauderdale in 1660 that Presbyterianism was no religion for a gentleman. Later in his reign he "always lamented that common and ignorant persons were allowed to read" the Bible, for "this liberty was the rise of all our sects, each interpreting according to their vile notions and to accomplish their horrid wickedness," but even without his Catholic sympathies – and liberty for Catholics meant liberty for sectaries – Charles was a generous man.

Of the more than 9,000 benefices, more than 2,000 were held by Presbyterians and nearly 400 Independents held benefices at the time of the Restoration. The Presbyterians had most to hope for. They were effectively the church in power during the inter-regnum, and their hope was that a compromise over their points of difficulty might allow them 'comprehension' within the restored Church of England – a full belonging which took account of their distinctive differences. The Independents (about to be known as Congregationalists) rested on the promise of toleration. So did the Baptists. The Quakers, as always, had most to fear. Even under Cromwell's benevolent dictatorship, they had known the bitterness of persecution. The combined numbers of all these groups must have amounted to many thousands, most of them of humble origin.

The King, as an immediate concession, appointed ten leading Presbyterians as his chaplains, and he also agreed to the setting up of the Savoy Conference, a meeting of twelve bishops and twelve Presbyterian ministers, to consider the possibility of compre-hension of Presbyterianism within the Church of England. It began its work in April 1661, and seemed doomed from the start. It was not a meeting of equals, as the King had intended and the Presbyterians hoped. The bishops from the start asserted their supremacy and subtly forced the Presbyterians into being sup-plicants. Nor did Baxter, the leading Presbyterian and a man of great gifts, acquit himself well. On the contrary, he was stiff and unyielding and allowed any possibility of success to slip from his grasp. The Conference dragged on until the strongly Anglican Parliament did its work for it.

This work has been called the 'Clarendon Code' after Charles' chief minister. It was not a code but a series of punitive measures against those who would not conform to the laws of the Church of England. It was in five sections. The first was the Corporation Act of 1661. It prohibited any, other than members of the Church of England, from holding any official civil or ecclesiastical posi-tion. The Act of Uniformity, 1662, spelt out in detail what the Church of England required of its clergy. First, all ministers who had not already been episcopally ordained were to be reordained. Secondly, ministers must declare "unfeigned assent and consent" to the Prayer Book in its entirety, as "in all things agreeable to the word of God." Thirdly, ministers were required to 'unswear' the oath they had sworn to the Solemn League and Covenant. In 1662, an Act was passed specifically against the Quakers, for they, remarkably, were the most feared and hated of all.

There were extremists, and authority made the eccentric violence of a few the excuse for persecuting the many. In 1661 there was an uprising, the last of its kind, by the Fifth Monarchy Men. As was noted in Chapter IV, this group was never numerically large or politically powerful. Thomas Venner, a wine cooper by trade, was one of their preachers. He had spent some years in Massachusetts but returned to England where his preaching led him to the Tower. On release, he took up preaching again and set out with fifty ill-armed followers to set up the reign of Jesus. A number were killed by troops and the leaders arrested. It was a pathetic fiasco. Venner was hanged, drawn and quartered. The movement was crushed. Its importance lay in the blame such incidents conferred on others. It was well known that the Fifth Monarchy Men had close associations with the Quakers. It was forgotten that pacifism was a part of the true Quaker faith, though it is also true that at least some Quakers were prepared to fight. The vast majority of all the non-conforming Protestant groups wanted nothing of the King and Parliament except the right to worship God in their way. The Act against the Quakers nevertheless proclaimed severe penalties for meeting, and transportation for a third offence.

One of the excuses for the next part of the Clarendon Code was a series of relatively minor insurrections in Yorkshire and Durham. The Conventicle Act of 1664 was a temporary Act made more adamantine by the Conventicle Act of 1670. It made illegal, gatherings for religious purposes of five or more persons over the age of sixteen. A first offence led to a £5 fine. The third offence meant transportation, usually to Barbados. The 'Five-Mile Act' was the abbreviated name given to the Act for Restraining Nonconformists from inhabiting towns. Hereafter all preachers and teachers who refused the oaths, were forbidden to go within five miles of any town. These, and any who refused to attend worship at a parish church, were prohibited from teaching either as schoolmasters or private tutors under a penalty of £40. The Test Act of 1673 was an extension of the Corporation Act. It prohibited Nonconformists from occupying any government post – civil, naval or military.

From this time forward all excluded from the Church of England were referred to as 'Nonconformists' or 'Dissenters.' Both are negative terms. Such men chose not to 'conform' to the

John Wyclif (c.1328–1384)

The Burning of Master John Rogers Vicar of St Sepulchers & Reader of St Pauls in London

John Rogers (c.1500–1555). The first Marian martyr, burnt
4 February, 1555, from Fox's *Book of Martyrs*

Nicholas Ridley (c.1500–1555)

Hugh Latimer (c.1485–1555)

and portion of their in heritaunce
But tell them from me: that we feare
not men who can but kille, the bo
dye : because we feare that god who cã
cast both body and soule into vnquen-
chable fire. And tell them alsoe this.
That the more bloode the churche
loseth the mor lif and blood it gets
When the fearfull sentence pronounced againt the persecuters of the truth
is executed vpon them, I would then
gladly know, wheter they who go ab-
ont thus to sheade our bloode : or we
whose blood cyeth for vengeance. a-
gainst them, shall hau: the worst ende
of the staffe. We are sure to posses our
soules in everlasting peace, when soever we leav this earthly tabernacle : &
in the mean tyme we know that an
haire of our heade can not falle to the
grounde without the wil of our heaven
lye father : who of his greate mercye
loueth vs in, and for our Saviour Crist
Iesus, and that with a loue as farr pas-
ing the loue of a naturall father towarde
his children , as he who so loueth vs.
excelleth all earthly parents. This per-
suation

The penultimate page of the last Mar-
Prelate tract, found in John Penry's
possession when he was arrested

Heare o King, and dispise not the
counsell of the poore, and let their
complaints come before thee.
The King is a mortall man, not God
therefore hath no power over the immortall
soules of his subiects, to make lawes &
ordinances for them, and to set spirituall
Lords over them.
If the King have authority to make
spirituall Lords & lawes, then he is
an immortall God, and not a mortall
man.
O King be not seduced by deceivers
to sinne so against God whome thou
oughtest to obey, nor against thy
poore subiects who ought and must
obey thee in all thinges with body
life and goods, or els let their lives
be taken from the earth.

God Save the Kinge

Spittlefield
neare London.

Tho: Helwys.

Tract of Thomas Helwys of 1611, with
his personal message addressed to
James I

John Milton
(1608–1674), by
W. Faithhorne,
1670

Fresco of the embarkation of the Pilgrim Fathers, 1620

Oliver Cromwell
(1599–1658), after
S. Cooper

Satire of Cromwell preaching in a church

Richard Baxter
(1615–1691)

William Kiffin
(1616–1701)

Titus Oates
(1649–1705), by
R. White, 1679

R. White ad vivum   delin et Sculp

TITUS OATES.
Anagramma
TESTIS OVAT.

Judge Jeffreys
(1648–1689)

A QVAKER

With face of braʃʃe, this woman that you see
moʃt Impudently doth afirm, that ʃhee:
The mind of God, in all poynts, more doth knovv,
then from the Sacred Scriptures, ere could flovv,
Preʃumptuous vvretch: it vvere more fit that ʃhee,
at home ʃhould keepe, and mind hir hovvʃevviʃey.
And if more meanes to live on, vvorke for bread,
then idlye goaʃop vvith hir maʃet head.
Their light vvithin doth so pervayle,
it makes them hot about the fayle.
Except eʃpund that poynt doth cleare,
they could them ʃelve in peeces teare.

Quakers Satirized. A common charge against them was that they took women and girls away from their God-provided element, the home

George Fox (1624–1691) preaching at Market Cross, Carlisle, 1655

And the Magistrates Wives had said, That if I came there, they would pluck the Hair from off my Head; Nevertheless I went upon the Market-Cross, and there declared unto them That they should put away all Lying and Cheating, and keep to Yea and Nay and speak the Truth one to another. The Throng was so great, it being Market-day, that the Serjeants could not get to me, nor the Magistrates Wives come at me. I passed away quietly

G Fox his Journal. Carlisle 1655

Act of Uniformity; they 'dissented' from it. Collectively, therefore, such men and women will be called 'Nonconformists' in these pages. Individually, they were slowly assuming their individual identities – Presbyterians, Congregationalists, Baptists (of two kinds), Quakers, etc. 'Sects' or 'Sectaries' were loose terms to describe the minor groups – all excepting the Church of England, the Presbyterians, and the Congregationalists, though the latter were sometimes given those labels.

Vainly Charles tried to avoid the tragic results of these laws by asking Parliament to allow him by royal prerogative to exempt those he favoured. Parliament was implacable. On 24 August 1662, the Act of Uniformity came into force. By an embarrassing coincidence for the Church of England, it was the anniversary of St. Bartholomew's Day when thousands of Huguenots had been massacred in Paris in the sixteenth century. Puritan propagandists made much of that. Roughly a fifth of the clergy of the Church of England were ejected from their livings for conscience sake. They were as able a company as they were noble. Of the 1,603 ejected, 1,285 were University graduates. Of those who remained, some were men of principle; more than a few were men whose consciences were not tender, poor ornaments of any church.

The sufferings of many who left were great. Their flocks would be untended. Most had no means of support whatever. Some even lived by begging. The Act had left them no choice. To have offered themselves for reordination would have been to declare their original ordination invalid, and they could not subscribe to every word of the Prayer Book when they had so often found it conflicted with the Scriptures. Men of principle, how could they unswear the solemn oath of the Solemn League and Covenant? They moved into darkness. The only light that remained to them, many of them not knowing how they would feed their families, was the light of the gospel by which they had lived and which now was their only hope. It had always been God's practice, they could have argued to themselves for comfort, to bring good out of evil. That was one of the supreme messages of the Cross, that from the wickedest deed in history had come man's salvation. Yet in those dark days they could hardly have foreseen what possible good could come.

One good was the establishment of the Dissenting Academies – schools and colleges run by and for Nonconformists who were

denied access to schools and universities. Between 1663 and
1690 more than twenty flourished to produce men of the calibre
of Defoe (1660–1731) and Samuel Wesley (1662–1735), father
of John Wesley, Archbishop Secker (1693–1768), Bishop Butler
(1692–1752), and Isaac Watts (1674–1748). Philip Doddridge
(1702–1751), distinguished Congregationalist, was the Principal
of a Dissenting Academy in Northampton.

What could not possibly have been seen as an advantage at the
time was that, by their very ejection, the Nonconformists became
officially recognized. True, the recognition took the form of
making them second-class citizens, but at least they now had an
identity. This identity was to prove an immense force in the
history of England. The Puritan tradition was passed on in them.
The 'nonconformist conscience,' with its passionate concerns for
freedom of worship, standards of decency, love of learning, social
conscience, and personal religion, is observable throughout the
subsequent history of England. It wished to remain within the
ambit of the Church of England. When this was denied it, it yet
remained in the nation as the steel that stiffened its framework, as
its conscience in matters of social responsibility. Succeeding
centuries were to see the power of Nonconformity.

Penalties imposed on Nonconformists were relative to the
supposed political danger. The severest penalties were rarely
imposed after the Restoration. Persecution, however, there was,
and for all sections.

Among the Baptists, for instance, William Kiffin (1616–1701)
had been a member of Henry Jacob's church in Southwark and
had followed him from Congregationalism into Baptism in 1641.
In 1643 he had entered the woollen trade with Holland and, over
a period of years, had become very wealthy. Persecuted by the
ecclesiastical authorities until the interregnum, he lived at peace
under Cromwell's régime and was M.P. for Middlesex from 1656
to 1658. He was arrested in 1660, freed as no charge was brought
against him, twice unjustly arrested for plotting, twice successfully
had interviews with the King on behalf of persecuted Baptists,
and was wise enough to give the King £10,000 rather than, in
answer to a royal request, lend him five times that sum. Later he
was again arrested, this time for complicity in the Rye House Plot,
in which he had no part whatever, and lived to see two of his
grandsons executed for their part in the Monmouth rebellion. He

refused to deal with James II when the latter tried to buy his support by a promise of toleration. Kiffin offended no more than in being a Baptist. Colonel Hutchinson (1615–1664), another Baptist, had at least been one of Charles I's judges. It was for this, notwithstanding his exemplary life, that he was imprisoned and barbarously treated until he died in 1664.

Like Kiffin, Hanserd Knollys (c.1599–1691) was a distinguished Baptist. He had been a clergyman but resigned his living by 1636 and fled to New England to escape persecution. Left in peace during the interregnum, he also was arrested periodically during the Restoration, though his offence was only nonconformity. It was also on those grounds alone that Joseph Wright, a Baptist minister, spent twenty years in Maidstone gaol.

The most distinguished of all the persecuted Baptists was John Bunyan (1628–1688). It is interesting to speculate how much, if anything, we would have known of his life had he not become a famous author as well as a Baptist preacher. We would probably have known very little. By that token we may assume that there were other nonconformist preachers of Bunyan's devotion and selflessness and courage of whom we have never heard.

Bunyan's early ministry was noted in Chapter IV. He was imprisoned in 1660 and remained there for twelve years. He was released in 1672, imprisoned for six months three years later, and released again. He died just before the revolution of 1688.

His first work, *Grace Abounding to the Chief of Sinners*, 1666, written in prison, is an astonishing work which, had he written nothing more, would have given him an important niche in literary history. It tells the story of his conversion. It reveals the heart of the Puritan agonizing over his sins and struggling towards God. To such a man, a minor fault is a monstrous insult to his maker. There is no more honest or self-revealing document, nor a more moving description of a man's naked soul pleading with his God.

The first part of *Pilgrim's Progress* was written during his second imprisonment. This masterpiece is incomparable, for no one else has ever written as Bunyan did. He had no university education. He knew only one book – the Bible. It is as if he had saturated himself so deeply in it that his allegory, refined by his thought, had come from the heart of the scriptures and been reborn in a pure seventeenth century form. The allegory itself was no new thing. It had been used many times. What was new was Bunyan's passionate imagination working in the labyrinth of his own dealings with God and using the magnificent prose of the King James Bible to do it, the whole set in Restoration England. It is a sombre, frightening book; it was a sombre, frightening age. It was a mad world where those who cared most for the spirit of prayer were in the prisons, and those who cared most for the form of prayer were in the pulpits. His own soul's destiny was the subject of *Grace Abounding. The Life and Death of Mr. Badman* teaches through example and, as Greek tragedy did, through catastrophe. *Pilgrim's Progress* leads to the Eternal City, and Bunyan wrote it to take his readers on the pilgrimage with him. Few men knew suffering better than he. On the journey was much doubt and disappointment and suffering, but at the end of the journey was the Celestial City, and the trumpet would sound for them all on the other side. The story is as naïve as it is profound. The book, incredibly in that age, sold 100,000 copies by the time of Bunyan's death. Stranger still, and this is unique, it was a book initially read only by and to the poor and simple, which worked its way up to the most learned, and was finally accepted by them as a work of literary genius.

Bunyan the pastor tends to be forgotten because of Bunyan the author. He was a pastor of surpassing kindness. He was not bigoted in doctrine. "Christ, not baptism, is the way to the sheepfold," he said. He died through an illness brought on by his insistence on visiting sick members of his flock when he was ill himself.

Of the Congregationalists some, like John Owen, had private means, and exiled themselves on their estates. John Howe found shelter with a Puritan family. These two found comfort in their writings. Some others managed to support themselves in secular occupations. Many, however, lived pitiably. One layman, now old and blind and so distinguished that the authorities thought it wisdom to ignore him, lived in a cottage in Buckinghamshire. This was John Milton (1608–1674). He had started *Paradise Lost* before the Restoration, but had all the time in the world to finish it now and sell the rights for £5. The theme, the battle between heaven and hell for the soul of man, must have seemed an appropriate one. He had lived through the hopes of the godly rule, when man should have lived in obedience to God alone, and he had seen how man had failed to meet the challenge on earth. In his long, dark exile he, like Bunyan, voiced the Puritan's longings.

The Presbyterians had had the greatest hopes and therefore the greatest loss. Their great days during the interregnum would never, it seemed, come again. Some of them became Congregationalists. Most struggled on under the punitive laws which branded them Nonconformists when so few alterations could have made them conformers. The most eminent of them was Richard Baxter. In his *Saints' Everlasting Rest* of 1650 he wrote that one of the joys of heaven would be to "rest from all our sad divisions and un-Christianlike quarrels with one another." But on earth Baxter could not tamper with his conscience, and he refused the proffered bishopric. Just before the Restoration, Baxter had published his *Call to the Unconverted.* Now exiled, after a long life of faithful service he too wrote for his consolation, and that of others, *Now or Never.* Devotional literature indirectly owes much to the ejections of 1662, and historians owe much to Baxter's autobiography, which recorded these times. It was Macaulay who wrote: "If the debauched Cavalier frequented brothels and gambling houses, he at least avoided conventicles. If he never spoke without uttering ribaldry and blasphemy he made some amends by his eagerness to send Baxter and Howe to gaol for preaching and praying."

Most persecuted were those groups which seemed furthest from the laws of the Church. For instance, John James was a member of a tiny sect known as the 'Seventh Day Baptists.' "A poor, low, deformed worm" of a man, he had received little education and was no danger to anybody. His theme was the second coming of Christ and he was accused of treasonable language. It is very doubtful if he committed any offence at all, for his trial was a travesty of justice, but he was hanged, drawn and quartered in 1661. Most misunderstood of all and most hated were the Quakers. Their beginnings under George Fox were noted in Chapter IV though they were not a formal body until 1666. Everything about them was different and raised suspicions. They had no churches, no ministers, no sacraments, met in silence, would not pay tithes or make oaths, would not fight. Even the Bible was, for them, a secondary authority. They responded only to "inner light." Most trivial but most annoying to authority, they would not raise their hats to those above them, for all men were equal. Worse, they attracted to themselves fanatics like poor mad James Naylor, who proclaimed himself the Messiah and was hideously mutilated during the days of the Commonwealth. The King himself, however, appears to have had some sympathy for Quakers. To one group he said, "of this you may be assured, that you shall none of you suffer for your opinions or religion, so long as you live peaceably, and you have the word of a King for it." He was as powerless to keep his word over this as he was powerless to keep any other promise of toleration.

Their creed, totally consistent in itself, they clung to with fervour, and nothing would make them relinquish it. They met openly and scorned secrecy. When haled before a magistrate they automatically refused to take an oath and just as automatically were imprisoned. No set term was ever fixed and some remained for years in prison. George Fox himself spent most of the years of the Restoration there. Prisons were intended as places of punishment. They were always cold and damp, sometimes unlit. All manner of vermin and insects infested them. Disease spread rapidly. The prisoners were often fettered with irons on wrist and leg. Rarely, a gaol-keeper was thought remarkable because he was kind. Most were brutal. Beatings and starvation were a normal part of life. There was no inspection and no appeal. In 1662 there were many Quakers in prison, some authorities estimating the number as high as 4,500. The lowest estimate is 1,300. It is certain a great many died in prison, perhaps more than 400. In 1672 hundreds of Quakers still lay in prison. It would be difficult to exaggerate their sufferings in these foetid, disease-ridden prisons where so many died. Death was no enemy. Life was intolerable. All their hopes were fixed on heaven, where they had been promised everlasting happiness and their inner light would be needed no more in the light of the presence of God. No wonder they longed for death.

When, as occasionally happened without high governmental authority, Quakers were released from prison, they went immediately to their meeting-house and there waited in silence with the door unbarred for the soldiers to call and take them back to prison. It was unnerving for authority, the total lack of resistance, and over a period of time it brought toleration, for in the end there is nothing one can do against this measure of determination coupled with non-resistance. It was Quakers more than any other

group who were transported. Their third offence meant transportation and they were as willingly packed, living cargo in a
prison-ship, fettered hand and foot, as they had been packed into
English gaols. Some went to America, some to Barbados.

William Penn (1644–1718) was the son of Admiral Penn
(1621–1670), who had become a Royalist with the Restoration.
William was converted to Quaker practices while at Oxford and
had been expelled from the University. After a continental tour he
seemed 'cured,' but reverted to his Quaker beliefs and from that
time held them for life. He suffered solitary confinement in the
Tower for eight months after he wrote a book in defence of the
Society of Friends, was tried a second time but acquitted by his
own brilliant defence, imprisoned for a further six months and left
alone after that, more particularly because he inherited a great
fortune on his father's death and became a friend of the King. It
was the King who chose the name Pennsylvania for the tract of
land which Penn was given in discharge of a debt owed by the
government to his father. In 1682 Penn sailed to America to
found his new colony, and there became Governor, though he
returned to England frequently. Among the articles of the colony's
constitution was the solemn promise: "That all persons living in
this province, who confess and acknowledge the one almighty and
eternal God to be the creator, upholder and ruler of the world,
and that hold themselves obliged in conscience to live peaceably
and justly in civil society, shall in no wise be molested or prejudiced
for their religious persuasions or practice in matters of faith and
worship; nor shall they be compelled at any time to frequent or
maintain any religious worship, place or ministry whatsoever."
Unlike some settlers, Penn established warm relationships with the
Indian inhabitants. Persecutions only strengthened the Nonconformists. The Quakers met openly, in defiance of consequence.
The other groups met secretly. Curious devices were used to
conceal their meetings. Look-outs were posted. One minister
arrived to preach with a fork over his shoulder, an innocent
labourer going to work. Some congregations prepared meals, so
that a service could be turned into a communal meal when the
mayor's officers walked in. Their defiance and courage were
equal.

Charles' first attempt at a Declaration of Indulgence, one
which Parliament had angrily refused to consider, had been

in December 1662, only five months after the ejection of the Nonconformist incumbents. How much he had sympathy for those ejected we do not know. There was always suspicion that Charles' real concern was freedom from the laws for the Catholics. Certain it is that Charles, who had received many kindnesses from them during his exile, was sympathetic to Catholics, and certain it is that he died in that faith and was a secret Catholic by January 1669. Little reference has been made to the persecution of Catholics in these pages, which varied considerably. Like the Nonconformists, they suffered in relation to their apparent danger to the State. The time was to come when Charles' support of Catholics became almost impossibly difficult. Meanwhile, he had other things to trouble him.

Bubonic plague had broken out fitfully in Europe from the middle ages onward, but the huddle of unhygienic houses and the primitive sanitation of seventeenth-century London encouraged an unprecedented epidemic in 1665. The court fled. The wealthy closed their houses and moved to safer parts. The poor were left to die. Most of the established clergy left, their flocks uncared for when they most needed help. In some weeks thousands died. The recently ejected Nonconformist ministers took over the deserted churches and duties. Baxter records it: "And when the plague grew hot most of the conformable ministers fled, and left their flocks in the time of their extremity, whereupon divers Non-conformists, pitying the dying and distressed people that had none to call the impenitent to repentance, nor to help men to pre-pare for another world, nor to comfort them in their terrors, when about ten thousand died in a week, resolved that no obedience to the laws of any mortal men whosoever could justify them for neglecting of men's souls and bodies in such extremities, no more than they can justify parents for famishing their children to death. And that when Christ shall say, 'Inasmuch as ye did it not to one of these, ye did it not to me,' it will be a poor excuse to say, 'Lord, I was forbidden by the law.'" At the risk of their lives as well as at the risk of law, these men did duties for which their conforming brethren had been paid, but had fled.

After the plague came the fire of London in 1666, and it was not only fanatics who saw in two cataclysmic tragedies the wrath of God against the profligacy of the court. Others, who saw a Catholic plot in every event, convinced themselves that papists had started it. Indeed, one madman who had nothing to do with it, insisted on being hanged for his crime. More than 13,000 houses were destroyed, and old St. Paul's was only one of many churches to become charred embers. What the King could do he did, but London would never be the same again.

Charles' younger brother and his eventual successor was James, Duke of York. James had been educated as a Protestant but had become a Catholic in 1668. In January 1669 Charles told his brother not only of his own conversion to Catholicism, but also a plan he had been evolving in his mind for some time and one that Parliament must never know. It was a secret treaty with France, negotiated personally through his sister, the Duchess of Orleans. England was to support France against Holland in exchange for a large subsidy to raise an army and re-equip the navy. Part of Charles' bargain was that he should lead England back to Rome, and part of the French bargain was to lend him, if necessary, French troops to help him accomplish this. This agreement, perhaps the most perfidious of all Charles' actions, was the 'Secret Treaty of Dover'.

It was well for Charles that his secret plan never became known. With great cunning he encouraged Buckingham to make a second treaty with France, this public version omitting the religious clauses which, had they been found out, would certainly have cost Charles his throne. It was a remarkable piece of political duplicity. In fact Charles never received the promised money, did relatively little to aid France in the war against Holland, and made what profit he could by trading with both sides.

It seemed urgent to him, however, to get toleration for the Catholics and in 1672 he made his second Declaration of Indulgence, this time by assertion of his royal prerogative and without consulting Parliament. By virtue of his 'supreme power in ecclesiastical matters' he suspended all penal laws against 'whatsoever sort of nonconformists or recusants (Catholics)'. Places were to be licensed for the public worship of Nonconformists under approved 'teachers', and Catholics were to be allowed to worship in their own houses. It was generous, but it was ill-timed and the way he did it ill-judged. The English of the seventeenth century feared papists, hated France, and had already beheaded a king for arbitrary power. Two days later Charles declared war on the Dutch. The Duke of York distinguished himself at the drawn battle of Sole Bay, but it was obvious that the King could not press the war without money. He was heavily in debt with his personal and court expenses and the navy, long allowed to fall into disuse, was a bare match for the skilled Dutch sailors. Parliament stated its terms. The King should have almost all the money he needed (£1,200,000 for three years) provided he withdrew his Declaration of Indulgence and also passed a Test Act so that only members of the Church of England could hold public office, civil or military, which included commands in the army and navy, and directly affected the Duke of York.

Charles bowed to the necessity. He had no choice. The Nonconformists and Catholics alike, freed from prison and tolerated at last, were dragged back to prison. This time, at least for a while, their treatment was sometimes harsher, for they had been given their liberty with reluctance. There was a curious identification between Catholics and Nonconformists in the public mind. Both, it was thought, were seditious. The Catholics were plotting to make England Catholic and the Nonconformists were plotting to turn England into a republic. There was enough truth, however little, in each charge to make the accusation seem plausible. The great majority of Catholics were faithful to England first and the Catholic world second, but there were always some who really were plotting – the Jesuits, in particular, had a well-earned reputation for it – and the 'Gunpowder Plot' of 1605 was within living memory. As for the Nonconformists, the vast majority of them also desired nothing more than to worship God in the way that seemed to them best, but among them also were some whose love of religious liberty included political liberty also. Nor was there a lack of recent minor rebellions by extreme Protestant groups. Both religious wings, therefore, lived under deep suspicion.

Nevertheless, for a few years after 1672 there was a degree of toleration that had not existed before, or at least persecution was not pushed to the uttermost. The laws were unchanged – indeed, the new Test Act made them harsher – but the local authorities began to weary of persecution, nor during these years was there any serious suspicion of seditious action. It was obvious that most of the prisoners of conscience were good men. The Presbyterians, after all, had helped in the Restoration. The Quakers were pacifists. What harm could they do? Little by little the laws were not enforced so rigorously. Penn, courtier and Quaker, helped ease the lot of some of the imprisoned Quakers, but his powers were limited. He could not prevent the King in 1675 from revoking the licences he had granted Nonconformists in 1672, and from closing conventicles. This new act of persecution almost brought union between the Presbyterians and the Congregationalists.

In 1676 the Earl of Danby, who had recently become Charles' chief minister, had a religious census made. Men and women over sixteen were counted at their places of worship. The result showed two and a half million Conformists, 108,000 Protestant Nonconformists and less than 14,000 Catholics. The figures, however, do not reveal the known concentration of nonconformity in London, nor do they reveal the rush to conformity when the census was announced. The only thing we can be sure of is that the true figures given for Nonconformists and Catholics were higher than those given, possibly far higher. The four largest nonconformist groups – Presbyterians, Baptists, Congregationalists and Quakers – were roughly equal in size, though the Presbyterians received more licences to build their churches by the King's permission in 1672 than the Baptists and Congregationalists combined.

It was unfortunate for Charles' desire for Catholic toleration that in 1678 the vile Titus Oates should have been believed when he told his series of lies. Oates had had a remarkable career. He had been expelled from a school, from a naval chaplaincy, from a university college, and from a Catholic seminary, probably for homosexual practices. False throughout, he had not even graduated from Cambridge, though he awarded himself a doctor's degree. The only genuine thing about him was his ordination, no credit to the Church that bestowed it. A compulsive plotter as well as a liar, he laid information that the Jesuits were planning to assassinate the King, massacre Protestants, and put the King's Catholic brother on the throne. Even if some Jesuits were involved in plots, it is extremely doubtful if any plot such as Oates revealed ever took place. He was plausible, and his genuine membership of a Jesuit community made him sound the more so. Oates, interviewed by the King, was proven a liar to the latter's satisfaction, but the King was a clever man. The London mob were neither reasonable nor clever and were also eager to believe any ill of the Catholics. Word spread quickly.

Oates had made his first formal deposition before a Westminster magistrate, Sir Edmund Berry Godfrey, who only a few days later was found murdered in a ditch by Primrose Hill. Face downwards, he had been pierced with his own sword, though an inquest proved he had been transfixed after his death. There was immediate panic. The mystery of the magistrate's death has never been resolved, but as far as the populace was concerned it was no mystery – it was more bloody work by the papists. Terror spread through London. Innocent Catholics were arrested without cause, their houses attacked, their businesses burned. Men went armed. Galloping horses were seen by night. Groups of hooded monks were alleged to be roaming the countryside.

Oates, aided by another clergyman, Israel Tonge, his dupe, swore away reputations and lives. They were fêted as the saviours of England and they lived at public expense. They gave accounts of treasonable letters they had seen, conversations they had over-heard, suspicions they had long nourished. The gullible believed them, and in an atmosphere of maddened fear, the authorities persecuted savagely and relentlessly.

Oates cunningly named Edward Coleman, the Duke of York's Secretary and a convert Catholic like his master. With almost incredible carelessness, Coleman had failed to destroy corres-pondence which was certainly of a plotting nature and could easily be construed as treason. Grave suspicions surrounded the Duke himself, already a focus of dislike, but though Coleman could undoubtedly have implicated James, not with murder but with seditious correspondence, James' name was never mentioned. Coleman died horribly – he was hanged, drawn and quartered – but bravely. Of all those who died because of the 'Popish Plot,' he was probably the only one who was guilty even of a hint of treason. Some thirty-five died, some priests, some nobles. One of them, Oliver Plunkett, an Irish Archbishop, was a man of sanctity. Of all the judicial murders, his was the most disgraceful. Many suffered persecution, and for a long time no Catholic was safe. Pepys himself was arrested and committed to the Tower, presumably because he had made the error of marrying a French wife.

Charles could do nothing but watch, helpless. James he sent to Scotland. It was inevitable that an 'exclusionist' party should arise, a Protestant move to exclude James from succeeding his brother because of the Duke's Catholic faith. It was widely believed that Mary of Modena, James' second wife, was a daughter of the Pope. The bitter battle over exclusion lasted almost until Charles' death. So determined was Charles about the succession that he even gave up his pleasures for a while and devoted himself to state concerns. His formidable opponent was the Earl of Shaftesbury. The Exclusion Bill, which made it unlawful for any Catholic to be King of England, was passed by the Commons and narrowly defeated in the Lords.

The problem for the exclusionists was a substitute for James. There was no purpose in excluding a Catholic if there was no suitable Protestant as an alternative. In fact there was an alternative and a son of the King, albeit a bastard one. The Duke of Monmouth was the natural son of Charles by his association with Lucy Walter. Born in 1649 and recognized by his father, Monmouth grew up a handsome, pleasure-loving extrovert, an admirable horseman and huntsman and an able and brave soldier. He would, many thought, make a good king. At any rate, he was a Protestant, and that was what chiefly mattered. Monmouth began to find flatterers in his company. In the summer of 1680 he made a progress through the west of England, and everywhere the 'Protestant Prince' was greeted with joy by Church of England supporters, nervous of their King's religion, and especially by Nonconformists.

In 1683 the clumsy 'Rye House' plot was formed to murder the King and his brother and place a Protestant on the throne. It failed. Monmouth was deeply implicated but fled and hid. Whether he was party to attempted murder or only willing to occupy the throne should there be a sudden vacancy is not known. Within a little while, though others were executed, he sought his ever-forgiving father's favours, and they were reconciled. He then fled abroad and awaited brighter days.

Charles II ceased to rule for three years before his death. The virtual ruler was James. As Charles lay dying, James gave orders. Father Huddleston hurried up the back stairs to assist the King into a Catholic heaven.

James II (1633–1701) was fifty-one when he became King in 1685. He reigned for less than four years, and it took him considerably less time than that to alienate all support. It should not have been so. He was a hard-working and deeply religious king, and he was an honest one, at least by Stuart standards. His disastrous reign had elements of tragedy, for what went wrong was as much because of his virtues as his vices. Had he had the deviousness of his brother, had he been less honest, he might have kept his throne. It was a total honesty or a monumental tactlessness, which ever way you look at it, that was a chief cause of his undoing. Charles had kept his Catholic principles to himself; James heard mass with open doors in the chapel of his Palace at Whitehall on the second Sunday of his reign. Charles inherited a belief in his divine right but was skilful in concealing it; James let it be known, in season and out of season, that he would assert his royal rights at God's command, whatever mere men said. Charles sought toleration but bowed before the storm he roused, and submitted; James demanded instant toleration. Charles endured all manner of men as his advisers; James, a Catholic, chose Catholics for as many high offices as he could. This was bitterly resented, and the more so in 1685 when Louis XIV finally revoked the century-old Edict of Nantes, the charter of Huguenot rights, and a flood of Huguenot refugees flooded to London to embarrass the King with proof of persecution by continental Catholics and horrify the English that the King could support a religion which approved murder, rape, and pillage on a colossal scale. Charles controlled Parliament by alternately appeasing it and dissolving it; James detested Parliament and made his detestation obvious.

It was James' conviction that loyal Anglicans and loyal Catholics had much in common, but that Nonconformists were republicans at heart. There was an element of truth in it, but he might as truthfully have said that loyal Nonconformists had much in common with loyal Anglicans and Catholics. The truth that was in the charge, however, would appear when Monmouth landed in the West.

James was as ambitious as he was self-confident. He saw himself, not merely as the champion of England, but as the arbiter of Europe. Over him would dawn a golden age. Trade would flourish, the Empire would expand, he would order all things, absolute power having been given him by God. There would be religious liberty for all his subjects. This was his vision. His immediate policy was more cautious. He believed that while religious persecution was in itself wrong it would be politic for a while, because of his distrust of Nonconformists, to forbid them to organize themselves into churches or worship publicly. William Penn became his friend and used his influence with the King to alleviate the sufferings of the Quakers. To this body alone therefore the King showed tolerance. As pacifists, after all, they would hardly harm him. He relieved them of the payment of fines in 1686 and in 1687 he freed 1,600 of them from prison. It was an untypically generous act for which many historians have sought ulterior motives. One probably need look no further than Penn's friendship and the Quaker doctrine of non-resistance, which by this time and through Penn's mediation, would be known at Court.

Any sign of kindness in James was surprising in the light of his choice of George Jeffreys as Lord Chancellor in September 1685, a man notorious for his cynical sadism. By this time the panic of the Popish Plot was over and calmer minds began to doubt if there had been any plot at all. All the evidence seemed to come from one source and a tainted one – Titus Oates. It was in May 1685, when he was still Lord Chief Justice, that Jeffreys tried Oates for perjury and found him guilty. Of his guilt there was no doubt, and it is difficult to feel any sympathy for a man whose lies had led to more than thirty innocent men being executed. However, Jeffreys never considered the effects of his barbaric sentences, or that they might have exactly the reverse effect of the one intended. Among other punishments, he sentenced Oates to so severe a flogging – he was unconscious for most of it – that the odious perjuror received sympathy. Miraculously, for the flogging was probably intended as a death sentence, Oates survived. Another of Jeffreys' victims was the now aged Richard Baxter, whom Jeffreys taunted and insulted. It was clearly a joy to Jeffreys to have a famous Nonconformist of seventy in his power. Baxter's offence was to have protested against the persecution of the Nonconformists in his paraphrase of the New Testament. Baxter appeared the same day that Oates was pilloried and flogged, and he asked for time to prepare his defence. "Not a minute," said Jeffreys. "I can deal with saints as well as sinners. There stands Oates on one side of the pillory, and if Baxter stood on the other the two greatest rogues of the Kingdom would stand together." When Baxter's counsel tried to address the jury Jeffreys broke in with "This is an old rogue, a schismatical knave, a hypocritical villain . . .!" He called Baxter a dog and said he should be whipped, and had arranged with the jury to find the old man guilty. Baxter was fined and imprisoned and only because the other judges overruled him was Jeffreys prevented from ordering him a flogging as well. Under Jeffreys, persecution reached the highest peak it had known for years. Nonconformists everywhere looked for a saviour from a Catholic king who persecuted his Protestant subjects through barbarous laws and a barbarous Lord Chancellor.

In these circumstances Monmouth's hopes revived, in spite of the hatred he inspired in his uncle, now King of England. The sycophants who surrounded Charles' bastard son assured him that if only he would declare himself the Protestant contender for the throne all England would rise to his banner. He believed them, but never resolutely enough to become a formidable usurper. On 11 June 1685, he invaded England with three small ships and eighty-two officers. Some of the officers were dissolute friends, some were old Cromwellian veterans, some were professional plotters, like Ferguson, a Nonconformist preacher whom Macaulay described as "violent, malignant, regardless of truth, insensible to shame, insatiable of notoriety, delighting in intrigue, in tumult, in mischief for its own sake." The company, ill-prepared and seriously lacking in experience of warfare at top level, landed at Lyme and proclaimed "The Good Old Cause," that is, Protestantism. The hope was to enlist all men of strong Protestant opinion, and the West was chosen because here Nonconformity was strong and Monmouth already known and popular. Ferguson's speech contained such gross exaggerations and lies that only simple people could believe in it . . . "The life of the Duke of York hath been but one continued conspiracy against the reformed religion and the rights of the nation. For whoever considers his contriving the burning of London . . . his fomenting the Popish Plot, and encouraging the murther of Sir Edmond Berry Godfrey . . . And whereas the said James . . . hath poisoned the late King . . ." Such absurdities as these damaged the just points of his speech, which were that under James, Protestants were being daily persecuted while Catholics were given favoured posts at Court, and that James, if he could, would turn England from Protestantism to Catholicism while Monmouth would give Protestants the toleration for which they longed.

If many of the leaders were rogues, those who joined Monmouth in England were for the most part humble, good men who saw his cause as God's cause. There was John Coad, a God-fearing carpenter of Dorset, who was in the County Militia and had taken an oath to fight for the King. What should he do now? "The hellish oaths and ribaldry of many of that company strengthened my resolution in going off. But the two opposites of my apprehension were plainly popery and slavery, and Protestantism and liberty; to contend for the former and oppose the latter was directly against my principles and conscience." There was Nathaniel Wade, a young Bristol lawyer, who remembered the rapturous start of what these men looked on almost as a crusade: "Now were the hearts of the people of God gladded, and their hopes and expectations roused that this man might be a deliverer for the nation . . . Now also they hoped that the day was come in which the Good Old Cause would revive again." There was Henry Noon, a Congregationalist of Axminster, whose church called him after he died in a skirmish, "a pious and lively Christian." There was also the strange Thomas Phook, a Quaker, who offered help from his band of "Clubmen."

There were also men as fierce as was Samuel Storey, the Scots Nonconformist, who addressed aldermen cowering in the mayor's house at Taunton: "The Duke of York, whom you call King, poisoned his brother . . . He is introducing popery, tyranny and arbitrary government – witness poor Oates, who was the saviour of the nation and its first sufferer (a reference to Oates' punishment for perjury). You are for the church of England, gentlemen, I am a Dissenter. We Dissenters shall be first brought to the stake, but depend upon it, you will follow."

If this sounds extravagant, it did not seem so then. Men had been burned for their beliefs in living memory, and hanged, drawn and quartered more recently. Thousands at that moment lay in prison for their religious principles. At any rate, many joined Monmouth and most of them were humble, upright men whose cause was religious liberty.

The rebellion was a series of disasters. The first was the Earl of Argyle's simultaneous attempt to invade Scotland, expel the bishops, and reinstate the Kirk. News of its total failure reached Monmouth, who at that point contemplated flight. The second disaster for Monmouth was James' unexpected power and speed in opposing him. A royalist Parliament had voted him great sums of money to annihilate Monmouth. The King's army was experienced, well-led, well-equipped and resolute. The Earl of Feversham, an unpopular but able Frenchman, was in command,

John Churchill a resentful second-in-command who coveted the chief post. Colonel Kirke, a blood-thirsty rogue whose ferocious troops were known as the lambs from their insignia and facetiously, from their brutal habits, also ranked high. James had instructed his army to arrest all disaffected and suspicious persons, especially 'Nonconformist ministers and such as served against our father and brother.' He also instructed that a pardon should be offered for all except the ringleaders who would lay down their arms and surrender to him. Another of the disasters that beset Monmouth was the number who accepted the King's offer. Many deserted. The last disaster was the Battle of Sedgemoor, when Monmouth risked all by an attack at night and was routed. He was found in a ditch and arrested, pleaded in vain for his life, and died by the axe, the executioner so clumsy that even five blows failed to sever his head. A worse fate was in store for his followers.

Judge Jeffreys was sent down as the instrument of retribution. His hatred of Nonconformity, his natural cruelty, his bullying of witnesses and insulting of defendants, his automatic choice of the maximum penalty possible, all these things made him suitable for James' vengeance.

About 5,000 rebels fought at Sedgemoor. Several hundred, probably, were hanged untried by Kirke. Some escaped abroad. Some escaped more locally by means of bribes, and fourteen turned King's evidence. In all, 1,400 were brought to trial. Of those tried, a handful were acquitted, another handful obtained the royal pardon and a larger number bought their freedom. More than a few died in prison. Of those left, 849 were transported and 330 hanged, drawn and quartered. The scale and horror of the revenge appalled the nation.

Jeffreys' first case was a widow, Dame Alice Lisle, seventy years old and deaf, probably senile too. She was charged with harbouring John Hicks, a Nonconformist preacher and an alleged rebel. As he had not yet been tried, she could only in justice be charged with harbouring a Nonconformist. Jeffreys cared nothing for justice. During her trial he took opportunity to curse all Nonconformists. "There is not one of those lying, snivelling, canting Presbyterians, but one way or another had a hand in the rebellion. Presbytery has all manner of villainy in it . . . Show me a Presbyterian and I'll show thee a lying knave." He brow-beat the jury into a verdict of guilty and sentenced her to be burnt at the stake. An appeal to the King, who had to acknowledge her rank and dared not risk a London burning for so slight an offence, led to her beheading instead. Elizabeth Gaunt, a Baptist, was also charged with harbouring a rebel, but could not plead gentility. After a brave speech, she died at the stake. In Dorchester, there were 302 prisoners. Jeffreys considered a trial for each one was a waste of time. They were told that the merciful King would spare their lives and execute only the officers and chief offenders. It was therefore in their interest to plead guilty. Accordingly 272 of them pleaded guilty and Jeffreys promptly sentenced over 60 to be hanged, drawn and quartered and the rest to be transported. Of the 30 who pleaded not guilty, 29 were executed like the rest, and one was acquitted. Minor offenders, on Jeffreys' instructions, were whipped through every market town.

The ghastly punishment for treason was just to be half-hanged. If the executioner was merciful, the victim was cut down in a faint; if not, he was still conscious. His genitals were cut off, his bowels hacked out and burnt before his eyes and he was then beheaded, his body divided into four quarters, the remains boiled in brine, tarred for preservation against the weather, and hung up on gibbets in prominent places as a warning to others. Some of Jeffreys' instructions to the sheriffs, if current report is to be believed, are too disgusting for repetition.

They died with wonderful courage. Captain Sampson Lock, a Congregationalist minister, wished to preach his last sermon with the rope round his neck. He was told there was no time for it. Captain Annesley, as the rope was put round his neck, said that if he had a thousand lives to spare they would all be sacrificed for so good a cause. John Holloway of Lyme said to his escort as they led him to his death, "You seem to be brave fellows, but if I were to have my life for fighting the best five of you, I would not question it." Captain Kidd, the last of twelve to die at Lyme, and who had watched the horrible deaths of eleven before him, said a prayer and died bravely. Of William Hewling, nineteen, another of that group, the officer in charge said, "I believe that if the Lord Chief Justice were here, he would not let him die." At Taunton a group waiting to die, prayed and sang hymns when the ropes were round their necks "with heavenly joy and sweetness". Among them was Benjamin Hewling, brother of William, who had died at Lyme. Strenuous efforts had been made to save his life, and Churchill had been sympathetic to the appeal. The King would not listen. "The marble of this mantelpiece," said Churchill, standing by the fire, "is not harder than the King's heart."

Jeffreys returned to London, leaving behind him orders which would ensure that the West country, for months to come, had the dismembered bodies of some of its most devout citizens displayed in every public place. Sickened by the barbarities reported from the West, the city was seething with discontent. It was typical of James that, knowing this, he yet made his Declaration of Indulgence by royal decree in 1687. To "all our loving subjects" permission was given to worship "after their own way and manner" provided the meetings were peaceful and not secret or seditious. The clergy were to read it from the pulpit on four successive Sundays. It was much to ask. Effectively they were to announce the removal of their own privileges. Revolt was in the air. James had already thrust Catholics into Church of England benefices. He had promoted four Catholic lords to the Privy Council. He had revived the Court of High Commission, the more easily to deal with difficult ecclesiastics. Was he really intending to destroy the Church of England? Many believed so. Many also believed that he saw no limit to his arbitrary power. He was as dangerous as his grandfather had been, possibly more so. The Church of England, loyal so far, began to have doubts about the price they would have to pay for loyalty. Destruction, perhaps?

The Nonconformists could only gain. All they had ever asked for would be given and the only thing asked in exchange was loyalty to James and support of his policy. The Nonconformists in fact were asked in a personal appeal by the King to join the Catholics as a balance against Anglican power. They were sorely tempted. The persecutions had recently been so bitter that it was a matter of common sense to accept the offer. The Nonconformist ministers met to discuss the matter. They decided that however much it was a matter of sense to accept the King's offer, it was a matter of conscience to refuse it, and it was a refusal they sent back with the Court attendant to the waiting King. "It were better," said Dr. Williams, for Nonconformists "to be reduced to their former hardships, than declare for measures destructive of the liberties of their country, and that for himself, before he would concur in an address which should be thought an approbation of the dispensing power, he would choose to lay down his liberty at his Majesty's feet." That was the message the King received, a great shock for him and an immense credit to the Nonconformists.

Seven bishops refused to read the King's Declaration. He arrested them and put them in the Tower. They were visited there by ten Nonconformist leaders in a gesture of sympathy. The judges acquitted the bishops. The King abruptly reversed his policies and blunder succeeded blunder. Negotiations with William of Orange had been secretly made by the King's enemies. James found he had no friends left. Even members of his family deserted him. He fled, was captured before he could get far, but tactfully allowed to escape again, this time for ever.

Ironically, he was probably happiest, in his morbid conscience-stricken way, when in exile: "I was never truly happy till I was convinced that it is impossible to have content in this world but by despising of it." His laws had taught his Nonconformist victims that. A lady of the French court had summed up James: "Our good King James is a brave and honest man, but the silliest I have ever seen in my life; a child of seven would not make such crass mistakes as he does. Piety makes people outrageously stupid." Piety was not James' downfall, though under his reign thousands of his subjects suffered for their piety.

It was another irony that little more than three years after Monmouth's death another fleet invaded England – with 600 ships instead of 3 and 15,000 soldiers instead of 82 – and this invasion gave to England almost everything that Monmouth had promised. James' unique combination of ineptness, miscalculation, arrogance and stupidity had united England as nothing else could have done.

The Nonconformists greeted the 'Glorious Revolution' with hope. William was a Protestant. They had been persecuted by Protestants as well as Catholics, however, and it was wise to be cautious. It seemed unlikely that they would be called to endure more suffering than had been meted out by their recent King or his brutal creature Jeffreys, now locked up in the Tower, where he died. Yet from the terrible years of persecution they had grown in power and strength. History was to show that, like the primitive church on which they had modelled themselves, their sufferings would carry them into a future of proselytizing power. The glorious revolution was for them a glorious dawn of freedom.

CHAPTER VI

Toleration, Decline and Revival

WILLIAM III (1650–1702) AND MARY II (1662–1694) were offered the crown of England jointly in February 1689. William's mother was a daughter of Charles I. He was Stadtholder of the Dutch, a soldier of great personal courage, the chief Protestant champion against the power of Catholic France, and that crusade was the consuming passion of his life. Mary's claim to the throne was greater, for she was the daughter of James II and Anne Hyde. She had been brought up as a strict Protestant and was deeply loved both by the Dutch and the English. She was the devoted wife of a man who was never loved in England. With all his great qualities William was cold and reserved, spent a considerable part of his reign fighting abroad, and seems to have made little effort to win his people's affection. Together they set an example of happy married life. They gave a moral tone to the court which it had lacked since the days of Cromwell. Decadence was no longer acceptable.

Nevertheless, though rulers in name they were not rulers in fact as their predecessors had been. They had been named rulers out of due succession by the most powerful men in the country. Hereafter, real power belonged more and more to Parliament, less and less to the King. The tyranny of James II convinced Parliament that it was wise to vote William money on an annual basis. By this simple expedient, power shifted decisively from King to Parliament. Further, during the reign of William and

110

Mary, Parliament strengthened its position by passing laws to define and limit the power of the King.

It was only a few years before the Glorious Revolution that the terms 'Whigs' and 'Tories' came into use. Whigs were really Scottish outlaws and Tories Irish rebels, but the names, first used in contempt, stuck. Tories were gentry, hereditary landowners of long standing, rulers by tradition. They were high churchmen, asserted the rights of the king, and had doubts about William's right to the throne. The Whigs were wealthy merchants who bought their land, recently ennobled peers, Puritans and Nonconformists. They asserted the rights of Parliament against the king. Both parties could have dangerous elements against the crown, for some Tories were Jacobites, who hoped for the Stuarts to return, while some Whigs were republicans. There was bitter hostility between the two parties for generations. The party system began in rancour: in rancour it remained.

Nonconformists now had effective representation, therefore, in Parliament, but their fortunes would fluctuate with the ascendancy of one party or the other. The King's own personal views yet counted for something, and William came to the throne with credentials that looked excellent for Nonconformists. The Dutch tolerance of religion was famous. Generations of English had fled to the Netherlands to escape persecution. The number of religious communities – some tiny sects – was great. While the leading Church was the Dutch Reformed one, the fruit of Calvin's work, it was not an official state religion. William was therefore technically a Nonconformist until he took the English crown. His personal conviction was strongly Protestant and Calvinist, and he was an enemy of persecution for religion's sake. He told the Scots that he was "never of that mind that violence was suited to the advancing of true religion." When he received the crown of Scotland and was asked to take the oath pledging him to destroy all heretics, he said: "I will not lay myself under any obligation to be a persecutor." The European Protestant champion, a devout man personally, a hater of religious bigotry, William seemed to Nonconformists a man sent of God.

Mary was not less devout than William; she was more so. There was much of the Puritan about her. It was she more than William who kept the court pure, for though he was at least suspected of infidelity, no taint ever damaged her name. Mary, with William's support, sent directives to magistrates to implement the laws against morals, especially against drunkenness. It should be remembered that this was the beginning of the age of Hogarth, when the purity of the court was in stark contrast to the rottenness of life outside it. Whoring, gambling and drunkenness were widespread and overt. Mary's attempt to reform public morals was brave, but many in England could remember the days of Cromwell's Generals and their attempt to enforce morality by law. In 1692 Mary was behind a new attempt to reform public life by a series of laws governing Sabbath Observance. Her attempts failed as dismally as Cromwell's. Thereafter, she taught by example.

It was not the fault of the monarchs that Nonconformists received little more liberty after the Glorious Revolution than they had received before it. Had William and Mary owned the power to help them they would have used it. Their throne, however, depended on walking a religious tight-rope. Their personal views meant conflict with the Anglicans. If William's sympathies were with a presbyterian system, he was now 'Defender of the Faith', and the faith included the theories of apostolic succession and episcopal ordination. The faith by implication also included the importance of vestments and rites. High Anglicans liked William as little as they liked James. Indeed, some of them preferred James. Many of them early showed their total disapproval of William and Mary by refusing to swear an oath of fidelity to them on the grounds that they had sworn an oath of loyalty to his predecessor, the man he had usurped. These men – called Non-Jurors because they would not swear an oath – were given months to consider their position, were cajoled and encouraged to change their minds. They were implacable, and after about a year they were ejected.

On the one hand one admires the tenderness of their consciences and their heroism in taking a step which meant loss of all livelihood. On the other hand, one regrets that so many – there were some 450 in all including the saintly Bishop Ken (1637–1711) and others almost as distinguished – left the Church for so poor a cause. James had proved himself an impossible king. One wishes that his series of blunders, coupled with the fact that he fled his country, would have allowed the Non-Jurors to feel that their oaths had been absolved. Not only, ejected by their own decision, did they leave the Church that so badly needed them; they also, or some of them, were involved in Jacobite plots for decades to come.

All the Nonconformists gained from William and Mary was goodwill and the protection of the Toleration Act. This Act was so vital a part of the future of Nonconformity that it needs to be considered in a little detail. No man or woman who took the oaths of allegiance and supremacy and also accepted the declaration against transubstantiation (so proving himself no Catholic) should be compelled to attend his parish church or be prosecuted for worshipping in another licensed place of worship. Further, any person who disturbed worship or caused damage in licensed Nonconformist premises could be prosecuted. Thus much, and little more, was given to Nonconformists, unless they occasionally conformed, by attendance at the parish church and taking the sacraments there. Otherwise they were banned from public office and from the two Universities. Nonconformist ministers who wished for a licence had to subscribe to at least 34 of the 39 Articles (those which could be omitted concerned ceremonies, the Book of Homilies and Ordination Service). Since the whole tone of the Articles was Calvinistic, Arminians had to satisfy themselves that they could be interpreted in an Arminian sense.

Special arrangements were necessarily made for Quakers, who would not take oaths as a matter of conscience. They were freed from oaths but had instead to declare solemnly against transubstantiation, give a confession of faith in the divinity of Christ and the Holy Spirit, in the inspiration of the Old and New Testaments, and also promise loyalty to the government. For Unitarians, however, whose beliefs prevented them from subscribing to the general method for Nonconformists or the particular one for Quakers, there was no protection.

Had it been successful, the Nonconformists might have profited from a move made on their behalf. This was a Comprehension Bill introduced into the House of Lords. The purpose of the Bill was to modify the ecclesiastical establishment of the Church of England to include Nonconformists. It was well intended, but it was an abortive attempt. Clergy would be required, not to subscribe to the 39 Articles, but instead to give a general approbation to the "doctrine, worship and government of the Church of England as by law established, as containing all things necessary to salvation", and a promise "to preach and practise according thereunto." The Bill failed for a variety of reasons. From the establishment side there was reasonable hostility. The 39 Articles many considered the bulwarks of the Church. A "general approbation", they judged, would open the door to all manner of creeds, all manner of ecclesiastical practice. It was hard enough already to get conformity; the new system would introduce nonconformity as the essence of the Church. It is more surprising that Nonconformists themselves were for the most part indifferent to the Bill. Their motives for the indifference were complex. In the first place, some in conscience could not subscribe to the idea of episcopacy and clearly this would be part of the general approbation. Others, who might have accepted episcopacy, found themselves, paid by their own flourishing congregations, far better paid and honoured than they would have been in the establishment. Others clung to the particular doctrines of their own separated churches and thought a general approbation an insult to the doctrines they held. Still more felt that they could not trust the Church of England; long experience of bitter persecution had taught them that promises were not always fulfilled. Overall, many believed that the measure of liberty they had found outside the establishment had been bought at a great price; it could not be lightly thrown away. The Bill failed.

Nonconformists, whatever infringement of their liberties the law still demanded, were flourishing. Between William and Mary's accession and the end of the century, a mere twelve years, 2,218 meeting-houses were licensed, and a further 2,140 during the first 20 years of the eighteenth century. Nonconformity was becoming a powerful force in the country, represented in Parliament, tacitly approved by the King and Queen and adopted by the mighty as well as the lowly, though in general it was more for the lowly. As long as William and Mary reigned and the Whigs were in power, Nonconformity was content. Unfortunately, it was not a long reign. Mary died in 1694 and William in 1702. They were succeeded by Anne, Mary's younger sister, long alienated from her.

Queen Anne (1665–1714) reigned for twelve unhappy years. She was worn out by seventeen pregnancies, none of which produced an heir to survive infancy; she had married a Danish Prince whom she loved but everyone else treated as a joke; she was obsessed by her devotion to Sarah Jennings, later Duchess of Marlborough (1600–1744), with whom she quarrelled incessantly. Anne was a Tory, Sarah a Whig, and it was only Sarah's domination over her during much of the reign that saved the Nonconformists from greater persecution, for Anne hated them.

Battle was joined early in Anne's reign over the issue of occasional conformity. It had long been acceptable for Nonconformists to hold public office within the law by taking the sacrament once a year in the parish church. It was clearly in the Tory interest to prevent them doing it so that the Whig Nonconformists would cease to be magistrates and members of Parliament and their power reduced. In 1702 the first attempt was made. The Queen supported it and ordered her poor husband George, although a Lutheran, to vote for the 'Occasional Conforming Bill'. It is recorded that he did what he was told but muttered "My heart is vid you" to the leaders of the opposition as he did so. This attempt foundered in the House of Lords, and further attempts failed also. Not until there was a Tory majority in Parliament was such a bill likely to succeed.

Political rancour was great. The real issue at stake was not really occasional conformity, or not for many. The question was one of political power. For Nonconformists, however, it was obvious that the passing of the Bill would be a prelude to further persecution, as indeed it proved. Dr. Henry Sacheverell (c.1674–1724) was a bigoted High Churchman and Tory, a man whose views were so extreme that even his own party had doubts about him. He came of Nonconformist stock, but few men have ever abused Nonconformists so violently. He also detested Whigs and Low Churchmen (the descendants of the Puritans who had remained in the Church of England). His pamphlets and sermons poured vitriol on his enemies. In 1702 he launched a crusade against Nonconformists. Occasional conformers he called "these crafty, faithless, and insidious persons who can creep to our altars and partake of our sacraments". From his London pulpit, St. Saviour's, Southwark, the stream of invective caught the notice of leading Tories, and he was invited to preach from prestigious pulpits.

Sacheverell's principles inspired others. One of his earlier pamphlets inspired an imitation so extreme that even Sacheverell would have hesitated to own it. This was the anonymous pamphlet of 1702 entitled 'The Shortest Way with Dissenters'. The ferocious work recommended that the only way to deal with Nonconformists was to massacre them – another St. Bartholomew's Day. Only total extermination would rid the nation of these pernicious people. Some high Tories approved it and warmly applauded the unknown author. Moderates were disgusted and Nonconformists horrified. It was soon discovered that the work was a hoax and came from the pen of Daniel Defoe (c.1661–1731). It was a caricature of High Church bigotry. Defoe was arrested, and charged with libelling the Church by misrepresenting its opinions. He was fined, imprisoned, his tract was publicly burned, and he was sentenced to the pillory for three days. The latter punishment, intended as a public humiliation, was made a triumph by the great crowds that gathered to protect him, to garland him with flowers, drink his health and read the noble 'Hymn to the Pillory' which he had written for the occasion. The work was sold in thousands to help him pay his fine.

Defoe was born a Nonconformist and educated at a dissenting academy. He planned first to become a Nonconformist minister but abandoned the idea and then went into the hosiery business. He travelled abroad, embraced Monmouth's cause when the Duke invaded England, and was lucky to escape with his life. Some of his class-mates were butchered by Jeffreys. By about 1700 he had settled in London as a journalist, and defended William of Orange in a satire entitled 'The True-born Englishman', 1701. He made a contribution to the current religious dispute in a pamphlet of 1702, 'Enquiring into occasional Conformity', in which he argued that if Nonconformity was just, then occasional conformity was a sin; alternatively, if occasional conformity was just, then Nonconformity was a sin. The pamphlet proves how deeply the Nonconformists were themselves divided on the issue. It was his anonymous work, however, and his punishment in the pillory that followed it, that gave Defoe notoriety and made him perhaps the best known Nonconformist of his age. 'The Shortest Way with Dissenters' was no service to Nonconformity; it only exacerbated the bitter division between Anglican and Nonconformist. Some of his later works of fiction were masterpieces; *A Journal of the Plague Year*, 1722, *Moll Flanders*, 1722, and especially his best known book, one of the most famous works of English Literature, *Life and Strange*

Surprizing Adventures of Robinson Crusoe, of York, Mariner, 1719.
His reputation was tarnished in his lifetime by his apparent
political inconsistencies – he served both Whig and Tory
governments. His imaginative genius survives in his novels.

Dr. Sacheverell was not amused by Defoe's wit. In November
1709, he used the pulpit of St. Paul's to preach the most incendiary
sermon till then. Nonconformists were all rogues; toleration was
an error; the Revolutionary Settlement had been a disaster; occasional conformity was a scandal and an offence to God. The
sermon included a personal attack on the Bishop of Salisbury.

Offensive as the sermon was, it was an error to prosecute
Sacheverell. Such a man is better treated with the silence of
contempt. Almost overnight the bigot became a martyr and
London mobs, knowing little of the issues involved, roamed and
rioted in his support. Nonconformists were abused and attacked.
Several Meeting-Houses were burned down, including Thomas
Bradbury's. The trial in 1710 was a political forum, more an
acrimonious parliamentary debate than an attempt to determine
guilt or innocence. Sacheverell acquitted himself tolerably well,
though the strong suspicion was that Bishop Atterbury had written
his defence, for Sacheverell was no scholar. The verdict, which
excited national interest far beyond the importance of the case,
was guilty, but the punishment so light – public burning of the
offending sermon and three years' suspension from preaching –
that both sides claimed victory. More mobs rioted and more
Nonconformist property was damaged. It is probable that the
impeachment of Sacheverell was an important factor in the over-
throw of the Whigs at the next Parliamentary election.

It followed inevitably from a Tory victory that the attempts to
oust Nonconformists from public office could at last be successful.
In 1711 the Occasional Conforming Act became law. No person
could continue to hold public office or trust who attended a place
of worship licensed under the Toleration Act during the time of
holding it. Any offender was fined £40, and the Act provided as an
unpleasant and un-English addition that the sum of money was to
be paid to the informer.

Worse was to come. In 1714 the Schism Bill passed through
Parliament. This vicious Bill sought to suppress all Nonconformist
seminaries and schools. In future all teachers and tutors were to
be licensed by a Bishop, must conform to the Anglican liturgy,

and take the sacrament in the Church of England at least once a year. This ensured that no Nonconformist could teach. If a teacher attended any church other than the Church of England he was liable to three months' imprisonment and disqualified from teaching.

Henry St. John, Viscount Bolingbroke (1678–1751), had introduced the Bill. It would have denied Nonconformists the right to educate their own children as they wished, and would have effectively destroyed them as a body. It is extraordinary that Bolingbroke cared little or nothing about religious distinctions. His aim was entirely political. It was a challenge thrown at his enemy, Robert Harley, Earl of Oxford (1661–1724), who came from a Nonconformist background. Since Tories were now the strongest party, nothing could prevent the Bill, disgraceful as it was, from becoming law – nothing, that is, except the death of the Queen. No monarch ever died more conveniently. Anne died on the very day when the Bill should have become law. As the leading Nonconformists appeared to offer George I an address of welcome, Bolingbroke sneered at their black Geneva gowns. "Is this a funeral?" he asked. "No, my lord," answered Thomas Bradbury (1677–1759). "Not a funeral, but a resurrection."

Anne reigned over an age of elegance and the arts flourished. Kneller, Grinling Gibbons, Steele, Addison, Pope and Wren adorned it. It was an age of battle, of Marlborough's victories, of colonial expansion, of speculation. It was also an age, and increasingly so, of moral rottenness. External elegance seemed, ironically, to accompany inward corruption. It became fashionable to treat religion with scant respect. Enthusiasm was considered in bad taste. Good breeding consisted of affecting lukewarmness about spiritual matters. George I (1660–1727) succeeded to Tory domination, but the Jacobite rising of 1715 brought a reaction of sympathy for the Whigs, and Tories did not have power again until the reign of George III.

George I never expected to be King of England, though it was the 1701 Act of Settlement that had prepared the way. At least fifty-seven cousins were passed over in his favour because he had proved himself the most hearty of the European Protestants who opposed Louis XIV. Never popular in England, never able to master the language, he did not even bring a Queen with him, for his wife had been imprisoned for life under suspicion of adultery, and her alleged lover murdered. He brought instead two mistresses, Mademoiselle Schulenberg, a placid and brainless woman of whom one historian said, "the only thing that brought her to life was the scent of money", and Madame Kielmansegge. Even more than William and Mary, George was King by Act of Parliament, not by divine right. The Act that had made him King also circumscribed him with laws to contain his powers. Parliament was now in charge, and George did not interfere.

Corruption in public and decadence in private life increased. Sir Robert Walpole (1676–1745), effectively England's first prime minister, made immorality a matter of policy. For him, every man had his price, and self-interest was the governing principle. Even Nonconformists became contaminated by the subtle poison. Their price for support of the government was a bribe known as the 'regium donum', an annual sum of about £1,000 from the exchequer to assist widows of Nonconformist ministers. The cause itself was admirable, but that it was kept secret and caused embarrassment when it was revealed proves it was accepted as a bribe. It was a sad falling-off from the ethical standards of earlier generations. In 1734, just before the general election, a body called the 'Dissenting Deputies' was formed to take political action for the rights of Nonconformists. Walpole promised his support for the body in return for support for his party in the election. He duly won the election, but failed to do anything to help Nonconformists. The Dissenting Deputies eventually did much good, but the deal with Walpole was not the action of men who had died at the stake for their beliefs, or of those who had refused James II's offer of protection in return for support against the Anglicans. The whole country seemed affected by the corruption of the age. Even among the descendants of the Puritans came a stagnation of their spiritual life.

There were yet good and great men among the Nonconformists, some of whom became famous, not for their preaching or pastoral powers but for their written works. Such a man was Matthew Henry (1662–1714). His father had been ejected in 1662 and Matthew had rejected the law to become a minister in his turn. He was a Presbyterian. In 1687 he became Minister of the Church in Chester and from 1704 devoted himself to the mammoth task of commentaries on the Old and New Testaments. The work was scholarly enough, but the emphasis was on the practical and spiritual aspects rather than the critical, and the style was English and idiomatic. I had great popular appeal for generations, though by his death he had only got to the end of the Acts of the Apostles.

Isaac Watts (1674–1748) was another Nonconformist whose greatness long survived him and lives to this day. His father had been in prison for his Nonconformity. Isaac was educated at the Dissenting Academy at Stoke Newington. A Congregationalist, he was first at Mark Lane Chapel, then at Pinner's Hall and in 1708 moved with the congregation to Bury Lane. Four years later, when his health was broken, he was invited by Sir Thomas Abney (1640–1722), one of the founders of the Bank of England, to join his household for a visit while Isaac got back his health, and there he stayed for the remaining thirty-six years of his long life. He wrote educational manuals, devotional works, philosophical works, religious poetry (his *Horae Lyricae*, 1706, earned him a place in Johnson's *Lives of the Poets*), and some 600 hymns. Luther was a great hymn-writer, but Calvin had proscribed all music in his services except metrical psalms and canticles. The tradition of English Puritanism had followed Calvin, and it was a very long time before innovators dared to break Calvin's embargo. Watts was not the first to break it but he was the first able one. He wrote in a simple and vivid style. His best hymns are superb. Among his most famous ones are 'Come let us join our cheerful songs', 'I'm not ashamed to own my Lord', 'Jesus shall reign where'er the sun', 'Awake our souls, away our fears', 'There is a land of pure delight', 'Give me the wings of faith, to rise', 'Before Jehovah's awful throne', 'Join all the glorious names', 'Our God, our help in ages past', and 'When I survey the wondrous Cross'. All these hymns and many more were sung first by Congregationalists, then by other Nonconformists, and over a period of time became part of the whole Christian heritage.

Philip Doddridge (1702–1751), another Congregationalist, and influenced by Watts, was the son of a merchant, and the grandson of a Lutheran Minister. He was orphaned young, refused an invitation from the Duchess of Bedford to educate him for orders in the Church of England, was educated at a Dissenting Academy, and became instead a Congregationalist Minister. A considerable scholar, in 1729 he opened his own Dissenting Academy in Northampton while also Pastor of Castle Hill Congregational

Chapel in the same town. His Academy produced Nonconformist Ministers. He taught in English, a rare approach then, but his frequent absences led to indiscipline in the college. In 1745 he published *The Rise and Progress of Religion in the Soul*, a series of powerful addresses which were influential in their day. He was a fearless man who risked the displeasure of his congregation many times. He invited George Whitefield to his pulpit; he defended James Peirce (c.1674–1736), whose theological views most found heretical; he passionately desired to unite all Nonconformists. Doddridge also founded a charity school in 1737 and helped found the county infirmary in 1745. He was one of the greatest men of his age. In his many labours his deep spirituality shone. Doddridge is best remembered for his hymns. He used Watts as his pattern but never achieved Watts' greatness. His hymns are still sung, however, and the best-known include 'Hark the glad sound, the Saviour comes', 'Ye Servants of the Lord', 'Ye humble souls that seek the Lord', 'O God of Bethel, by whose hand', 'O happy day, that fixed my choice', and 'See Israel's gentle Shepherd stand'. He contracted tuberculosis and was sent by friends to Portugal where it was hoped the climate would cure him. The help came too late; he died and was buried in Lisbon.

One of the leading Congregationalists of his age was Thomas Bradbury (1677–1759), already briefly mentioned. It is symptomatic of the times that he was political pamphleteer – an extreme Whig – as well as Nonconformist divine. From 1707 he was Minister of New Street Church, near Fetter Lane. He is alleged, on Queen Anne's death, to have preached from the text II Kings 9:34: "Go, see now this cursed woman and bury her, for she is a King's daughter". He was an uncompromising Calvinist, violently opposed to the mildly Unitarian views of James Peirce. It was over the dispute that Nonconformists waged over Peirce's theological position that Nonconformity splintered and broke up. For a while there had been warm relationships between them.

Within the main Church body, Deism became fashionable. This was the belief (noted briefly in Chapter IV) that there is a personal God who created the Universe but he is detached from the world he made and has given no revelation. Natural religion alone is the hope for those who do not accept the Christian revelation. Deists also believed that priests had corrupted religious truth. It was a short step from this position to no effective religion at all. Such a theological position was typical of this age. Reason seemed a more acceptable principle of life than revealed religion. When Bishop Butler (1692–1752) said to John Wesley, "Sir, the pretending to extraordinary revelations and gifts of the Holy Ghost is a horrid thing – a very horrid thing", he was voicing the religious attitude of many of this period. Dr. Johnson defended the expulsion of the six students of St. Edmund's Hall, Oxford, whose only offence was to be more religiously zealous than others, with the words "Sir, that expulsion was extremely just and proper. What have they to do at a University, who are not willing to be taught, but will presume to teach? Where is religion to be learned but at an University? . . . I believe they might be good beings; but they are not fit to be in the University of Oxford. A cow is a very good animal in the field; but we turn her out of a garden". Dr. Johnson also was speaking for many of his age. Enthusiasm was ungentlemanly. Too much concern in matters religious was vulgar. Only in such an age could Dr. Trapp have published his strangely, if scripturally-titled tract, 'The Nature, Folly, Sin and Danger of being Righteous over-much'.

If some of the giants of the age accepted Deism, and great numbers accepted its ethos without being over-concerned with the theological niceties, it is no wonder that Unitarianism spread rapidly among the Nonconformists. On a strict interpretation, many do not consider Unitarianism a branch of Christianity inasmuch as it denies the divinity of Christ. A modern summary of Unitarian faith lists the Fatherhood of God, the brotherhood of man, the leadership of Jesus, the victory of good, the Kingdom of God, and the Life Eternal. While Christ's pre-eminence is acknowledged, and he is considered the world's greatest religious teacher as well as the supreme prophet of righteousness, he is not acknowledged as the son of God; he is wholly human, not divine.

Isolated Unitarians have been mentioned before, but during this age the cause became numerous and powerful. Thomas Emlyn (1663–1741) is considered the first Unitarian Minister in England as opposed to lonely predecessors who had no following. He was educated at two Dissenting Academies and was briefly at Cambridge. He became domestic chaplain to a Presbyterian lady in Belfast and somehow obtained a preaching licence though not in orders. In 1688 he left Ireland for London. He preached Unitarian doctrines and was arrested, fined and imprisoned.

James Peirce (c.1674–1736) of Exeter, mentioned above, caused disputes at the same period by mild Unitarian views and was locked out of his own church. He set up elsewhere and some of his congregation followed him. Other congregations were set up, particularly from the Presbyterians. The new Churches multiplied rapidly. Unitarianism rejected orthodox theology but substituted no coherent alternative. Some of their Ministers held only a vague humanitarianism. The best of them were excellent, godly men, and, notwithstanding what appears to the orthodox as missing the heart of the matter, in imitation of Christ, human, not divine, they went about doing good.

Such a man was Dr. Joseph Priestley (1733–1804) distinguished scientist and Unitarian Minister. His eminence in chemistry, his championship of Nonconformity against unjust laws, and his life of Christian service marked him out and brought lustre to Unitarianism. He was not alone in supporting the French Revolution, nor in suffering the indignation of the mob when that movement, set up to remove tyranny, became as tyrannous in its turn.

It has been said that Nonconformists, by the middle of the eighteenth century, had lost in zeal what they had gained in respectability. There is much truth in it. Numerically they could prove great progress. They could also prove political power. They were organized and confident and prepared to fight incipient persecution. The 'Dissenting Deputies' had been formed to fight the Test and Corporation Acts. Nevertheless, Nonconformists were not what they were. No longer starving in prison, they had become half-hearted under persecution. They were self-satisfied. It is a commonplace that a cause is strongest under persecution, but it is still sad to see the descendants of the Protestant saints and martyrs so emasculated.

It would be unfair to single out the Nonconformists for being spiritually dead; the whole Church was asleep. Hume said that England had "settled into the most cool indifference with regard to religious matters that is to be found in any nation of the world", and Bishop Butler said, "the deplorable distinction of our age is an avowed scorn of religion in some, and a growing disregard of it in the generality". Christianity in England had almost ceased to count.

The spark of living religion never died, though it was difficult to see it. A group of men of like mind, no apparent connection between them, were struggling towards a vital personal religion. There were Vincent Perronet (1693–1785) in Shoreham, William Grimshaw (1708–1763) in Haworth, John Berridge (1716–1793) in Cambridge and then Everton, and there were three men in Oxford who, with others, formed a tiny religious society, derisively called the 'Holy Club' by their enemies, in their joint quest for God. These were George Whitefield (1714–1770), John Wesley (1703–1791) and Charles Wesley (1707–1788).

The Evangelical Revival really began with George Whitefield. He was the son of a publican of Gloucester. He got to Oxford as a despised 'servitor', a man whose poverty compelled him to be College servant as well as undergraduate. The College, Pembroke, was the same one that Dr. Johnson had left only the year before, compelled to leave because of poverty even greater than Whitefield's. Whitefield joined the 'Holy Club' or 'Methodists' (both terms of ridicule, the latter destined to be adopted by Wesley's followers) and was deeply influenced by it. Very early in 1735 he had an experience of God which totally altered his life. In 1736 he was ordained deacon and during his year as a curate he began his astonishing career. He was a preacher without peer.

He was, in all probability, the greatest preacher of the post-apostolic age. Stories about him are legion. In his first year of preaching he was alleged to have driven fifteen men mad, and the report drew the response from the Bishop of London, "I wish he would bite some of my clergy." The great actor Garrick pronounced him a genius, and said Whitefield could make men weep or tremble by his varied pronunciation of the word "Mesopotamia"; he made Benjamin Franklin, the determined American statesman, who had attended a sermon by Whitefield and resolved the preacher would not get a farthing for a collection the visitor disapproved, empty his pockets into the plate, copper, silver and gold. It was said of him, "his face was language, his intonation music, and his action passion." Even Chesterfield, rake and cynic, was not proof against Whitefield's power. As the preacher told of an old blind man, deserted by his dog, tottering on a cliff edge, his Lordship lost control. "Good God!" he shouted, "He's gone."

Whitefield could be intensely dramatic, as when he ordered the Archangel Gabriel to pause in his flight while he urged his hearers to let news of their conversion be carried to God, or when he put on his 'condemning cap' to damn lost souls. Yet Whitefield was no actor; he was utterly sincere, and his whole life proved it. It was the power of his conviction and the power of his imagination joined to the great gifts of the orator that made him so outstanding, and the effect was the same on the fashionable as on the poor, who, never having heard the Gospel message before, flocked in thousands and wept as Whitefield preached.

After a visit to Georgia, in which he established schools and projected the foundation of an orphan house, Whitefield returned to England to be ordained priest and found church doors barred against him. Many clergy detested his 'enthusiasm'; others feared the effects of his preaching on simple people, for reports of insanity and convulsions grew; others were frankly jealous of a young man, barely out of College, who could fill churches and thrill congregations, when they could not muster a handful.

In 1739, therefore, Whitefield preached in the open air and flouted church order. Thereafter, he saw the need for lay preachers and encouraged their efforts, ignoring the laws of his Church. He judged that the spiritual needs of the people outweighed rules and regulations, and he preached to all who would hear him, irrespective of their church allegiance. Anglicans and Noncon-formists were all one to him; they were all souls to be saved.

He itinerated, ignoring parish boundaries. He visited Wales and there met Howel Harris (1714–1773), who was to become the principal founder with Whitefield of Welsh Calvinist Methodism. He met and became the intimate friend of Selina Hastings, Countess of Huntingdon (1707–1791). Converted to 'Methodism' by her sister-in-law, she was the first member of the nobility to be affected by the religious revival, and her influence was great. Exercising her right as a peeress to appoint as many chaplains as she liked, she appointed Whitefield as one of them, William Romaine (1714–1795) as another, and her circle of religious influence embraced the Wesleys, Berridge, Grimshaw, Isaac Watts, Howel Harris, already noted, and John Fletcher (1729–1785), Augustus Toplady (1740–1778), Henry Venn (1725–1797), Rowland Hill (1744–1833), and Martin Madan (1726–1790). Moravians, Congregationalists and Presbyterians were among her friends, but most were ministers of the Church of England whose lives had been altered by a sudden conviction of personal salvation and a desire to share this experience with others.

The Countess built a chapel for Whitefield to preach in, and chapels in Brighton and other fashionable centres, in the hope that the godliness of the Revival might be heard by the ruling classes. In 1768 she opened a training centre for ministers of the Gospel, with Fletcher as its President. In 1779, however, when she opened yet another chapel in London, this time at Spa Fields, her rights were challenged by a clergyman. Was there no limit to the rights of a peeress to build places of public worship wherever she wished? The case went against her, and she was therefore forced to license all her chapels under the Toleration Act as Nonconformist places of worship. Thus was formed, not by her wish, for she was a faithful member of the Church of England, 'The Countess of Huntingdon's Connexion', an unintended addition to Nonconformity. It was another sad reflection on the times. Too much zeal for religion had forced out of the Church of England some of its most devoted supporters. It would not be long before an even larger body would be obliged to follow.

Whitefield spent part of his time in England, part in America. In the latter, he was responsible for the foundation of some 150 Congregational churches and the revival of many Presbyterian ones. Though his ordination could not be taken away, Whitefield was effectively a Congregationalist, except that labels meant nothing to him. It was during his seventh visit to America – some of them lasted several years – that Whitefield died and was buried, at his own wish, under the pulpit of the Presbyterian Church in Newburyport.

John Wesley was the greatest man of his age. Born at Epworth, Lincolnshire, he was the son of the rector, a somewhat unlovable and feckless man, a Bible commentator and poet, a high church-man and Tory. John Wesley's mother, however, was a woman of genius. Both parents were of nonconformist stock. Wesley was educated at Charterhouse (he entered the year of George I's accession) and at Christ Church, Oxford. An excellent scholar, he left his College to act as his father's curate from 1727–9, but returned to Oxford on his appointment as Fellow of Lincoln College and here, taking over the leadership of the 'Holy Club' which his younger brother Charles had founded, he plunged into what he later believed to be a spiritual blind alley. He devoted every moment of his day to spiritual exercise. He rose at four for private prayer, was assiduous in attendance at College Chapel, studied the Scriptures, visited prisoners, the sick and the poor, gave away every farthing he could spare, spent hours with Charles and Whitefield and the other members in self-examination, but found no lasting peace with God for he was relying on his own righteousness. Persuaded by Whitefield to go to Georgia, he found another blind alley in his missionary zeal; his time there was disastrous. His stiff high church principles caused offence, he had an unhappy love affair, and he returned to England in despair. His only gain had been the friendship and advice of Moravians, whose fellowship he sought again on his return. For the second time he found he had been struggling to God through his own works.

On 24 May 1738, not long after his brother Charles had been converted, Wesley had an experience which changed his life. In his own words: "In the evening I went very unwillingly to a society in Aldersgate-Street, where one was reading Luther's preface to the Epistle to the Romans. About a quarter before nine, while he was describing the change which God works in the heart through faith in Christ, I felt my heart strangely warmed. I felt I did trust in Christ, Christ alone for salvation: and an assurance was given me, that he had taken away *my* sins, even *mine*, and saved *me* from the law of sin and death". Wesley had discovered that holiness is the fruit of faith, not faith the fruit of holiness. Having flung himself totally on God's mercy, having admitted his total worthlessness, Wesley found his peace, and there followed from this experience an almost incredible life of service.

During the remaining fifty-three years of his life he travelled nearly a quarter of a million miles, most of it on horseback. He preached some 5,000 sermons each year. Within the Church of England he organized religious societies through the British Isles and in the American colonies. He trained devout laymen to become travelling preachers. He wrote many books and edited hundreds more. In the end, but by accident, he had founded a new great branch of Nonconformity, had revitalized the Church of England, had strengthened every existing Nonconformist Church, and he had changed the face of England.

Whitefield had found it easy to ignore Church discipline. Wesley found it extremely difficult. In preaching out of doors

he said he had "consented to be more vile". He had the utmost
difficulty in persuading himself that lay preachers were necessary.
Having done these things, however, and been convinced that they
were God's will, he did them to the uttermost. He preached in
fields, barns, at cross-roads, on mountain-tops, in city streets and
market-places; he even used his father's tomb as a pulpit. When it
became impossible for him to get men ordained for ministry in
America, he reluctantly ordained them himself – a Superinten-
dent, Thomas Coke, and two Presbyters. Charles, ever a more
cautious churchman than his brother, was horrified and wrote on
the subject:

> How easily are bishops made
> By man or woman's whim!
> Wesley his hand on Coke hath laid,
> But who laid hands on him?

John Wesley had long passed the point at which any barrier or
criticism could prevent him from doing what he believed his task
to be, spreading Scriptural holiness. "The world is my parish", he
had said, in defence of his refusal to observe parish boundaries.
He had been attacked by mobs many times, stoned and arrested;
vicious pamphlets had vilified him; his followers were harried,
their property damaged, their meeting-houses burnt.

It was Wesley's organizing genius that gave permanence to his
work. His followers were divided into 'Classes' of twelve or
fourteen members each, and the concern of each group was to
foster its faith through prayer, Bible study and spiritual examination. 'Bands' were groups of ten who knew themselves to be
'justified'; 'Select Bands', the highest spiritual category, were for
those 'made perfect in love', a phrase referring to Wesley's
doctrine of Christian perfection. Self-discipline was the heart of
membership, but Wesley always stressed that salvation by faith
was the first step – without it, all self-discipline was worthless, as
his own had been.

There had always been a barrier between Whitefield and the
Wesleys. Though they had so much in common and worked
so closely together and took each other's advice, yet a great theological gulf divided them, for the Wesleys were uncompromising Arminians and Whitefield was an uncompromising Calvinist.
As long as Whitefield lived the two leaders agreed to differ as

gentlemen, and minimized their difference for the sake of their vital agreements. On Whitefield's death in 1770, however, the Methodist Conference (it had met annually from 1744) declared its Arminian faith and condemned Calvinism. This move effectively split the Evangelical world apart and turned some of the best men on each side into furious pamphleteers. Bitterness poisoned relationships between those who for years had been struggling as fellow-workers for the souls of the unloved. On one side were the Wesleys, John Fletcher, and Wesley's travelling preachers; on the other was the Countess of Huntingdon and almost all the other clergy of the Church of England. Wesley had summarized a tract of Toplady's, a defence of predestination, in these words: "The sum of all is this: one in twenty (suppose) of mankind are elected; nineteen in twenty are reprobated. The elect shall be saved, do what they will; the reprobate shall be damned, do what they can. Reader, believe this, or be damned. Witness my hand, A— T—." Wesley then left the dispute to his lieutenants. In acrimony the Calvinist cause was certainly victorious. Toplady and Rowland Hill spat venom against, in Hill's words, "Wesley's ragged legion of preaching barbers, cobblers, tinkers, scavengers, draymen, and chimney-sweepers". The battle of ideas, however, moved towards Arminianism, for long before the turn of the century most of the Calvinists were talking about "moderate Calvinism", a compromise against their own iron doctrine.

Charles Wesley itinerated with John for some years, but married and settled happily in Bristol to a resident ministry. This was a great grief to the celibate Berridge, who mused over the marriages of his three friends: "Matrimony has quite maimed poor Charles, and might have spoiled John and George, if a wise Master had not graciously sent them a brace of ferrets." As far as Mrs. John Wesley is concerned the description is tolerably accurate, but it is probably unfair to Mrs. George Whitefield, of whom we know little. Certainly Charles was happy. His chief contribution to the Evangelical revival was as a poet. He was the greatest hymn-writer of his age. Many of the 6,000 hymns he wrote are long forgotten; a considerable number are in daily use today. For Christmas there is 'Hark, the herald angels sing'; for Easter, 'Christ the Lord is risen today'; for Ascension, 'Hail the day that sees him rise'; for Whitsuntide, 'Lord, we believe to us and

ours', 'Granted is the Saviour's prayer' and 'Away with our fears';
for Trinity Sunday, 'Hail! Holy, holy, holy Lord'. There is 'Jesus,
Lover of my soul' and 'Love divine, all loves excelling', and there
are hundreds more.

Charles Wesley could put a doctrine into a couplet:

> Our God contracted to a span,
> Incomprehensibly made man.

He could contemplate the mystical:

> Ah! show me that happiest place,
>   The place of thy people's abode,
> Where saints in an ecstacy gaze,
>   And hang on a crucified God.

He could write with sublime simplicity for little children:

> Loving Jesus, gentle Lamb,
>   In thy gracious hands I am;
> Make me, Saviour, what Thou art;
>   Live Thyself within my heart.

He could stress the depth of divine love and the personal nature of
salvation:

> Throughout the world its breadth is known,
>   Wide as infinity;
> So wide it never passed by one,
>   or it had passed by me.

He could make his verse thrill with happiness:

> And my heart it doth dance at the sound of his name

or urge weary humanity on its road to heaven:

> Come on, my partners in distress,
> My comrades through the wilderness,
>   Who still your bodies feel . . .
>   .   .   .   .
> To patient faith the prize is sure,
> And all that to the end endure
>   The cross, shall wear the crown.

The Father shining on his throne,
The glorious co-eternal Son,
     The Spirit, one and seven,
Conspire our rapture to complete;
And lo! we fall before His feet,
     And silence heightens heaven.

Charles, with John or alone, accompanied doomed felons on
their hideous journey to death in an open cart. Side by side felon
and clergyman sat on the coffin and sang the hymn Charles wrote
for that journey – identifying the doomed man with the penitent
thief:

Canst thou reject our dying prayer
Or cast us out who come to thee?
Our sins, ah! Wherefore didst thou bear?
     Jesus, remember Calvary.

O might we, with believing eyes,
Thee in thy bloody vesture see
And cast us on thy sacrifice.
     Jesus, my Lord, remember me.

For his conversion and his brother's Charles wrote a hymn of
triumph through faith:

Where shall my wondering soul begin?
     How shall I all to heaven aspire?
A slave redeemed from death and sin,
     A brand plucked from eternal fire,
How shall I equal triumphs raise,
     Or sing my great Deliverer's praise?

Some of Charles' greatest hymns, 'Come, O Thou Traveller
unknown,' for instance, are virtually unsingable, too long,
too intense, too personal for congregational singing. For the
most part, however, it was part of his genius to know what the
Classes – and these were the people for whom he wrote – could
sing and learn from. The Evangelical faith comes strongly
through his hymns, and his Arminian theology with it. Every
single line of this hymn is an affirmation of Arminianism, a denial
of Calvinism.

Father, whose everlasting love
　　Thy only Son for sinners gave,
Whose grace to all did freely move,
　　And sent him down the world to save:

Help us Thy mercy to extol,
　　Immense, unfathomed, unconfined;
To praise the Lamb who died for all,
　　The general Saviour of mankind.

Thy undistinguished regard
　　Was cast on Adam's fallen race;
For all Thou hast in Christ prepared
　　Sufficient, sovereign, saving grace.

John Wesley, in his Preface to their hymnbook, had informed those who wished to reprint their hymns (and usually without acknowledgment) that "they are perfectly welcome so to do, provided they print them just as they are. But I desire they would not attempt to mend them – for they really are not able." It was sound advice. There were many scribblers of hymns in the eighteenth century and one or two able writers as well as Charles Wesley. Among the latter were, ironically, the two most fierce rivals in the Calvinistic controversy. The Calvinist Toplady wrote 'Rock of Ages, cleft for me', and the Arminian Thomas Olivers (1725–1799) wrote 'The God of Abraham Praise'.

In Olney, Buckinghamshire, lived John Newton (1725–1805), ex-slave-trader and Evangelical Minister of the Church of England, and with him lived the poet William Cowper (1731–1800), struggling with mental problems and resting on the strength and assurance of his friend. Between them they published a hymn-book. Newton's hymns included 'How sweet the name of Jesus sounds' and 'Glorious things of Thee are spoken'; Cowper's, 'Hark, my soul! it is the Lord', 'O for a closer walk with God', 'God moves in a mysterious way', and 'Sometimes a light surprises'.

John Wesley had much of sanctity in him, but John Fletcher was the undisputed saint of the Revival. Swiss in origin, he was Vicar of Madeley in Shropshire for twenty-five years. He established Methodist societies throughout his neighbourhood and tried to suppress brutal sports. Magistrates, publicans and clergy organized mobs to harry him. He was attacked many times. In the end his love broke down all opposition. Alone among the protagonists of the Calvinistic Controversy he wrote in love. Wesley justly said of Fletcher's 'Checks to Antinomianism', "One knows not which to admire most – the purity of the language, the strength and clearness of the argument, or the mildness and sweetness of spirit which breathes throughout the whole". "His whole life," said his biographer, "was a sermon." It was true. In Switzerland on a holiday, Fletcher handed round the simple daily lunch to his circle of friends with the words of the sacrament. Only a saint could have done it without blasphemy. George III was impressed by some of Fletcher's political pamphlets and wanted to honour him. The King sent an official to ask Fletcher what he wanted. Church preferment? Or could the Lord Chancellor reward him? Fletcher answered, "I want nothing, but more grace". Wesley knew Fletcher's value and designated him as his successor, but the Vicar of Madeley predeceased him. His Vicarage is virtually unchanged. On the wall can be seen the hollow where the breath of his prayers wore away the plaster.

The Evangelical Revival affected the whole Church. It started in the Church of England, but it was too big for that Church to contain. Whitefield was not the only one to act outside it when his flouting of church discipline closed almost every door. His converts joined the Church of England, Congregationalism and Presbyterianism. Rowland Hill had been ordained deacon, but no bishop could be found to ordain him priest. He built his own church, Surrey Chapel, in 'the devil's territory' of London, and it was administered as if he were a Congregationalist. Berridge, Vicar of Everton, rode rough-shod over the rules and was nearly imprisoned for refusing the bishop's instructions to stop preaching in other men's parishes.

It was Wesley himself, however, whose position in the Church was the most critical, for he left a great empire at the time of his death in 1791. There were 71,688 members of his classes in Great Britain, 5,300 in foreign societies, 42,265 in North America, a total membership of 119,253, and these figures do not include thousands more adherents. Though Wesley died imploring his followers to remain in the Church of England, it was his own decisions which had made it impossible. Successive moves he had made removed his followers from any possible reabsorption in the establishment. He had followed Whitefield in field-preaching and encouraged his followers to do the same; he had adopted extempore prayer; he had appointed lay preachers in great numbers; he had organized his followers into religious societies, and held local and national conferences; above all, and if there were no other impediment this would have been enough, he ordained men as Ministers. This last point was absolute. "Ordination was separation", said Charles Wesley, but John, astonishingly, could not see it.

Methodism was a new branch of Nonconformity very soon after Wesley's death. The loss to the Church of England was incalculable, but they could be excused for not seeing it that way. The whole movement was tainted with 'enthusiasm'. No doubt some of Wesley's new converts were irritatingly critical of their parish church. No doubt also some of Wesley's lay preachers were tactless. Rank mattered much in the eighteenth century, and most of the lay preachers came from a rank that would never have been ordained. The first of Wesley's lay preachers, Thomas Maxfield, did great damage to the Evangelical cause by preaching strange doctrines which John Wesley had to repudiate. Further, however much Wesley insisted on attendance of his people at the parish church, and however much he forbad meetings during service hours, there was an inevitable clash of loyalties. It must have been infuriating for a parish priest to minister to a flock each Sunday whose real allegiance they felt to be their Class-meetings on weekday evenings.

It is true, however, that some of the Church of England clergy stayed firmly within the Church of England and kept their flocks there. Such men were Henry Venn (1725–1797), his son John (1759–1813), Joseph Milner (1744–1797) and his brother Isaac (1751–1820), all members of Cambridge. It was at Cambridge that Charles Simeon (1759–1836) was importuned by John Berridge to break church rules as he had done, and spread the Gospel across the land in the earliest tradition of the Evangelical Revival. Simeon refused, choosing rather to use his great influence exclusively in the mother church. This decision helped to establish Evangelicalism in the Church of England as a distinct body which was to be an immense force for good, not only for the Church but for the world.

The Evangelical Revival was a resurgence of Puritanism. J. R. Green the historian said of the movement, "Puritanism won its spiritual victory in the Wesleyan movement, after the failure in the previous century of its military and political struggles." There is much truth in it.

It was noted in Chapter III that the stresses of the Puritans were the supreme authority of the Scriptures, preaching, lecturing, Lord's Day observance, the religion of the home, and the permeation of every aspect of life by religion. These stresses were as strong during the Evangelical Revival. The Bible was their guide. Bible study was an essential part of a new convert's way of life, and it was because so many children could not read the Bible that Wesley anticipated the Sunday School movement in getting his helpers to teach children to read. Illiteracy was no impediment to life in those days, but it might be an impediment to eternity. In middle- and upper-class families twice-daily prayers became the rule, the reading of the Scriptures being the centre of each service.

It was through preaching that the Gospel had been spread. It was through sermons delivered in the highways and byways that the thousands of converts had been brought to Christianity. Preaching, therefore, in all its aspects became the most important and the longest part of an Evangelical service. In the early days of the Revival, and especially when they were addressed to crowds out of doors, sermons were usually 'Gospel' sermons. It was said of Whitefield, "His 30 or 40,000 sermons were but so many variations on two key-notes. Man is guilty, and may obtain forgiveness; he is immortal, and must ripen here for endless weal or woe hereafter". Berridge gave his own advice on constructing a sermon. A Gospel minister should begin by "laying open the innumerable corruptions of the hearts", then "declaring every transgression . . . deserving of death," wait until "your hearers are deeply affected" and then "wave the Gospel flag . . . that his blood can wash away the foulest sin."

Observance of the Sabbath was vital to the Evangelicals. Since the Restoration the English Sunday had reverted to being a day of debauchery. Most of the devil's work, the Evangelicals judged, was done on the Lord's day. From towards the end of the eighteenth century there was a conscious effort to purify the day, societies were founded to compel Sabbath observance by law, and these attempts were one of the fruits of the Evangelical Revival.

Similarly, Evangelicals began with the religion of the home, but spread the family wider and wider. All the leading Evangelicals were passionately concerned about family religion, most were practical educationalists and founded schools and colleges, most made special provision for children, all stressed that religion should begin in the home. Wesley's Class system not only encouraged the religion of the home but created artificial family units which clung together for spiritual help and as a concomitant material help as well. Classes were families of God; fellowship was essential to the Christian life. Experience of the unconverted led the Evangelicals into two wider channels of service; social concern and missionary enterprise.

The condition of the poor was a shock to those who preached outside the churches. Good parish clergy, good Nonconformists had always cared for the poor of their parish or neighbourhood, but there were never enough good men to go round and there were great areas – especially in Wales – where there was no ministry. The unloved, the unwanted, the outcasts of society were precious to Christ. He needed their souls and he cared for their bodies. The Evangelicals began in self-help and moved on to the organization of relief.

The Sunday School movement was an important aspect of social concern. Robert Raikes (1735–1811) was an Evangelical layman of the Church of England. In 1780 he had founded a Sunday School. The idea was not new. An account of this experiment appeared in the *Gloucester Journal* in 1783. "Farmers, and other inhabitants of towns and villages," stated the report, "complain they receive more injury in their property on the sabbath, than all the week besides. This in a great measure proceeds from the lawless state of the younger class, who are allowed to run wild on that day, free from any restraint. To remedy this evil, persons duly qualified are employed to instruct those that may have learned to read, are taught the catechism, and conducted to church". The inducement was a realistic one; if wild lawless youth could be occupied on Sunday and educated as well, the nation would profit. Evangelicals of all church groups took up the challenge and the work grew at an astonishing rate. By 1810 there were more than 3,000 Sunday Schools established in

Britain and nearly 275,000 scholars had passed through the schools. Joseph Lancaster (1778–1838), a Quaker, introduced a method of teaching the underprivileged, a monitorial system, which for many years allowed an education for some of the poorest.

Another social concern was the deplorable state of the prisons of the day. John Howard (1726–1790) was a friend of John Wesley's, a Congregationalist, who moved easily between the Church of England and Nonconformity. He inherited wealth and used it to campaign for prison reform in Parliament. A brief and accidental imprisonment in a Continental gaol had taught him early what imprisonment meant. When he had achieved a measure of success in England, he tried to alter conditions in foreign prisons also. A generation later Elizabeth Fry (1780–1845), a Quaker, was to continue Howard's work, especially for women prisoners.

The abolition of slavery was also largely due to the Evangelicals. The Quakers supported abolition as a body. The dying Wesley wrote to William Wilberforce (1759–1833): "Oh be not weary in well-doing. Go on in the name of God, and in the power of his might, till even American slavery, the vilest that ever saw the sun, shall vanish away before it." Wilberforce battled for it in Parliament and won the final battle in the year of his death. Others who were deep in social concerns and were associated with Wilberforce, members of a group scoffingly called 'The Clapham sect', were Zachary Macaulay (1768–1838), father of the historian, Thomas Clarkson (1760–1846), James Stephen (1758–1832) and the redoubtable author, Hannah More (1745–1833). It is difficult to find any cause of social concern in which the Evangelicals were not involved. It was an extension of their beliefs, and a vital one. The championship of the unprivileged by the Evangelicals was one large factor in the nineteenth-century rise of Chartism and the Trade Union Movement. It was the Evangelical Revival, and especially the foundation of Methodism, that trained the working classes in democracy.

In times past Puritans had fled abroad to escape persecution. Evangelicals resolved to go abroad in their turn, this time to carry the message of the Gospel across the world. Whitefield and Wesley had been abroad themselves and knew the needs. Both had sent individuals. The first Church to organize a Missionary

Society, however, was the Baptist Church. William Carey (1761–
1834) was a remarkable man. Born in Northampton, his father
kept a small school where William gained a modest education
before being apprenticed to a shoe-maker. In 1783 he became
a Baptist, and three years later was chosen as Minister of
the Baptist congregation in Moulton. He had completed his
education entirely by his own labours. Carey joined the movement that led to the formation of the Baptist Missionary Society
in 1792. In his cobbler's shop he pinned home-made maps of
the world on the wall and to the thump of his hammer he heard
an insistent voice, "Cobbler, while you mend your shoe, We
have a soul as well as you." In 1793 he sailed to India with his
wife and a colleague, the first missionaries of the society. He
settled in Serampore with two others, and there he eventually
translated the Scriptures into twenty-six languages, including
Chinese, and founded a school for the training of Indian
Christians. His chief work was neither translation nor education,
however. He went to India to spread the Gospel, and this he did
for over forty years.

The London Missionary Society was founded in 1795, a Society
formed by Evangelicals of all denominations, though most of its
funds and its ministers were Congregationalist. The next year
two Scottish Missionary Societies were founded. In 1799 a group
of prominent Evangelicals in the Church of England founded the
Church Missionary Society. Methodists had long been in the
field, but the Wesleyan Methodist Missionary Society was not
founded until 1818.

Theologically, the Evangelicals emphasized and almost isolated
the doctrine of personal salvation. It was a very practical theology.
Most of their leaders had experienced years of depression and
frustration struggling towards an acceptance of God's love. The
acceptance had come in a blinding moment of illumination.
Congregations, adherents, children were therefore taught to pray
for this experience, without which there would be no spiritual
progress, without which all works and service were totally vain.
Wesley alone taught new doctrine – that of Christian Assurance
and that of Christian Perfection. Both doctrines were stages, he
believed, in the imitation of Christ. He never claimed that he had
experienced the latter doctrine himself; it was, however, realizable
on earth.

The dour Calvinism of previous centuries, one of the hall-marks of the earlier Puritans, was fast waning. Though a considerable number of the leaders of the Evangelical Revival were Calvinists, the Revival helped kill the doctrine. The whole of Methodism was Arminian, and long before the turn of the century, most Evangelicals of the establishment were talking of 'moderate' Calvinism, which was not really Calvinism at all, for Calvin's creed was absolute and could not be compromised. It is nevertheless true that at least one branch of Nonconformity, Calvinist in theology, flourished at this time. During the early eighteenth century unitarian views had spread among the General Baptists who were, it will be remembered, Arminian in their theology. Dan Taylor (1738–1816), under the influence of the Evangelical Revival, organized those who remained and were of an orthodox and evangelistic spirit into a New Connexion, strong, spiritually keen. Simultaneously, the Particular Baptists experienced a spiritual renewal, and they reorganized themselves under the somewhat confusing title of 'General Union of Baptists', Calvinist in thought, and not to be confused with the General Baptists, who were Arminians.

All branches of Nonconformity were reinvigorated by the Revival, and a new Church, Methodism, came into being, while the presence of a strong Evangelical party in the Church of England ensured its influence there. (As a matter of convenience, the term 'Evangelicals' in future will refer to that body in the Church of England only.) The battle for greater liberty for Nonconformists, however, had been in progress long before Methodism was a distinct Church.

It was not only necessary to fight for greater liberty. It had been found necessary to fight even for the rights that the Toleration Act had given. The City of London, in the middle of the century, had found a cunning means to extort money from Nonconformists. A law had been passed that any man who refused to stand for the office of sheriff should be fined, and fined more heavily still if he were elected and refused to serve. Since sheriffs had to be communicants of the Church of England, and since most Nonconformists would refuse to communicate for conscience sake, the City raised £15,000 in six years by this device. In 1754 the City elected three successive Nonconformists who refused either to serve or to pay. The case went to law, and thirteen years later

Lord Mansfield gave judgment for the Nonconformists. It was no crime, he said, to be a Nonconformist, and persecution was 'against natural religion, revealed religion, and sound policy.' The conduct of the City of London was a violation of the Toleration Act.

This Act, it will be remembered, required Nonconformists to accept almost all the 39 Articles if they wished to be licensed as Ministers. For Unitarians this was impossible, and it troubled the consciences of many other Nonconformists. A repeal of this part of the Toleration Act was therefore attempted, the substitution of a declaration of faith that the Scriptures contained a revelation of the mind and will of God being the proposal. The first attempt passed the Commons with ease but was blocked in the Lords, notwithstanding Lord Chatham's defence of Nonconformity. He had seized on a phrase of the Archbishop of York, who had called Nonconformist Ministers men "of close ambition". "They are so, my lords," said Chatham, "and their ambition is to keep close to the college of fishermen, not of cardinals, and to the doctrines of inspired apostles, not to the decrees of interested and aspiring bishops. They contend for a Scriptural and spiritual worship; we have a Calvinistic creed, a Popish liturgy, an Arminian clergy. The Reformation has laid open the Scriptures to all; let not the bishops shut them again. Laws in support of ecclesiastical power are pleaded which it would shock humanity to execute. It is said religious sects have done a great mischief when they were not kept under restraints; but history affords no proof that sects have ever been mischievous when they were not oppressed and persecuted by the ruling Church." Not until 1779 was this modest repeal law and, once this was achieved, Nonconformists began battle for the repeal of the Test and Corporation Acts, but this battle would not be won until the nineteenth century.

The nineteenth century was a time of rapid expansion for the whole Church of God. The eighteenth century had begun in limited tolerance for Nonconformity, but a spiritual torpor had afflicted the whole Church. A little before the middle of the century the Evangelical Revival had rekindled the flame of religion, and by the turn of the century it had spread through the British Isles and beyond. The nineteenth century was to see the work consolidated and expanded.

CHAPTER VII

Expansion and Consolidation – The Nineteenth Century

ENGLAND CHANGED RAPIDLY IN the nineteenth century. Revolutions abroad (the American War of Independence and the French Revolution, followed by the French wars), brought to some Englishmen fellow-feeling that England itself needed change, but to most, and increasingly as the bloody aftermath of the French Revolution shocked the world, horror and panic. Simultaneously, the economic revolution that the Industrial Revolution brought in its wake altered the whole face of England. It brought extremes of wealth and poverty, the rise of the middle classes and a corresponding rise of the desperately poor, exploitation of labour, overcrowding of cities, the desertion of the country and migration. It also brought the policy of laissez-faire. Yet another revolution in all but name was the Evangelical Revival.

Traditionally the older Nonconformist bodies were liberal in outlook and initially they supported the revolutionary spirit. It was noted in Chapter VI how Joseph Priestley the Unitarian had his house sacked by the mob and fled to America. Dr. Richard Price (1723–1791), a friend of Priestley with similar views, died too soon to suffer a similar fate. His support of the American colonies and his condemnation of the war would have branded him traitor. Liberty had become a dangerous belief. Nevertheless, it was not merely fear which swept most Nonconformists into an anti-revolutionary fervour; it was the logic of events. In France the destruction of the State had meant the destruction of religion and if, to Protestants, the Catholic Church was corrupt, at least it was preferable to the rule of reason, Anti-Christ in disguise.

There was a marked distinction between the attitudes of the old Nonconformists and the Methodists. If the former were traditionally Whigs, the latter were founded by a Tory. Wesley's despotic rule was high Tory, and he roundly condemned the rebellious colonies. Their duty was to their King. The Methodist Conference, long after Wesley's death and even as some of their number were moving further and further left in their political views, sent an annual address of loyalty to the King, proof that they were untainted by republican views or revolutionary fervour.

Nor were relationships warm between the old Nonconformists and the Methodists. The older groups had won their identity in prison, on the scaffold, at the stake. They had fought their way through persecution to acceptance and even to respectability. They had become a force to be reckoned with. The Methodists, on the other hand, did not know at this time whether they wanted to be members of the Church of England or a new Nonconformist body. Many of their preachers were of the earth, earthy. It was some years before Nonconformity, with Methodism as one branch, was a recognizable whole, and this only became possible when Methodism rejected the possibility of reabsorption in the Church of England.

For the first half of the nineteenth century, Methodism was divided on the issue. Indeed, it was impatience with the slowness of the separation that led to the first secessions from Methodism, and the formation of new Churches. Only the Oxford Movement and the conversion of its most distinguished member to Roman Catholicism ended all hope of reconciliation. Methodists were utterly resolute in their Protestantism. If the Church of England was not only Catholic but toying with Rome, then Methodists must be Nonconformists.

There is a hint of their equivocal position in 1820, when the annual Methodist Conference was concerned at the first fall in numbers since the movement began: "Let us ourselves remember, and endeavour to impress on our people, that we as a body do not exist for the purpose of party . . . Let us therefore maintain towards all denominations of Christians . . . the kind and catholic spirit of primitive Methodism."

Jabez Bunting (1779–1858) was almost a second founder of Methodism. The movement needed a strong leader after Wesley's death and for years it struggled without. His enemies called him "the premier of Methodism who never went out of office, whoever might do so, having never been appointed." This was unfair inasmuch as he held the annual appointment of President of the Methodist Conference no less than four times, certain proof that he was desired as leader. Bunting not only ruled Methodism by the sheer power of his personality for over forty years; he equipped it with a constitution which detached it from its Anglican parent and set it on its own feet for a separated future. Friendly to the establishment as well as to Nonconformists, he set the course for the whole movement. Like Wesley, he was a Tory; like Wesley, he was a benevolent dictator. Tirelessly zealous for political and religious freedom as well as the spiritual welfare of half a million people, "his sole revenue" was "a furnished house, coals, candles, and £150 per annum." Hated by some in his lifetime for his ultra-conservatism as well as his autocracy (he flatly refused to conduct the funeral service of a Methodist luddite shot while breaking into a mill in 1812, and in 1827 was alleged to have said that Methodism was as opposed to democracy as it was to sin), he yet served his Church magnificently, and deserves more generous treatment than historians have granted him.

It was not hatred of Bunting, however, that led to the first secessions from Methodism. The root cause, as has been noted, was impatience with Methodism's allegiance to the Church of England and an anxiety to be as 'free' as the Nonconformists. Alexander Kilham (1762–1798), as soon as Wesley was dead, led the opposition to those who wanted to adhere to the Church of England. A fiery preacher and a vigorous pamphleteer, intolerant of Methodist leaders over him whom he called "persecuting Neros", he refused to resign and was finally expelled by the Conference of 1796. The next year, with a few others, he formed the 'Methodist New Connexion' with a membership of some 5,000. Its only differences from its parent body were that each church was autonomous and more power was given to lay members.

A second splinter group, the 'Primitive' Methodists, were formed in 1810. The leaders were Hugh Bourne (1772–1852), a remarkable man of humble origins who, self-taught, even grappled with Greek and Hebrew, and William Clowes (1780–1851), a

potter. Bourne, whose church views were basically Congregationalist, founded a Chapel for his converts. The work was blessed by
the Methodist Conference, who adopted it into their system, but
Bourne found it impossible to conform to Methodist discipline. He
had 'Camp Meetings', an idea borrowed from America, revival
meetings in the open air. Bourne justified them, not least because
they so closely followed Wesley's own example; the Methodist
powers condemned them on the grounds that they led to dangerous
emotionalism and were an affront to the government, which disliked large public meetings. Bourne and Clowes there fore formed
their own Church. The Primitive Methodists flourished. Their
rule was similar to the parent body except that, like the
'Kilhamites', they gave greater power to the laity. They were
particularly successful in rural areas, and with the very poor. Forty
years after their foundation they were more than 100,000 strong.

Yet another secession was led by William O'Bryan (1778–
1868). He was a Cornishman and a Methodist local preacher who
refused to stop preaching outside his own area and was expelled,
readmitted, and expelled again. In 1815 the Bible Christian
Society was formed, with O'Bryan as its President. No body could
contain such a man. He demanded the perpetual presidency of
the Society and absolute power in decision-making. When this
was refused O'Bryan left, and used his considerable preaching
gifts in Canada and America. In his place the gentler and abler
William Thorne became President and under his influence the
Society grew in numbers and influence. These godly people were
strongest in Cornwall where the eccentrically brilliant Billy Bray
(1794–1868), a home-spun evangelist of genius, furthered the
cause. From its beginnings Methodism had fostered leadership
and preaching by women; the Bible Christians were the first to
appoint itinerant women preachers on equal terms with the men.

The last big secession from what by this time was called
Wesleyan Methodism was through James Everett (1784–1872), a
bitter pamphleteer who hid in anonymity and by a series of vicious
attacks on Bunting and the Methodist leaders did great damage to
the parent body. Two seceding groups, one of them formed by
Everett, joined in 1857 to form the 'United Methodist Free
Churches'. By the end of the century Wesleyan Methodism was
still very much larger than the other groups, and by 1932 almost
all the splintered Methodist Churches were one again.

Methodism had, by imperceptible degrees, moved a considerable distance from its founder's intention. For Wesley, the heart of worship was the Holy Communion held in the parish church. The Class meetings and the preaching services were 'extras' – spiritually of great value, but not the essence of the worship of God. Before the middle of the nineteenth century, the preaching service, with the sermon as the main ingredient, was Methodism's chief way of worship. This was an inevitable corollary of Methodism's choice in accepting Nonconformity. Long before the end of the nineteenth century, Methodists had given up their compromise of having their own Holy Communion but being married and buried in the parish church. They were now totally one with the Nonconformists, 'chapel' as opposed to 'church', and they accepted the historical titles that belonged to their Nonconformist brethren – Protestants, Puritans, Dissenters, Nonconformists, and, finally, Free Church men and women.

All branches of Nonconformity expanded in the nineteenth century. The 1851 census, which showed that almost half the number of churchgoers were Nonconformists, revealed other statistics – for instance, that Wesleyan Methodists represented 1 in 9 of churchgoers who attended their church on Sunday mornings and 1 in 4½ of those who attended on Sunday evenings. By the end of the century this proportion was greater still. Building had to keep pace with attendance. Between 1801 and 1873 4,210 new Anglican churches were built, an increase of one third, while 20,000 non-Anglican chapels were built in the same period, a ten-fold increase. In 1801 the Baptists possessed 652 buildings; in 1851 they owned 2,789.

If great in numbers, Nonconformists were for the most part low in popular estimation. Many of them, especially the Methodists, came from lower social strata than the Anglicans, and were despised for it. In the fiction of the day they were often caricatured. Mr. Chadband, for instance, Dickens' creation in *Bleak House*, is a smug, unctuous hypocrite. He is introduced as "a large yellow man, with a fat smile, and a general appearance of having a good deal of train oil in his system". His manner of conversation is a skit on a popular type of pulpit oratory which Dickens records "widely received and much admired". "Peace be on this house!" says Chadband. "On the master thereof, on the mistress thereof, on the young maidens, and on the young men! My friends, why do

I wish for peace? What is peace? Is it war? No. Is it strife? No. Is it lovely, and gentle, and beautiful and pleasant, and serene, and joyful? O yes! Therefore, my friends, I wish for peace, upon you and yours." Nauseous as the style is, it was not particularly Nonconformist. Indeed, it is the very style that Martin Mar-Prelate mocked nearly 300 years before from the mouth of an enemy of the Puritans. It would be recognizably Nonconformist, however, in that preaching itself was a Nonconformist passion.

Charlotte Brontë more gently mocked clergy both in the establishment and outside it, but it was the latter who suffered most. In *Shirley* Church battles with Chapel in a school-feast procession. "The fat Dissenter who had given out the hymn was left sitting in the ditch. He was a spirit-merchant by trade, a leader of the Nonconformists, and, it was said, drank more water in that one afternoon than he had swallowed for a twelvemonth before." The charge here is hypocrisy, with an underlying implication that a spirit-merchant had no business with spiritual concerns. No doubt some of the Nonconformists were smug and self-satisfied, critical of others, proud of being 'the sweet selected few', over-zealous in matters of little importance, the victims of spiritual pride. No doubt also some of the men and women plucked from the gutters by the Evangelical Revival were slow to learn the ways of society and were disliked more for being 'upstarts' than for their religion. Equally, they themselves, as they rose in society, sometimes confused social with spiritual progress.

If they were despised by some they were also respected. Many Anglicans had a sneaking suspicion that Nonconformists with their puritanical ways, their regular chapel attendance and extra spiritual exercises, had somehow found a better path to God. Hardy expresses it well in *Far from the Madding Crowd* on the lips of the inn-keeper. "We know very well that if anybody do go to heaven, they will. They've worked hard for it, and they deserve to have it, such as 'tis. I bain't such a fool as to pretend that we who stick to the Church have the same chance as they, because we know we have not."

The working-class movement owed much to Nonconformists in general and Methodists in particular. Chartism and Trade Unionism were nurtured, accidentally in large measure, in Non-conformist Chapels. It was at the chapels that working men were encouraged, after conversion, to share their experience with others, to preach, to become educated, to lead in Chapel affairs, to become thrifty, to value the freedom to worship as they chose. This process, designed for spiritual advancement, could equally be of value in the material advancement of one's fellows, and a God of love and justice and mercy could only bless the attempts of his servants to obtain fair wages for the sweated poor.

The Tolpuddle martyrs were Wesleyan Methodists, three of them local preachers. It is sad to remember that the Methodist leadership did nothing to help them, not even offer aid to the families of the transported men. In 1834, official Methodism would not countenance political agitation for its members. The poorest Nonconformist group was the Primitive Methodist one, and it is not surprising that it was from their ranks that the labour leaders came. They knew better than any the injustices of the age, the dreadful conditions of the poor, the pittances for heavy labour, the social gulf that divided the indigent from the affluent. They took their preaching gifts to the political arena. It is recorded of Joseph Capper, the Chartist leader in the Potteries, that he had "a tongue like the sledge-hammer he used in his shop," of Tommy Hepburn, the leader of the Durham miners, that he "could be heard at one time by 40,000 people, and always carried the multitude with him." Joseph Arch (1826–1919) began life as a hedge-cutter, founded agricultural trade unions, and rose to be a member of Parliament. Thomas Burt (1837–1922), the miners' leader, rose higher still. He served under Gladstone as Parliamentary Secretary of the Board of Trade, became a Privy Councillor, and lived to be Father of the House of Commons. Local union groups are called 'Chapels' to this day. The term came from the Nonconformity of the pioneers.

There were Wesleyan Methodist leaders too. Joseph Stephens (1805–79) was a Methodist minister who resigned to give himself entirely to Chartism. He was imprisoned for eighteen months for his political agitation but philosophically observed, "To a man who has slept soundly with a sod for his bed and a portmanteau for his pillow . . . there is nothing so very, very frightful in a moderately good gaol, as gaols are now." He preached all his life, no less after his resignation from that calling. Henry Broadhurst (1840–1911) was a stonemason who at one time was employed on the clock tower of Big Ben. He also became a labour leader and M.P.

Nonconformity came under even heavier pressure than the

establishment, over the controversy that followed publication of Darwin's *Origin of Species* in 1859. It seemed to many that religion was being undermined by science. A bible-based authority was more vulnerable than episcopacy. If the account of the creation as given in Genesis was not true, how could the Scriptures be trusted? Biblical criticism as a serious study seemed the work of the devil. A moving account of the turmoil can be seen in Sir Edmund Gosse's *Father and Son* (1907). It is autobiographical, and describes how Sir Edmund's father, Philip Gosse, an eminent zoologist and a Nonconformist, struggled with problems to which his science had one answer, his religion another. There were years of bewilderment during which the basic question was always, "Is the Bible true?"

For some, 'true' meant literally true in the fullest sense. There was a Garden of Eden, there was a man of Uz whom God allowed Satan to persecute, there was a man called Jonah who was swallowed by a whale, God did instruct Abraham to sacrifice his son, and God did harden Pharaoh's heart. For others, 'true' meant literally true part of the time but sometimes true in a symbolical or allegorical and spiritual sense as opposed to a literal one. When, at a later date, some biblical scholars began to question Christ's miracles, the wise men and the virgin birth and, it seemed, almost every line in the Bible, divisions of opinion became bitter. The divisions remain to this day and cut across other divisions. The great majority of biblical scholars of all denominations no longer accept the Bible as literally true throughout, though a substantial number of 'fundamentalists' or 'conservative evangelicals' – terms used for those who claim the Bible to be the literally inspired word of God – remain, especially as a powerful minority in the Church of England, and in the smaller and newer Free Churches, American importations for the most part.

The strength of Nonconformity lay principally in the power of its leaders, particularly its great preachers. The Victorian age was an age of preachers, and young Nonconformists grew up assiduous sermon-tasters. Even as children they were expected to attend chapel twice on Sundays, and in those days a half-hour sermon would be a very short one. Wesley's itinerating system and the exchange of ministers between pulpits in other denominations as well as encouragement of lay preaching by all the churches, meant variety and opportunity for comparison. Popular preachers were in heavy demand, and an eminent name meant overcrowding or even exclusion for those who did not arrive early enough to get a place. Buildings were made larger and larger, but never seemed to be large enough to hold the sermon-hungry crowds.

Of the Congregationalists, R. W. Dale (1829–1895) of Birmingham was outstanding. A preacher at sixteen, he was not encouraged to make the ministry his profession, but taught instead for some years. Barred by his religion from Oxford and Cambridge, he graduated instead at London University in philosophy and obtained first-class honours and a gold medal. He was minister of Carr's Lane Chapel, Birmingham, from 1852 until his death more than forty years later. He achieved eminence in the city. His preaching powers drew crowds, and his intellectual ability, combined with moral passion, forced him into the city's political life. A forthright liberal, he was the close friend of Joseph Chamberlain. Dale, through his chairmanship of committees, was the effective head of political and educational policy in Birmingham. He refused offers of higher-paid posts elsewhere in order to minister to his own adopted city, spiritually first, but because of that socially too. Scholar and writer as well as preacher, his powers as a controversialist were so great that Matthew Arnold called him "a brilliant pugilist." In those days the Nonconformists found no difficulty in being politically active as well as ordained. Almost all (Jabez Bunting being a notable exception) were liberals. They looked upon political activity as their Puritan forebears had, as a natural extension of their religion.

Another Congregational giant of a very different kind was Joseph Parker (1830–1902). He was born in Hexham, the son of a stone-mason. He first preached for the Wesleyan Methodists when his family, brifly disenchanted with their own chapel, had sought spiritual help elsewhere, but returned with them after a while. He served in Banbury for four years, and for eleven in Manchester, where he became a great power in the city, but it was in London that he became famous. He was appointed minister of the Poultry Chapel in 1869, but five years later, minister and congregation moved to magnificent new quarters in the City Temple. His reputation as a preacher drew crowds, the eminent as well as the humble, and clergy of all denominations attended his services (sometimes in disguise) to try and understand his magic. Gladstone admired him. He had, says one biographer, "a will of adamant and a soul of fire." Another lists his qualities: "impressive appearance, regal personality, commanding voice, impeccable diction, and histrionic manner." Parker had a streak of eccentricity and a streak of arrogance, but he also had a preaching gift which few could equal.

Thomas Binney (1798–1874), another Congregationalist, was minister of the Weigh House Chapel in London. Like so many Nonconformists, he was in part self-taught and, having acquired scholarship by the most difficult means, prized it the more. Chairman of the Congregational Union, he was an able scholar and controversialist, world traveller and hymn-writer. He always told the truth as he saw it without the slightest regard for the effect it would have. One of his most celebrated sermons contained a denunciation of the Church of England: "It is with me a matter of deep serious religious conviction that the established church is a great national evil; that it is an obstacle to the progress of truth and holiness in the land; that it destroys more souls than it saves; and therefore its end is devoutly to be wished by every lover of God and man." The Church of England was reasonably furious. It is much to Binney's credit, and to that of the Church of England, that Dean Stanley esteemed him enough to attend his funeral. Binney was a lovable man and a fine Christian as well as a fierce polemicist.

Robert Hall (1764–1831) was educated in part at J. C. Ryland's school in Northampton. All branches of Nonconformity had families which, generation after generation, served their Church. The Rylands were a Baptist dynasty. Hall was one of the great oratorical preachers of the first half of the nineteenth century. He ministered in Cambridge, Leicester and Bristol. One of his hearers describes his power: "From the commencement of his discourse an almost breathless silence prevailed . . . Not a sound was heard but that of the preacher's voice – scarcely an eye but was fixed upon him – not a countenance that he did not watch, and read, and interpret . . . As he advanced and increased in animation, five or six of the auditors would be seen to rise and lean forward over the front of their pews, still keeping their eyes fixed upon him. Some new or striking sentiment or expression would, in a few minutes, cause others to rise in like manner; shortly afterwards still more, and so on, until long before the close of the sermon, it often happened that a considerable portion of the congregation were seen standing."

Hall could also be caustic when occasion prompted. He called himself "not a Calvinist in the strict and proper sense of the term." A self-important member of his congregation once had the temerity to complain that the minister was not preaching frequently enough on predestination. Robert Hall looked him steadily and carefully in the face and said, slowly weighing each word, "Sir, I perceive that nature predestinated you to be an ass, and what is more, I see that you are determined to make your calling and election sure."

Robert Hall was the champion of open against closed communion. "No man, or set of men," he argued, "are entitled to prescribe as an indispensable condition of communion what the New Testament has not enjoined as a condition of salvation." He was powerful in defence of freedom of the press in 1793, and published in 1819, after seeing the starving conditions of the stocking makers of Leicester, an appeal on their behalf. He was a champion of liberty, a typical representative of the 'Nonconformist conscience.'

Pre-eminent among the Baptist preachers of the second half of the century, pre-eminent among all Nonconformists, was C. H. Spurgeon (1834–1892). Born of Congregational stock, Spurgeon was converted in a Primitive Methodist Chapel, but became a Baptist in 1850. In his first ministry an old minister called him, in approval, "the sauciest dog that ever barked in a pulpit." At twenty-two he was the most celebrated preacher of his age, and caricature and ridicule were thrown at him because of his youth. Largely self-educated, he had learned enough to preach and write with authority and hold his own in controversy. His second appointment was to London where he immediately filled an almost empty church. Exeter Hall was hired but proved too small, so the congregation moved to Surrey Music Hall, which could take 10,000 people, until a permanent building could be completed. At a special service in the Crystal Palace Spurgeon once preached to 23,654 people. In 1861 the Metropolitan Tabernacle, built at a cost of £31,000 and capable of holding a congregation of 6,000, was completed. There Spurgeon preached to the end of his life, thirty years later. Twice every Sunday and once every Thursday he held over 5,000 people gripped by his preaching. Gladstone and Ruskin worshipped with him. Whitefield was perhaps a greater preacher, but he never had a settled ministry.

He could repeat his sermons endlessly. Spurgeon, on the other hand, had to deliver three lengthy sermons weekly (he preached every Thursday) to a discerning congregation who would be swift to note a repeated phrase or idea. Spurgeon's was a phenomenal achievement.

He had great oratorical gifts, though he was unimpressive in appearance. He "substituted naturalness for a false and stilted dignity, passion for precision, plain homely saxon for highly-Latinized English, humour and mother-wit for apathy and sleepiness, glow and life . . ." One authority thought Spurgeon's preaching had a special appeal for those who had missed all the prizes of life. "The perseverance of the saints is a doctrine without meaning to the majority of Christians. But many a poor girl with the love of Christ and goodness in her heart, working her fingers to the bone for a pittance that just keeps her alive, with the temptations of the streets around her, and the river beside her, listened with all her soul when she heard that Christ's sheep could never perish. Many a struggling tradesman tempted to dishonesty; many a widow with penury and loneliness before her, were lifted above all, taught to look through and over the years coming thick with sorrow and conflict, and anticipate a place in the Church Triumphant."

The crowds flocked to him all his life, but it is difficult to isolate the various gifts that made his preaching so appealing. He took risks that few would take today, no-one else at that time. Jokes of all kinds, especially puns, he loved; he mimicked from the pulpit; he assured his congregation more than once that he hoped that evening to smoke a cigar to the glory of God. Yet these are little things. Perhaps his greatest appeal was his sheer passion for the work, a longing to save souls, a conviction that to offer Christ was the most important work in the world. Spurgeon loved people with all his heart.

He preached Calvinism insistently and caused offence by attacks on Arminianism, but he said himself to Archbishop Benson, "I'm a very bad Calvinist, quite a Calvinist – I look on to the time when the elect will be all the world." He prayed more than once, "Lord, hasten to bring in all thine elect, and then elect some more," and J. C. Carlile wrote, "illogical as it may seem, Spurgeon's Calvinism was of such a character that while he proclaimed the majesty of God he did not hesitate to ascribe freedom of will to man and to

Philip Doddridge
(1702–1751)

George Whitefield
(1714–1770)
preaching, by
J. Woolaston

John Wesley
(1703–1791), by
John Jackson

John Wesley (1703–1791) preaching on his father's tombstone in
Epworth Churchyard

John Bunyan
(1628–1688)

Daniel Defoe (1661–1731) in the pillory, after Crowe

Thomas Bradbury
(1677–1759)

Isaac Watts
(1674–1748)

R. W. Dale
(1829–1895)

John Clifford
(1836–1923)

H. P. Hughes
(1847–1902)

William Booth
(1829–1912)

William Carey
(1761–1834) with a
convert

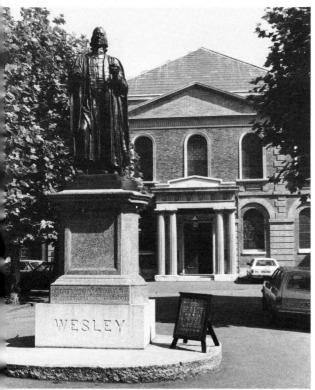

Wesley's Chapel, City Road, today

Jabez Bunting
(1779–1858)

C. H. Spurgeon
(1834–1892), by
Alexander Melville

insist that any man might find in Jesus Christ deliverance from the power of sin."

Controversy Spurgeon rarely shrank from. He bitterly hurt the Evangelicals of the Church of England by an attack on them for belonging to a Church that taught the absurd doctrine of baptismal regeneration. Over another controversy he broke with the Baptist Union in 1887. No ascetic, for in his later years he lived in some style in Norwood, he was yet generous to a fault and he left behind him an orphanage, a training college for ministers and a colportage association.

Alexander Maclaren (1826–1910) was a very different type of man who lacked a number of the gifts ministers are expected to have. Natural shyness made him a poor pastor. He hated statistics, organization, advertising, and all but the simplest music. His dress was unclerical and his ways unconventional. Spurgeon thought him a "dangerous man". In 1858 he was appointed to Union Chapel, Manchester, and there he remained for forty-five years proving that he had a genius for exegetical preaching. "He had an extraordinary gift of analysing a text," said one critic. "He touched it with a silver hammer, and it immediately broke up into natural and memorable divisions, so comprehensive and so clear that it seemed wonderful that the text should have been handled in any other way." In the Bible-based church tradition of Nonconformity, this great gift made Maclaren outstanding in his age. The tradition of Nonconformist preaching today is much more commonly to relate the subjects of the day to religious investigation, and often to use a biblical text merely as a hook on which to hang a sermon about the relevance of Christianity. Maclaren, as an expository preacher, was the most gifted example of an approach almost obsolete.

A third outstanding Baptist minister was John Clifford (1836–1923). He was the son of a factory-worker who received little education in his youth but made up for it by an insatiable thirst for knowledge for the rest of his life. His ministry was entirely in London. He was called "the uncrowned king of militant Nonconformity." Esteemed in all branches of Nonconformity as well as in the Church of England, Clifford gained a national reputation for his liberal views, which he saw only as Christ-inspired principles. Lloyd George said of him: "There is no man in England upon whose conscience I would sooner ring a coin than John Clifford's." A historian said of him: "By insisting that Christianity had to do with the whole of life, economic, civic, national and international, he was a pioneer in directing the thoughts of Free Churchmen to the social implications of Christianity." Perhaps Clifford's main contribution to his time, however, was his conviction that there was no real conflict between religion and science. He had no fear of biblical criticism nor of 'modern thought'. Theology for him was a progressive science. New light and new knowledge of God were acceptable from any source.

Of the Methodists, Jabez Bunting reigned supreme as long as he lived, but in the second half of the century others rose to eminence. W. M. Punshon (1824–1881) was both a great pulpit orator and church statesman. As preacher he drew huge congregations, especially during his years in London. He then spent five years in Canada organizing and preaching and presiding over the annual conferences. Canadian Methodism owes much to him. From 1875 to 1881 he was secretary of the Missionary Society, for by this time Methodism was a world church and Methodists abroad vastly outnumbered those in the British Isles.

The greatest Methodist of the second half of the nineteenth century was Hugh Price Hughes (1847–1902). In him Welsh and Jewish blood combined to make a fiery prophet. He was a liberal by conviction and it was largely under his influence that Methodism's long conservative or neutral tradition dramatically changed. Hughes preached the social gospel. Christ went about doing good, and his greatest concern was for the sick and sad and suffering. It was not sufficient merely to succour them; if their plight was the result of human injustice or negligence or apathy then laws needed changing, the idle needed stirring, the public conscience must be roused. Hughes was an evangelist who saw that the implications of salvation demanded social action, and it was of him, and in particular of his protest against men in public office whose private lives were immoral, that the phrase 'the Nonconformist conscience' was first used.

Hughes was no innovator in doctrine. Indeed, he was totally in accord with Wesley's theology, and a sacramentarian so strongly as to believe that to take the bread and wine was a symbol of mystic participation in the life of Christ and brought a special blessing. This view kept him apart from the older Nonconformist groups, but his liberalism and his warm friendship with other churches brought him and Methodism with him closer into the Nonconformist fold. He was principally responsible for the formation of the National Council of the Free Churches in 1896. All Nonconformist Churches were invited to be members, save only the Unitarians, for Hughes deliberately described the body as "a Nonconformist Parliament for our common objects, composed of those who believe in the divinity of our Lord, Jesus Christ."

England in the Victorian age was a country composed of the wealthy and the miserably poor. Between them lay the new middle classes who had effectively forced on the others a new class structure to replace the old aristocratic hierarchy of the eighteenth century. There was hostility between the strata, and it had effectively arisen from revolution, the Industrial one, and fear of revolution, the American and the French. Hughes during the second half of the century saw the utter squalor and degradation of the poor and applied his Christian principles. "Let us once realize the sacredness of every human being," he said, "however poor, however ignorant, however degraded, and tyranny becomes impossible, lust becomes impossible, war becomes impossible." He started 'Central Halls'. Every great city needed one, said Hughes. It was to be first a church and preaching place, but it must also be the centre from which social work could start.

Hughes got his way. His own social centre was St. James' Hall, Piccadilly, and he chose the site because of its "strategic and spectacular value". In imitation of his example central halls soon followed in all major cities, and philanthropic work spread from them. The century was closing as they were built and Hughes the prophet wondered how the Methodist Church could meet the huge expenses of the twentieth century. As President of the Methodist Conference in 1898 he launched an appeal to raise a million guineas. Almost incredibly, he succeeded, and in imitation of his appeal the other Nonconformist Churches set their targets too.

Politically, the most powerful Nonconformist in the House of Commons was John Bright (1811–1889), a Quaker. Most famous for his work in repealing the Corn Laws, he also fought against Church rates and capital punishment, and for an extension of the factory acts. He was an apostle of free trade, but also the Nonconformist conscience in office. Not since the days of William

Penn had there been a political influence of Bright's stature. He declared his religion openly and loudly and constantly. "When I look back to the history of this country, and consider its present condition," he said to the Commons early in his career, "I must say that all that the people possess of liberty has come not through the portals of the cathedrals and parish churches, but from the conventicles which are despised by honourable gentlemen opposite. When I know that if a good measure is to be carried in this House it must be by men who are sent hither by the Nonconformists of Great Britain – when I read and see that the past and present state alliance with religion is hostile to religious liberty, preventing all growth and nearly destroying all vitality in religion itself – then I shall hold myself to have read, thought, and lived in vain if I vote for a measure which in the smallest degree shall give any further power or life to the principle of state endowment." In that age Bright knew that tens of thousands of Nonconformists agreed with him. Never, except during the brief period of the Commonwealth, was Nonconformity so powerful, and it was never to be so powerful again. Well might Lord John Russell say, "I know the Dissenters. They carried the Reform Bill; they carried the abolition of slavery; they carried free trade; and they'll carry the abolition of church rates." "In the long run," said Lord Palmerston, "English politics will follow the consciences of the Dissenters."

Though Presbyterians remained dominant in Scotland, the English Presbyterians at this period were relatively few. This was in part because, as has been noted, many of them had embraced Unitarianism, and possibly also because Calvinism, the heart of their doctrine, was becoming ever less acceptable to most. Church of England Evangelicals by this time talked of "moderate Calvinism" or had totally discarded the teaching. A few Nonconformists clung to it, often as inconsistently as Spurgeon. Calvinism as a creed had virtually vanished by the end of the century.

It was also the nineteenth century that saw the flood and ebb of Unitarianism. Among its distinguished followers were James Martineau (1805–1900) and Joseph Chamberlain (1836–1914). Martineau, of Huguenot descent, was teacher and author. After a series of minor appointments he became professor in Manchester New College, and later Principal. Among his theological writings were defences of Unitarianism. He became best known for his attempts to harmonize religion and the 'modern thought' of the Victorian age, and was influential in his age both because of his persuasive power and his admirable character. Chamberlain was a distinguished political leader who held high office and twice resigned over matters of principle. He was Colonial Secretary from 1893 to 1903. The appeal of Unitarianism, with its rejection of the orthodox doctrine of the Trinity, was obvious. The moral teachings of Jesus were accepted and followed, but the paradox of three in one and one in three and the consequent divinity of Christ were 'irrational' and therefore unacceptable. To an age struggling with science apparently in conflict with religion, with the infallibility of the Scriptures apparently in doubt, the Unitarian solution must have seemed a welcome compromise. It flourished only a while, however, for it was only a short step from total disbelief. A faith that rejected the difficult essence of Christian dogma was always liable to lapse into agnosticism.

The Moravians, whose teachings had helped Wesley, and for whom he kept a life-long affection, led their quiet and pious lives in England as well as Germany throughout the century. They produced one distinguished hymn-writer, James Montgomery (1771–1854), who wrote 'Hail to the Lord's anointed,' 'Prayer is the soul's sincere desire' and the Christmas hymn 'Angels from the realms of glory.'

A number of new branches of Nonconformity were founded in the nineteenth century, some attracting few adherents and of short duration, others of greater importance. The earliest and least of these were the 'Sandemanians' or 'Glassites'. It was a minor Scottish high Calvinist sect influenced by Robert Sandeman (1718–1771) and his son-in-law John Glas (c.1725–c.1800) which began in the eighteenth century in Scotland, but a London branch appeared early in the nineteenth century. The sect was exclusive, the rules of membership strict, and numbers always small, though American Churches of this denomination survived until the 1880s.

Edward Irving (1792–1834) was a Scottish Presbyterian who was minister to a London Presbyterian congregation. In the 1820s he became obsessed by the prophecies in the books of Daniel and Revelation, and preached of the second coming of Christ and the end of the world. He introduced the early Church gifts of prophesying, speaking with tongues and healing by faith.

His church accepted his teaching, which caused a furore in London. The Presbyterian Church rejected him for heresy, but he formed his own Church in 1832 and called it the 'Catholic Apostolic Church', though his followers were usually called 'Irvingites.' For a while it had a following, especially among the fashionable and wealthy. Such millenarian sects are a common phenomenon. The Churches, or Disciples of Christ had their roots in the eighteenth century, for they appear to have been formed from remnants of other Churches, Glassites and Baptists, for instance. They also have a connection with Alexander Campbell (1788–1866), a Scottish evangelist who emigrated to America. They became organized into the Churches of Christ about 1842. The Church government is congregational in pattern. From 1920 an ordained ministry was trained in Birmingham. In 1981 the reformed churches of Christ became part of the United Reformed Church in Great Britain.

The Plymouth Brethren or Darbyites began about 1825 when a young man who was reading for orders in the Anglican Church, A. N. Groves, met friends in Dublin for spiritual reflection. They met for Holy Communion every Sunday; they spent much of their time in silent meditation after the way of the Quakers; also after the conclusion of the Quakers they decided that war was unlawful. These meetings would have been only a matter for the private spiritual lives of the men concerned had it not been for the interest of J. N. Darby (1800–1882). Though an ordained priest of the (Anglican) Church of Ireland, he detested establishment and resigned his curacy in 1828. Groves never took orders; the brethren agreed that no ordination was necessary to preach the Gospel. They left Dublin and made Plymouth their second centre. At first the movement was confined to a few men who were dissatisfied with the aridness of their own Churches, especially educated Anglicans, but converts began to gather from the very poor and those totally outside any Church. The initial emphasis had been on extreme simplicity in living, carried almost to asceticism, coupled with a total reliance on the Scriptures. Over a period of time interpretation of Scripture became very literal ("every word of Scripture," said Darby, "is from the Spirit, and is for eternal service") and was followed by absorption in prophecy after the manner of the Irvingites. Since Christ's second coming was imminent, preparation for it demanded separation from this world and all its tawdry amusements. Other churches, they believed, had become tarnished by worldly contact, and were to be avoided. All creeds were to be rejected, for the Holy Spirit would guide true Christians by inspiration. The Church became bitterly divided, in part on the permissibility of mixing with Christians who were not members of their group. Darby himself proved an intolerant man. George Müller (1805–1898), a warm and lovable man who pleaded for tolerance, said of the dispute that, beginning "with universal communion Darby ended with universal excommunication". The breach between them was never healed. Plymouth Brethren flourished, though the Church had no central organization, and their missionaries worked across the world, but they were 'open' or 'closed' brethren, tolerant and loving to others or exclusive and anxious to avoid contact except to convert. Unlike other branches of Nonconformity, Plymouth Brethren studiously avoided political activity, for the function of the Christian is to save men and women from this world. Nevertheless, some of the greatest social reforms in nineteenth-century England were begun by 'open' Brethren.

William Booth (1829–1912) founded a Church in the nineteenth century, and his foundation was to grow into a world-wide organization, respected and admired by all. He began life in awful poverty. His first occupation was an apprentice to a pawnbroker. Converted in 1844, he joined a group of revivalists and offered the love of God to those who had scarcely known any love in their lives. In 1849, desperate for work, he went to London and there once again found himself assisting a pawnbroker. He almost starved himself trying to save money to send to his mother and family. He had briefly been a Wesleyan Methodist local preacher and now became a minister, successively, of two of the Methodist splinter groups which were later to become the United Methodist Church. Neither could hold him. He had a single-minded passion for the evangelism of the destitute. His independent approach was a necessity. Only he, who had suffered from hideous poverty and did not shrink from filth and vermin, from drunkenness, and every form of violence, from diseased prostitutes and dying paupers, from every evil that man's inhumanity and lusts could cause, only he and those who were prepared to follow him wholeheartedly could begin to take Christianity there.

In 1855 William had married saintly Catherine Mumford. He

made as wise a choice as Wesley made a disastrous one. Catherine Booth was William's equal partner. In 1861 William severed his connection with Methodism and became an independent revivalist. In 1865 William and Catherine launched their 'Christian Mission' and it was not until 1878 that William referred to it, by metaphor, as 'a volunteer army'. Bramwell, his son, rejected the name. He was, he said, a regular soldier or nothing. Thus the name 'The Salvation Army' was adopted, with Bramwell as chief organizer. William accepted military titles and uniforms only grudgingly. He never really liked them. He agreed, however, that for those days both titles and uniforms made for instant recognition, and especially in the early days the Salvation Army needed that. It was calumnied. Armed mobs were paid to break up its meetings. The money of brewers bribed rogues to attack unarmed men and women because they preached against the evils of drink. The Salvation Army had its martyrs.

The poor and oppressed blessed the Army from the day it had begun, for they had had few champions. They had nothing to give: they could only receive. Booth therefore could only appeal for financial help from the middle classes, and in the end, when suspicion had died down, he got it. In 1890 H. M. Stanley published *Darkest Africa*, an account of his journey through equatorial Africa. The same year Booth, imitating that title, published *In Darkest England and the Way Out*. The late Victorians read it in amazement. It told them of life among the poorest people with whom they had no contact, nor wanted any. It was meant to shock. It was well that missionary work should spread across the globe, but it was equally necessary that the message of Christ should be preached in the English jungles and swamps, the festering slums of the great cities. Booth's first concern was to save the souls of the distressed, but he knew from personal experience that a man with an aching belly cannot even think about his soul. William and Catherine were social reformers because they were evangelists, not the reverse. The book made the point, and Victorian England poured money into a noble cause.

Booth was almost totally ignorant of theology. He could be autocratic. He was childlike and easily hurt. He disliked science and was nervous of philosophy. He was also a very great man whose achievement was to live and grow long after he was dead.

The Salvation Army was remarkable for many things, not least because the movement never grew 'respectable'. Several Churches before them had also tried to succour the most distressed – the Methodist Churches, for instance – and the older Nonconformist bodies had always found converts among the poorest strata of society. With the passing of time, however, the appeal of these Churches had become principally to the middle classes. The Salvation Army has never shifted from its original function of ministering to those in greatest need. Its selfless devotion has earned it what no other church has ever earned, the admiration of those with no personal interest in religion whatever. The Army spread through England, through the former British Colonies, to America, and so across the world. Perhaps the greatest compliment to its success was the foundation in 1882 of the Church Army, a Church of England organization of laymen and women based on the model of the Salvation Army. Like its model, the Church Army is highly active a hundred years on.

A number of other Churches or quasi-Churches were founded during the nineteenth century, some of them American foundations which missionaries brought to England.

The Christadelphian movement was founded in America in 1848 by John Thomas (1805–1871). It began in an attempt (like so many churches before it) to return to the beliefs and practices of the primitive church. It was Bible-based and fundamentalist in approach, though not totally so ("We look upon the devil as a telling representation of every manifestation of the wrongness of human hearts"). It rejected infant baptism, the doctrine of the Trinity, and orthodox views of the resurrection. A few, Christadelphians say, will be saved, the wicked will go to oblivion, and the unconverted and infants will not be raised from the dead. It is a very small group, utterly dedicated, and survives across the world today. There are no ministers, no ruling body, and each assembly runs its own affairs. The central concern of each 'ecclesia' is the second coming of Christ, which is expected to be in Jerusalem.

Mormonism or the Church of Jesus Christ of Latter-Day Saints is as vast a body as the Christadelphians are small. It was founded by Joseph Smith (1805–1844), who claimed divine revelations. After Smith's murder the leadership was taken by Brigham Young (1801–1877), who led Smith's followers to Salt Lake City, Utah, and there established an immense colony. The bizarre beliefs, based on Smith's revelations, are not Christian in any orthodox sense, but its followers show matchless devotion to their creed.

Christian Science, founded by Mrs. M. B. Eddy (1821–1910), who held that evil and disease can only be defeated by the individual's awareness of Spirit truth in his own mind, is not a Church and, to the orthodox, neither Christian nor scientific, but Christian Science 'Reading Rooms' sell Bibles and the works of Mrs. Eddy, and explain her faith. Yet another sect of American origin is the 'Jehovah's Witnesses', founded by C. T. Russell (1852–1916). Its followers claim not to be a Church and are against all forms of organized religion. They are concerned with the fulfilment of prophecy in some of the more obscure books of the Bible. Adventism is a form of millenarianism which has appeared during most ages, but especially during troubled times. The end of the world is prophesied on a given date, the date passes, the sect dwindles. Seventh Day Adventism was the largest of such groups and began in America in 1863. All of the groups listed above had some followers in England; none could be called a Free Church in the English sense. Still less is British Israelism, albeit of home growth, a Church. It is a theory – that the lost tribes of Israel somehow became the English people.

There is, and there probably always will be, a hinterland beyond the world of normal churches where the fanatics, the feeble-minded (on whom some dangerous sects prey) and the alienated, find comfort. It is, however, a little disconcerting to reflect that the abusive terms just used were once used of Congregationalists, Baptists, Quakers and Methodists.

There were two movements within the nineteenth-century Church of England which had effect on Nonconformity, and for this reason they demand brief mention. The first was the Oxford Movement, which began with a sermon by John Keble (1792–1866). Others were R. H. Froude (1803–1836), J. H. Newman (1801–1890) and, later, E. B. Pusey (1800–1882). The movement was an assertion of the divine origin and authority of the Church and a stress on its Catholic nature as opposed to its Protestant one. The message was spread through a series of pamphlets called 'Tracts for the Times'; ninety were published between 1833 and 1841. Naturally the teaching provoked hostility, for England had been fiercely Protestant ever since the reign of Mary I. The last tract caused the most offence in moving so close to Roman Catholicism as to be almost indistinguishable from it. The fears of the critics were confirmed when a group of Anglican priests resigned to seek acceptance in the Roman Catholic Church. Newman himself was among them and H. E. Manning (1808–1892), another able Tractarian. These two later became Cardinals.

The shock of the Oxford Movement and the apostasy of some of its members had several effects on Nonconformity, some of them already noted. There was no longer any possibility of Methodism returning to its mother Church; Nonconformity, positively Protestant, attracted converts from the establishment; Evangelicals of the Church of England began to feel they had more in common with Nonconformists than Anglo-Catholics, and in 1846 the Evangelical Alliance was formed to bind together Evangelicals of all denominations for fellowship and prayer; a new Church arose as a protest against the Catholicity of the Church of England.

The Church just noted was the Free Church of England, a flat contradiction in terms. It began in a dispute between a Tractarian Bishop of Exeter and an Evangelical Duke of Somerset. A curate called James Shore suffered between them and was imprisoned for three months when, as a priest of the Church of England, he preached in a Chapel of the Countess of Huntingdon's Connexion. The founder of the Church was Thomas Thoresby (1818–1883), Minister of Spa Fields Chapel. The Church had a close relationship to the Countess of Huntingdon's Connexion. It had a Presbyterian ministry, provision for episcopacy, and it accepted the 39 Articles and all the principles and practices associated with the Evangelical wing of the Church of England. The Church existed formally in 1863 and united with the Reformed Episcopal Church of America in 1927. The Free Church of England was never strong in numbers, but it had tenacity, and is well into its second century now.

The second movement with repercussions on Nonconformity was the Christian Socialist one. The leader was F. D. Maurice (1805–1872). He was the son of a Unitarian minister who himself came from a long line of Presbyterians. Maurice was ordained Anglican priest but was dismissed from a chair at London University because of alleged unorthodoxy. He laboured all his life to help the under-privileged and was among those who pioneered adult education and education for women. Others of the group were the great preacher F. W. Robertson (1816–1853) and Charles Kingsley (1819–1875), better known as the author of *Westward Ho!* and *The Water Babies*. The influence of these men was very little on their own Church, but markedly on the Nonconformists. Politically a bridge was formed across church barriers. The old liberal Nonconformist tradition welcomed the Christian Socialism which had sprung unexpectedly from a Church notorious for its conservatism.

Nonconformity, as was noted in Chapter VI, led in social and missionary zeal, strongly supported by the Church of England Evangelicals and the Christian Socialists. Sunday schools, prison reform, the abolition of slavery, the foundation of the missionary societies and the work of the Clapham Sect all had brief mention.

Today it is difficult to believe that abolition of slavery required courage, and especially in missionaries. White planters in Jamaica, for instance, hated the missionaries, whom they knew to be supporters of abolition. Their converts were flogged, their houses burned, chapels were destroyed, and the lives of the missionaries threatened. When William Knibb (1803–1845), a Baptist, returned to England on furlough he was urged to be cautious on the subject as there were fears on behalf of converts, and there were also strong commercial interests in England which supported slavery. Knibb would not listen to them. When a majority of the Baptists advised caution, and a few total silence on the subject, Knibb rose and said, "Myself, my wife, and my children are entirely dependent on the Baptist Mission; we have landed without a shilling; but if necessary I will walk barefoot throughout the kingdom, but what I will make known to the Christians of England is what their brethren in Jamaica are suffering." A few days later Knibb spoke at the Annual Society meeting of the Baptists, and began by saying that he appeared on behalf of 20,000 Baptists, the majority of whom would be flogged every time they were caught praying. His speech was passionate and angry. A cautious colleague tugged at his coat-tail, but Knibb pulled himself away and went on, "I will speak. At the risk of my connection with the Society, and of all I hold dear, I will avow this. And if the friends of missions will not hear me, I will turn and tell it to my God: nor will I desist till this greatest of curses is removed, and 'Glory to God in the highest' is inscribed on the British flag." Knibb won Baptist support, toured the country speaking from his personal experience, and the next year Parliament agreed to abolition.

The work of the missionaries in the nineteenth century can have no large place here, but it must be noted that a very large part of Nonconformist effort and resources as well as many of the most able Nonconformist ministers were sent abroad. Illustrious among an illustrious company were Henry Martyn (1781–1812) in India; Robert Moffat (1795–1883) and David Livingstone (1813–1873) in Africa; David Hill (1840–1896) and J. Hudson Taylor (1832–1905) in China; James Chalmers (1841–1901) in the South Seas. These great pioneers and many more spread Christianity through the whole world. For the most part, once they had landed in their particular country they became virtually independent, and necessarily so. Funds were sent out, but all the decisions as to their use rested with the individual missionaries. One appalling example of insensitivity among a home committee damaged missionary work by the Particular Baptists for ten years. William Carey, Joshua Marshman and William Ward lived communally to save expenses, reserved only the smallest allowance for their families and all died poor. They earned much between them, however, through their writings, through a boarding school, through College appointments and apparently owned wealthy property in the shape of the Serampore Mission. In fact it was this Mission, and Serampore College, which they later built with their own money, that received all their earnings. It was shameful that an ignorant, home-based committee could allege that these great men had "amassed extensive property, and thereby enriched themselves and their families, while they had been unmindful of the great cause to which they originally devoted themselves." Carey would not, and rightly, give up control of his foundations. "We are," he wrote, "your brothers, not your hired servants. We have always accounted it our glory to be related to the Society . . . and we shall rejoice therein so long as you permit us, but we will come under the power of none."

This sad episode was not typical. Most committees, most Nonconformists, gave generously and willingly to missionary work, and to home needs as well. Dickens caricatured the stupidly benevolent in the persons of Mrs. Pardiggle and Mrs. Jellyby. The former was devoted to a variety of excellent causes and so were her five boys: "Egbert, my eldest (twelve), is the boy who sent out his pocket-money, to the amount of five-and-threepence, to the Tockahoopo Indians. Oswald, my second (ten-and-a-half), is the child who contributed two and nine-pence to the Great National Smithers Testimonial. Francis, my third (nine), one-and-sixpence halfpenny; Felix, my fourth (seven), eightpence to the Superannuated Widows; Alfred, my youngest (five), has voluntarily enrolled himself in the Infant Bonds of Joy, and is pledged never, through life, to use tobacco in any form." The children are shown as mournful. Mrs. Jellyby, also "distinguished for . . . rapacious benevolence", neglects her family to provide missionaries for "Borrioboola-Gha, on the left bank of the Niger". The caricature is witty enough, but it is doubtful how many Mrs. Pardiggles and Mrs. Jellybys existed. Charity was desperately needed in that age, both at home and abroad. If the Victorians were slow in dealing with the root causes of the poverty and misery of their society, they were unfailingly generous in personal benevolence, and the Nonconformists most generous of all. As for Mrs. Pardiggle's miserable children, suffering under her 'rapacious benevolence', the great majority of the children of Nonconformists embraced their parents' creed and followed it, generation after generation. Nor is the implication that missionary support meant an ignoring of home needs – Dickens implies it more strongly elsewhere – a just one. Several of the Nonconformist groups, and notably the Primitive Methodist Church and, later, the Salvation Army, both specialized in helping the poorest of the poor and missionary zeal as well.

A striking example of the Nonconformist lead in social concern was their lead in providing orphanages. All branches of the Church provided them – Spurgeon's was one already noted – but three of them, each founded by a single person, became great national concerns. One of these men was Dr. T. B. Stephenson, a Methodist, who rescued Lambeth children and placed them in a home at his own expense. This work was to grow into the 'National Children's Home' which, when it was policy to keep children collectively in particular homes, had branches all over the country.

George Müller (1805–1898), already mentioned, was pastor, philanthropist, and leader of the open Plymouth Brethren. He was a German, was converted in 1825, and went to London in 1829 to train for missionary service among the Jews. Instead he ministered in England, and in Bristol, in answer to a need forced upon his attention, founded an orphanage. He refused a regular salary and starved himself to look after the children.

The most famous founder of orphanages, another Plymouth Brother, was Dr. Thomas Barnardo (1845–1905). Like Müller, Barnardo also began training as a missionary, in his case as a medical missionary to China, but also like Müller, found the greatest need for his talents at home. It was when he volunteered to assist with the cholera epidemic of 1866–7 that he became horrified by conditions in the London slums and was inspired to found his first home for destitute boys. His gifts were immense energy, organizing power, a genius for journalism and publicity (necessities for a man who needed to appeal to private purses) and, above all, total dedication to his cause.

In 1873 Barnardo converted a notorious Limehouse public house into a Church and coffee palace for men. In 1876 he built a 'village' at Ilford to make homes for girls in a less formal manner than his homes for boys. In 1882 he first sent boys to Canada, where their prospects of work were greater, and the next year made the same provision for girls. By 1886 he had begun to arrange boarding in private families for some of the children. His cardinal principle, faithfully observed, was, "No destitute child ever refused admission". By the time of his death Barnardo had admitted 59,384 children into his homes, had helped 20,000 to emigrate, and had assisted with food and clothing and family problems of 250,000 more.

It has been noted that the earliest Puritan traditions stressed the importance of scholarship, and that tradition was never lost. It asserted itself in the Dissenting Academies of the eighteenth century and it survived no less in the nineteenth century. Through the Religious Tract Society (founded in 1799) Bibles and Christian literature were provided. The interdenominational (but largely Evangelical and Nonconformist) British and Foreign Bible Society carried on the work. The British and Foreign Bible Society (1807, 1814) relied largely on Quaker and other Nonconformist help for their teachers. Nonconformists shared in the foundation of University College, Gower Street, and therefore in the foundation of London University. It was a Unitarian, Mrs. E. J. Reid (1789–1866) who founded the London Ladies' College, Bedford Square, a College for the higher education of women, in 1849. When Forster's education bill of 1870 was proposed some Nonconformists opposed it as its terms clearly favoured the Church of England. It was under Nonconformist pressure that a compromise (still unacceptable to some Nonconformists) was effected. It had also been the Nonconformists who had made the Sunday School movement grow so great when it nearly foundered at the beginning for lack of funds; Nonconformists set the example of teaching without any salary.

The lead in temperance (by which name total abstinence from alcohol was called) was another Nonconformist social contribution to an age which was more sottish than most. Drunkenness was bad in its own right, but greater evils sprang from it; wife-beating, child neglect, a whole catalogue of crimes. At first the Nonconformists themselves resisted the appeal (the Methodist Conference of 1840 ordered two ministerial candidates either to renounce their vow of abstinence or withdraw their candidature) but it was still Methodism that was first convinced of the evil of drink and, with the aid of such strong advocates as John Bright, not long before the other Free Churches accepted the view. Before the end of the century all the Free Churches were known as total abstainers. In course of time total abstinence became so exaggerated in its importance as to be considered almost an article of faith. Nevertheless, it was in its age a plea for moral decency that began it, and it could well be that its abandonment in some measure by the Churches that preached it has contributed to the great problem of alcoholism in the twentieth century.

As the nineteenth century began Nonconformists still lived under disabilities because of their religion. Throughout the century they fought tenaciously for equality within the law, and by 1900 they had won most, but not all, of the battles. It was only because they were numerically powerful, had brilliant speakers with political as well as Christian views, and were ably represented in the House of Commons that these things were possible.

In 1811 Lord Sidmouth's Bill to ban Methodist preachers but allow other Nonconformists to have a ministry was defeated chiefly by the intervention of the Archbishop of Canterbury, Charles Manners-Sutton (1755–1828). The hostility roused by the attempt made Nonconformity bitter and more aggressive, and in 1828 the Test and Corporation Acts were at last repealed. Important as this step was, it left a number of minor grievances. Edward Miall (1809–1881), Congregational minister, journalist, fighting reformer, and later a Liberal M.P., led an attack on Church rates from 1834 to 1836. During this period many chapel-goers refused to pay them. The property of some was confiscated; others actually went to prison. Not until 1868 were compulsory Church rates abolished. In 1837 a new Marriage Act allowed marriages to be solemnized "in any chapel or building properly registered for that purpose". Until then Nonconformists had to be married in the parish church, sometimes by a hostile incumbent. In 1844 the Dissenters' Chapels Bill became law. It confirmed the possession of buildings and any endowments on them in the name of those who had made use of them for twenty-five years. The same year, to pursue further freedoms, the British Anti-State Church Association (later called the Liberation Society) was formed with Edward Miall as one of its leaders. In 1866 the law requiring candidates for public office to declare their belief in the authenticity and truth of the Scriptures, and that they would not use their influence against the established Church, was abolished. In 1871 the doors of Oxford and Cambridge were opened to Nonconformists and Roman Catholics, and that year also Miall started a series of attempts to get the Church of England disestablished. As early as 1839 the Baptist Church had called establishment "a palpable departure from the laws of Christ, a gross reflection on His wisdom and power, and the most formidable obstacle in the land to the diffusion of true piety." By the middle of the century many thought disestablishment a probability within a year or two, and in the early 1870s Miall was confident of success. He would have been astonished could he have known that a hundred years later it was further away than ever. In 1880 the Burials Act removed another grievance. Hereafter, burial services by Nonconformists were allowed in churchyards. A whole century of reforms had given the Free Churches freedoms which to their ancestors would have seemed heaven on earth. The reforms also proved Nonconformist power.

The power had come in part by their joint associations for self-defence, but all the denominations had first drawn their world churches together. The General Presbyterian Alliance (its name was changed later – it was a union of the Presbyterian church in England and the United Presbyterians who joined to form the Presbyterian Church of England) first met in 1876; the first Ecumenical Methodist Conference was held in 1881; in 1891 the International Congregational Council met; in the 1890s the New Connexion of General Baptists merged with the mainstream

Particular Baptists, and the Baptist World Alliance was formed in 1905.

Most of the men named in this chapter were the great and distinguished of their particular Church. It is important to remember that the majority of the Nonconformists were names unknown to us – but they were legion. In many English villages a beautiful parish church had pride of position, but in the back streets, side by side and in rivalry, were a Wesleyan Methodist Church, a Primitive Methodist Church and a United Methodist Church, all of them square, ugly brick buildings, raised out of the pence of the poor. Some of the villages had all these and a Congregational and Baptist Church as well, while larger communities would offer a Unitarian or Presbyterian Chapel also, and every town, in addition to all these, had a Friends' Meeting-House and a Salvation Army Citadel. If the rivalry was deplorable, and it was, it also made for maximum effort in proselytizing, preaching, and social activity, including the giving of charity. The Victorian society and its class system were fundamentally optimistic. The greatest empire the world had ever known was the British Empire. England was immensely wealthy, and her power and prestige seemed to grow to limitless proportions. England was also fundamentally a Christian nation, and Christianity had spread from her to every corner of the world. Nonconformity shared in the pride and the optimism, and was very conscious of contributing to all that produced the pride. They felt that certain aspects of their society were attributable to them more than most – missionary zeal, the Nonconformist conscience that demanded high public and private morals, social concern. And by the end of the century they felt that they were almost accepted – but not quite, for Victorian Nonconformity was still conscious of being on a lower social stratum than the establishment, and to the Victorians, social class was everything. It was perhaps their very consciousness of an inferiority that made them so strong in character and so aggressive in fighting for their rights. By the end of the century they had got almost all their rights and they welcomed the challenge of the twentieth century with absolute confidence. All things augured well. The year 1900 would begin a century of ever-increasing evangelism, until there should be an ante-taste of heaven on earth.

CHAPTER VIII

Decline and Ecumenism –
the Churches Close Ranks

THE YEARS 1900 TO 1914 seemed to fulfil the extravagant hopes that the Free Churches had for their future. At least for this little space of time their world organizations flourished, their power and influence and confidence grew. They were not to know that the new century was to bring global war, upheavals of society, the use and abuse of atomic energy, racial conflict, a consciousness of a third world, new political dogma, industrial dispute, and all the concomitant problems that somehow in their train brought about a western world which made materialism its god and little by little pushed spiritual concerns, and the Church with them, into the background. The Free Churches – indeed all the churches – had perhaps been contaminated again by the worldliness which was their downfall in the early eighteenth century until the Evangelical Revival had roused them. Throughout their history, as persecution left them, the Free Churches seemed to suffer spiritually when they became respectable, acceptable, prosperous. It would be a facile explanation of their post-1914 decline, however, to suggest that they fell victims to their own lack of spirituality when the cataclysmic blows listed above beset them. There is truth, however, in the suggestion that their very confidence and optimism made them vulnerable to attack when the series of unexpected catastrophes struck their world. Sermons, hymns, addresses, and political speeches all seemed to herald a Christian

world, and especially in the new part of that world the Free
Churches were in the triumphant vanguard of Christ's conquering
army.

There was work to be done, however, before the world war.
The vital importance of education to Free Churchmen has been
amply demonstrated through the centuries, and the bitterness of
the Free Church struggles with government survived into the
twentieth century. Popular education had effectively begun with
the Sunday School movement. The 1870 Education Act had
angered the Free Churches. They argued that the state should
establish universal teaching exclusively in undenominational
establishments. Nor should it aid Church Schools (most of which
were Church of England ones) out of public funds, and so compel
Free Churchmen to pay for the education of children in schools
of whose religious instruction they disapproved.

In 1902 the new Education Act replaced school boards by local
education authorities, but left the dual system unchanged. The
Free Churches revolted. The Baptist John Clifford led the attack.
His campaign was one of passive resistance, and he urged those
who disapproved of the taxes to refuse to pay them. Many followed
his lead, and some had their goods confiscated. A few even went
to prison rather than pay. Nevertheless, the Act was the law and so
remained, for the liberals failed to repeal it in 1906. It is possible
that the Free Churches might have won this battle had their ranks
been undivided. In fact the Methodists, much the largest of the
Free Churches, were split in their views over the dual system.
Neither H. P. Hughes nor J. Scott Lidgett (1854–1953) felt the
issue was one on which to take such a stand as Clifford urged.
The Methodists, who had the greatest number of denominational
schools after those of the establishment, hereafter allowed them
to be handed over to the state and the objections to the dual
system never again became a battleground, however deeply some
still felt it an injustice.

Ecumenism, at least as far as Protestants were concerned (for
a papal declaration of 1896 effectively ruled out any hopes of
cooperation for generations) continued in the new century, and so
did the union of splintered Churches.

It was the Methodists who in 1907 began the first step towards
complete unity in England by a Union of three of their splintered
groups. Serious decline had not yet started, but this action was a

hint that the days of rapid expansion were no more, and it was wisdom to join closely related forces when the reasons for their distinctions were matters of historical significance only. Inter-Church collaboration, which needs no cynicism to be seen in part as another sign of a cessation of expansion, continued modestly up to the outbreak of the First World War. There was a world missionary conference, for example, in 1910. The divisions that had confused non-Christian converts began to heal. Churches which had operated in rivalry abroad as well as at home began to love with more understanding, and love their former competitors.

The conflict which began in 1914 changed the western world for ever. War before this had been to most men, who were remote from it, a glorious adventure. It was largely professional armies who were engaged, the aim had usually appeared patriotic, and God, it was assumed, was on the side of the British. Most Free Churchmen (though not, of course, Quakers) were happy to enlist and fight for their country. It took four years of horror, immense losses such as no one had ever believed possible, and the involvement of the whole nation in the war effort to make many doubt if war brought anything in its train but misery. Some blamed the Churches or Christianity or God for the suffering and losses. It is arguable that such people had more superstition than religion in them if their faith could be shattered by the results of the stupidity of man rather than God. It is certain that many turned their faces away from the Churches after the war. It is certain also that a generation of the youngest and fittest to carry on the work of their Church was wiped out. It is also certain that the loosening of family ties and the disruption of habit played a part in the Church losses which followed the First World War.

The great depression followed within a few years, and once again some turned away from an unjust God who killed their first-born and then left the rest to starve. William Booth had long before realized that it is almost impossible to worship God with an empty belly. It is even harder to worship him with no hope as well as no food. The Free Churches were still, for the most part, the humbler members of society. It was especially among their ranks that a loss of faith in God might reasonably be expected.

Intense nationalism is a key cause of war. The Free Churches felt this nationalism as much as the rest of the country, had won the war at so colossal a cost that it seemed hardly worth it, and now, deep in poverty and hopelessness, were busy losing the peace. If Church and State, being one, lost much, Chapel and State, linked by love rather than law, lost more. At least the establishment had tithes to support them; the Free Churches had never had anything except the coppers of many poor and a few rich, and the poor were now much poorer. Church and Chapel alike, during the period between the two world wars, ceased to be of importance to the British nation.

During the war J. H. Shakespeare (1857–1928), the Baptist pastor of St. Mary's Chapel, Norwich, pleaded for a close feder-ation of the Free Churches, and his lead in 1916 led to the formation of the Federal Council of Evangelical Free Churches, and Unitarians were as usual excluded. This movement later changed its name, after union with another federal movement, to the Free Church Federal Council. Shakespeare himself, however, early came under suspicion as leaning too far towards the Church of England in his anxiety for reunion. He published *The Churches at the Cross-roads* in 1918.

"The days of denominationalism," he wrote, "are numbered. There is nothing more pathetic or useless in this world, than clinging to dead issues, worn-out methods, and antiquated pro-grammes. The Free Churches have reached a stage in the religious life of this country when, if they are simply a denomination and not a united Church, they are doomed. They cannot reach the people or move them in their disunited state. If they would come together and bend their vast resources in unity to the one end, they would usher in a day of national religious awakening such as no living man has ever seen. It is no use concealing my conviction that reunion will never come to pass except upon the basis of episcopacy."

Shakespeare's book caused consternation among the Baptists, but the desire for union was echoed from the establishment itself. An 'Appeal to all Christian People' was issued in 1920 by the Bishops. Laws of 1919, which effectively were a small measure of disestablishment, allowed the Bishops what some of them had long desired, closer relationships with their Free Church colleagues and the possibility of reunion. They accepted that all who believed in Christ and had been baptized shared "member-ship in the universal church of Christ which is his body," and they appealed for new thought on the belonging together of Christ's

people. They specifically named Churches which were not episcopal as having been "manifestly blessed and owned by the
Holy Spirit as effective means of grace." Bishops hoped that it
might be possible to form a united church by mutual acceptance
of the Bible, the Nicene Creed, the two sacraments, and
episcopacy.

Shakespeare was already committed to the hope. The Conversations that the Bishops proposed, however, were rejected by the
Quakers, the Salvation Army, and the Unitarians. The Methodists
expressed guarded interest. Since the Baptists had initiated the
thought of unity through Shakespeare's book, it was reasonable to
suppose that most support would come from that Church. In fact
the Baptists would not follow their leader. A rival champion was
found in the aged John Clifford, who thought a loose but warm
fellowship preferable to unity of doctrine and practice.

In the 1926 Baptist Assembly, the President said that it was
impossible for Baptists to accept reordination. It would imply that
their ordination was not valid, and that the oneness of Christ's
Church "depended on the existence and powers of an order of
church officers." The formal reply to the Bishops said: "We
believe that this principle of the freedom of the individual church
under Christ has the sanction of Scripture and the justification of
history, and therefore we cannot abandon it without being false to
our trust. Moreover, it is plain to us that the headship and sole
authority of Our Lord in his Church excludes any relations with
the state as may impair its liberty . . . In our judgment the baptism
of infants subverts the conception of the Church as the fellowship
of believers . . .".

The Baptists judged that the world would be impressed less by
all Christians united in one ecclesiastical body than by the sight of
all Christians expressing common life in Christ by loving one
another and co-operating together. They saw no sin in differing
denominations provided they acknowledged one another as truly
within the Church of Christ. They deplored, not diversity, but
discord. They loved liberty, they said, more than uniformity. Nor
could they consider a unity which left out the Society of Friends
and the Salvation Army. There was then, and probably is now,
some division in the Baptists between those who felt themselves
Congregationalists in principle, and therefore Independent in
principle, and those who could see advantage in some stronger

form of connexionalism. Nevertheless, it was clear that the great majority of Baptists prized their historical Independency, for they were Congregationalists first and Baptists only because of one particular doctrine. Independency they saw as a logical outcome of their belief in the priesthood of all believers.

That was basically the stand the Baptists took. They followed Clifford's view. It was a tragedy for Shakespeare, who became autocratic and insistent and in the end had a total nervous breakdown. Nevertheless, he had made his conviction very clear, and the possibility of reunion at the cost of episcopacy was one that concerned the Free Churches increasingly as the century wore on. For the moment Shakespeare seems to have been relatively isolated in his stand and it was the Methodists, much later, historically closer to the establishment, who were most involved in the possibility of reunion. The Baptists seemed to have lost their interest in it through the controversy that followed the publication of Shakespeare's book.

Internal union in Methodism, already noted briefly, was achieved in 1932. Two of the three remaining Methodist bodies were eager for union. These were the United Methodist Church (itself a union of three smaller bodies) and the Primitive Methodist Church. These Churches, through their stresses (little distinction between ministry and laity, little concern about Church order, and a 'low' view of the Sacraments), were more in the tradition of historical Nonconformity than the parent body of Wesleyan Methodists, from whom they had seceded. The Wesleyans were more doubtful about union. Much more powerful numerically, they did not need the smaller bodies as the smaller bodies needed them. They also doubted the academic abilities of some members of the other churches, for their own entry system was formidably scholastic. The vote could not have been closer. The ministerial session of the Wesleyan Methodist annual conference required a 75 per cent majority for union to take place; a single vote decided it. Hereafter, the Methodist Church was one save for a few diehards who, fifty years after union, still struggle on as separated churches.

The Free Churches have not infrequently shown themselves unwilling to change their settled patterns. For some, and especially for Congregationalists, 'Free' meant autocracy within a particular church. It is no wonder that individual churches felt that to join a larger church order meant the denial of freedom to worship God in their own way, the very essence of their churchmanship.

The problems that the First World War brought in its wake were multiplied in the Second World War. The bombing of many Chapels, the shift of population, the destruction of the class system bequeathed by the Victorians and reluctant to die, the threat of nuclear power, the emergence of new towns, the rise of the welfare state – all these things brought new attitudes. Life-long habits were destroyed; social concerns replaced spiritual concerns in the minds of most; material prosperity became the natural goal; the Churches became ever less relevant; church attendance slumped.

The number of Church members, as opposed to occasional adherents, fell every year. The figures for the Methodist Church are as follows: 1939, 800,000; 1946, 745,000; 1961, 729,000; 1974, 550,000. There was an acceleration in loss in the 1960s.

The Free Churches agonized over the situation. Should they cling on to the pattern of worship handed on by generations of forebears, or should they adapt, modify, modernize? Had they failed because they were slow to make their services up to date? Most of the Free Churches fumblingly compromised, and in general pleased nobody. Their half-hearted attempts at 'modernism' offended the traditionally entrenched without attracting the young outsiders. England became more and more a secular society. It had long been a tradition – especially in the forces and in hospital – to name the Church of England as one's Church when it was in most cases the Church from which one stayed away – but it had been almost unthinkable to say 'atheist'. Increasingly it became acceptable to say 'agnostic'. By the 1960s Church attendance had slumped to less than 5 per cent of the population.

The Free Churches also lost something of their reputation as being the social conscience of the country. Militant teetotalism had been one of their hallmarks, but in 1974 the Methodist Conference found moderate drinking compatible with Christian ethics, and this was the end of a long process of debates. Sabbath observance was not so much abandoned as accepted as a lost cause, and another distinctively Free Church position has been all but abandoned. Nor are the morals of public men a matter, it seems, of deep concern, as they were in the days of Hugh Price

Hughes. Little by little the Free Churches came nearer in their ethos to that of the Church of England, and both had become, to most people, outward institutions of little relevance, which did mild good without disturbing the epicurean dreams of a materialistic society.

Wesley's class meetings were slowly abandoned until only the ticket of membership remained. Sunday schools lost numbers. Broadcasting and television became more attractive viewing than the Sunday service, the once obligatory proof of membership.

Not only did services become less well attended; week-night meetings for spiritual or political purposes attracted only the few. As far as the political meetings were concerned – and the Free Churches had been powerful in this area in Victorian times – there were other bodies more anxious to tackle such matters. There was in the early twentieth century a gradual alienation from the working classes. Middle-class respectability in the Free Churches shifted concern for social change from the originators of it. Though it was in the Chapels that the labour movement had started, that movement soon ignored its parent. Hostility replaced indifference. The last significant political leader in the House of Commons who lived his Free Churchmanship was Arthur Henderson (1863–1935). It seemed that the days of a powerful Nonconformity in the government were over.

Difficult times make those who suffer draw closer together, and since almost all churches were suffering equally from declining numbers, they began more consciously to close their ranks against the common enemies of apathy and secularism. In 1942 the British Council of Churches was formed to further common Christian action and promote the cause of unity. 'Christian Aid' is an organ of this body. In 1948 the World Council of Churches first met with representatives from 150 Protestant and Orthodox Churches. By the 1970s there were more than 260 member Churches from some 90 countries. Though the World Council of Churches had no legislative power, it formed associations that gave help in Christ's name to those who most needed it all over the world – material help, educational help, spiritual help. It has been criticized for giving material help that could have been misused, but has insisted that risks must be taken if starving people are not to die. These offspring of the World Council of

Churches have been a powerful source of good in the Third World.

In 1946 Archbishop Fisher reopened the question of unity. The Free Churches were invited to establish intercommunion with the Church of England by "taking episcopacy into their system." The Congregationalists and Baptists declined, courteously but firmly, and it was Methodism who agreed to exploratory conversations.

In matters ecclesiastical progress is always slow, and this is wisdom, for in such matters deeply-held beliefs, a faith almost in-born, a tradition of centuries – these are not easily modified. Slow as the progress seems, and the Conversations did not begin until 1955 or end until 1958, there is reason to suppose that even that time was not enough. Most of the twelve leaders from each side were convinced of the rightness of union, but it became clear later that grass-root opinion was not. In 1963 a Commission report proposed a method of Anglican-Methodist union in two stages. All twelve Anglicans agreed, as did eight of the Methodists. Both Churches accepted the report. The annual Methodist Conference of 1969 passed the proposals by the required 75 per cent majority as did the Bishops; the Lower House of the Church of England, however, failed to reach the required majority. In fact this vote was the predictable outcome of the divided nature of the Church of England. The issue was whether or not the 'Service of Reconciliation' was ordination. Some of the Anglo-Catholics, the High Church, claimed it was not, and was therefore inadequate for the purpose; some of the Evangelicals, the Low Church, saw the Service as a true ordination, which in their view was unnecessary. It seemed tragic to many that so much time and energy and love and prayer had ended in nothing, more especially as an overall majority clearly wanted the churches to be one. In 1972, therefore, opinion was tested a second time and a second time was passed by Methodism and the Bishops and failed because the Lower Anglican House could not find a sufficient majority. It is doubtful if, close as the voting was, opinion will be tested again for a generation, for a new and unexpected factor arose. Nearly a hundred years before, the Pope had ruled out all possibility of Communion with the Church of England. Pope John XXIII pronounced himself at least willing to talk about reunion with Protestants. It would be difficult for the Church of England to look in two directions simultaneously. Its Anglo-Catholic body would be more interested in union with the Roman Catholic Church; its Evangelical one with the Free Churches.

An ecumenical venture which succeeded was the union of the Congregational Church in England and Wales and the Presbyterian Church of England in the autumn of 1972. Presbyterianism in England, as opposed to Scotland, was never strong after the great secession into Unitarianism in the early eighteenth century. It will be recalled that the Church owed its foundation to Calvin and its churchmanship largely to John Knox. During the nineteenth century, as toleration increased, it was easier to form a Presbyterian system, and churches of this pattern began to flourish in England again. From Scotland and Ulster especially came families, often prompted by work that the industrial revolution had provided, to found more churches, and, in 1844 the Presbyterian Church in England was formed with seventy congregations. By 1972 there were 330 churches and some 70,000 members. The distinctive pattern of Presbyterianism was that authority rested in courts or councils of the Church. Each individual church was governed by a session (the minister and the elders) and a presbytery (minister, elders, and representatives from a wider grouping of churches) governed an area. Nationally the Church was governed by a general assembly (made up in its turn of ministers and elders of local churches).

Congregationalism in its organization could hardly be more different. It will be remembered that the first name used for Congregationalists was Independents, and the independence of each individual Church under Christ was the heart of this Church. Browne had suffered for it, Barrowe and Greenwood had died for it. There was no Vicar of Christ as in Catholicism, no monarch and Bishops as in the Church of England, no series of courts as in Presbyterianism. Each independent Church resolved its own affairs under Christ. It was centuries before a loose structure bound together these independent Churches (the national union of 1832), and it might have seemed that such a principle would have prevented this deliberately loose fellowship from ever joining a denomination with a formal organization.

Even in their doctrines of the Church, at least in earlier times, Presbyterians and Congregationalists differed fundamentally. Presbyterians, like Anglicans, believed in a national Church. For the brief period of the Commonwealth, when their power was greatest, they sought to establish a Church system in which it would be acknowledged that to belong to the state meant belonging to the established Church. Church and State should be one. The Congregationalists, on the other hand, believed in 'gathered' churches. They opened each church with a covenant, which bound that congregation to Christ, but that congregation alone. They never thought that all belonged to the Church; only those who gathered in that particular place in Christ's name.

The obstacles to union, therefore, were very great, but there was anxiety on both sides to bring it about. If the differences seemed formidable, the similarities in what mattered most were formidable too. Further, both Churches were relatively small, and their joint witness would be greater. An abortive attempt at union failed just after the Second World War, but early in the 1960s renewed attempts began, and after some nine years of discussion, the union was complete. It is true that a few Churches continued to assert their own independence, precisely as some of the Methodist Churches did after their union, but most Churches embraced the greater belonging that their union brought.

As the two Churches formally made common cause they declared their intention to explore ever wider unions. "The United Reformed Church," they said, "declares its intention, in fellowship with all the Churches, to pray and work for such visible unity of the whole Church as Christ wills and in the way he wills, in order that men and nations may be led more and more to glorify the Father in heaven."

The most recent attempt at a wider unity followed from this lead. The 'Churches' Unity Commission' came into being and in 1976 issued 'Ten Propositions' addressed to each separate Church. It proposed a Covenant which would bind all of them together. Each would, by this Covenant, recognize each other as members of the Body of Christ, and each other's ministers as true ministers of Word and the sacrament in the Holy Catholic Church. From this Covenant, if agreed, it would follow that all future ordinations of ministers would include elements of the episcopal, the presbytal, and the lay. Such an approach was considered a first step on the road to a more formal union, and might be a wiser way than the too hurried attempts at formal union between Anglican and Methodist which twice foundered. In fact, though four

Churches explored the matter (the Church of England, the Methodist Church, the United Reformed Church and the Moravian Brethren), the clergy of the Church of England finally rejected the scheme in 1982, while the other three Churches accepted it.

The agonizing of Free Churchmen over their falling numbers has led in the twentieth century to wider experiments than ever before. There was no need in the nineteenth century to offer anything but the spiritual fare that the congregations wanted. They proved what they wanted by the huge numbers in which they came, and by the extensions to existing chapels and the erection of more and more. Most of the Free Churches wanted a gripping preacher, with the sermon as the centre of worship, week-night meetings, hymns, scripture-reading, prayer, an occasional Communion Service, and a collection to keep the work going. When these crowds had departed, and would come, it seemed, no more, attempts were made to bring them back by varying the spiritual fare offered. Magic lantern shows, slide evenings, films and plays were all successively offered, first at week-night meetings, and later as part of services or even as a whole service. The suspicion of an 'age-barrier' began to prompt more ministers to experiment with guitar-groups and choruses. None of these things was new. Indeed, the Salvation Army had long used the 'devil's tunes' to Christian words to bring sinners to repentance. What was new was that the main branch Free Churches (Congregationalists, Baptists, Presbyterians and Methodists), now traditional in their approach, were experimenting also.

It had always been a well-known tradition for clergy of the Church of England to be teachers or scholars rather than parish priests, and totally acceptable for Congregational ministers to combine related professions to give them a tolerable income, but it was unthinkable before the 1980s that a Church would give an ordained minister permission to serve his ministry exclusively as a bus-driver. That, however, is precisely what Methodism did and justified, at least to the satisfaction of most. If the world would not come to the Churches, then the churches should get deeper into the world.

Nor was preaching by women a new thing, for most of the Free Churches had employed women preachers early in their histories, but ordination was another matter. Feminist movements had been active through most of the second half of the nineteenth century, and had successively stormed each bastion of male privilege. Very few professions remained closed to women by the turn of the century, and of these, because of ancient statute, priesthood in the Church of England was the most obdurate. The Free Churches needed relatively little persuasion – the less since they began to have few male ministerial candidates to fill their pulpits. Nevertheless, it was a late correction of a strange error, to wait centuries before half the world's population could qualify to become ordained pastors. The first fully ordained woman minister of word and sacrament was the Congregational Constance Coltman in 1917. The Church of England follows slowly behind.

The explosion caused by Bishop Robinson's *Honest to God* seemed to some experimental madness, and was yet another symptom and cause of uncertainty. His radical theology had an obvious appeal to those who had rejected from their lips and even from their hearts the *fides historica* handed down through the Churches, Free Churches as well as Anglican. Certainly not intended as such, the book seemed to some a reason for neglecting the out-of-date churches with their creeds and practices, and concentrating instead on the barest minimum of theology, on the person of Jesus Christ, and on social activity; to relieve the sufferings of others rather than cling to Church membership. It is arguable, and the book accepts it, that it is the lead of the Church that is most needed in the field of practical Christianity, but the danger to the churches of so radical an approach was seen in the increased doubts of their function both among ministers and their congregations. A secular theology not inspired by the churches could leave churches out in the cold, or perhaps, and more accurately, too cosy by their own firesides.

A number of strange churches or pseudo-churches founded in the last century, flourished in the twentieth, and notably the Mormons, who opened a Temple in Guildford and, backed by American resources, are opening more churches. Totally new churches have proliferated during the post-war years, many of them from America. Some are remarkable for the controversy they have aroused. Scientology is not a Church in any acceptable sense. The Church of Unification (more familiarly known as the 'Moonies') has probably aroused more controversy than any other, largely because of its exclusive nature. Its enemies claim that it commands both the minds and the bodies of its adherents, and that its claims order its members to have no further communication with their families, for the claims of the Church are absolute. Distraught parents have even appealed to the law to protect their children, and in more than one parliament, questions have been asked which suggest that many consider this Church a pernicious social evil. What evidence can be obtained suggests this alleged Church is not Christian, though some of its adherents distribute pamphlets from main branch Churches, so giving themselves a veneer of respectability.

The Oxford Group is not a Church but a movement. It was founded by Frank N. D. Buchman (1878–1961), who influenced a number of young men in the 1920s in Cambridge and then Oxford – hence the name, officially adopted in 1939. In 1938, however, Buchman launched the Moral Rearmament Movement, a heightening of the Group's purpose, which was to change the lives of young people and obtain a solemn commitment to Christ. The group had many enemies. Some claimed that the conversions were short-lived; others that Buchman was interested in the professional and upper classes only; others that some of the young assistants were sex-obsessed. The group did and does, however, have a good and great influence on many of its adherents. The work is always done by personal contact. A number of 'absolutes' are offered as a moral ideal. It is now an international movement with a headquarters in Caux, Switzerland, and it owns a theatre (the 'Whitehall') where plays, sometimes naïve in their appeal, show the results on human lives of moral rearmament.

While most Free Churches have lost in membership, one group, especially during the 70s, was remarkable for expansion. This group is the fruit of the Pentecostal Movement. There was no one founder. It was a movement which, like the Evangelical Revival of the eighteenth century, appeared to arise spontaneously in a number of men. W. J. Seymour, an American, in 1906 caused grave offence in a Los Angeles Church when he doubted if those who called themselves Christians were really so in fact unless they received the gift of the Holy Spirit as described in the second chapter of the Acts of the Apostles. When Seymour preached to certain members of the same congregation in their own homes the gift of 'tongues' (talking in a language incomprehensible to most in a kind of spiritual ecstasy) began to appear, and the Pentecostal Movement started in America then.

In 1904, in Cardigan Bay in Wales, a revival meeting led to frenzied outbursts which started a Revival in Wales. It became common practice during this revival to hear 'speaking in tongues'. The sermon became less prominent, a feeling of joy was stimulated by fiery preaching, singing and hand-clapping, and the presence of the Holy Spirit was felt in the strange language of the one 'possessed' by the Spirit.

This phenomenon, or one closely resembling it, was not new. There was, obviously, the example of Pentecost, but there were much more recent examples too. The preaching of Whitefield and Wesley (who actively discouraged it) was frequently accompanied by faints, screaming, shouting, and every form of hysteria. The same things happened during the second Evangelical Revival. The 'speaking in tongues' of the twentieth century is different in several ways. In the first place, some ministers and laymen claim the gift of interpretation, and can explain the apparent babblings of the one possessed. In the second place, the movement had, at least initially, wide influence in almost every Church. The Roman Catholic Church, the Church of England, and almost every Free Church has ministers active in Pentecostal Services within their own denominations. In the third place, the fruit of the Pentecostal ministry, which is arguably the only way to judge spiritual efficacy, is remarkable. Within long established churches a revival of religious fervour has followed. Lastly, a phenomenon which led to rapid increase in membership against a trend of almost a century suggests that Pentecostalism is meeting a need which most other Churches fail to meet.

While the movement had a marked effect on established Churches, it led also to the foundation of a new group. This group is 'fundamentalist' in biblical interpretation. The Apostolic Church, which was founded out of several Pentecostal groups just after the First World War, has its headquarters in Wales. It uses biblical words ('shepherd', 'prophet', etc.) to describe the functions of members of the congregation. Freedom of speech by members of the congregation is a feature of their services. Any member may stand up and 'prophesy'. In 1975 there were 191 congregations in Britain, with a total membership of some 4,000.

The Elim Pentecostal Church was one of the results of the

Welsh Revival. Two brothers, George and Stephen Jeffreys, began the work, but later parted company. Freedom of worship is encouraged to the extent that singing, clapping and speaking in tongues arise spontaneously as the Spirit dictates. There is as little organization as possible, since the Spirit is in charge. In 1975 there were 310 churches and 25,000 members.

The Assemblies of God has a definite date of origin, 1 February 1924. They are much the largest group with, in 1975, 541 Assemblies and a membership of about 60,000. This Church, even more than the others, was fed from existing denominations, some of whose members felt that worship had become dull, formal, lacking in emotion, irrelevant to the needs of the congregation. While this Church, and the others noted above, existed in tiny numbers for decades, the great impetus came in the 1950s. It was then that the movement spread through all Churches and also increased the membership of the separated Pentecostal Churches. In addition to the English Churches, there are a growing number of West Indian Pentecostal Churches – among others, the New Testament Church of God, the Church of God of Prophecy, and the Apostolic Church of Jesus Christ.

Binding together those Pentecostalists who wish to remain in their own churches, and not to become a member of a separated Pentecostal Church, is the Fountain Trust, an organization committed to revival and to the belief that it can come through the charismatic gifts which have been largely lost since New Testament times – speaking in tongues and miracle healing. The Trust was set up in the 1960s. The strongest response has come from a source which might seem the most improbable – the Anglican Church. There are now several Anglican Churches which are Pentecostal in outlook and practice. For the most part the Free Churches have looked nervously at Pentecostalism. Individually, a few ministers and laymen have become convinced of the wisdom of creating an atmosphere where 'speaking with tongues' has been encouraged; most have considered it dangerous emotionalism.

Pentecostalism is a reaction against the institutionalism of the churches. It is also a protest against the alleged stifling of the emotional part of man's nature in the conventional approach of the major churches. Both charges have at least some truth, though it is arguable that it is all but impossible for an institution to avoid becoming institutionalized and that a new Church founded to avoid the error must itself become institutionalized in time. The second charge probably has more truth in it, but emotionalism run riot is no substitute for religion, and the enemies of the Pentecostalists consider that the balance of intellect and emotion, if heavy on the first side in some other Churches, is dangerously heavy on the second side among followers of the charismatic movement. The most serious impediment to some Christians who consider the merits of Pentecostalism, however, though certainly not to all, is the unequivocal conservative evangelical approach of Pentecostalists to the Scriptures, their acceptance of miracle healing (rarely well attested), their belief (following their fundamentalism) that the Devil is a real being and constantly at war with God, and their belief in devil-possession and powers of exorcism. Cynics might argue that in an age of despair such marvels will draw the credulous; the wise are wondering why the movement has grown in an age of apparent spiritual torpor.

The twentieth century produced, even during so many years of dwindling numbers, some outstanding preachers and scholars of all denominations, though it is impossible to assess their merit when some have been dead so short a time, and some are still living. Among the Congregationalists, a term now virtually obsolete, was J. H. Jowett (1864–1923), a man who ministered both in England and in America. In England he was one of a series of great men who occupied Westminster Chapel (from 1918 to 1923), but he served as pastor of a New York Church for nine years. Such was his eminence that the Prime Minister's name was associated with the plea for Jowett's return to England in 1918 to help the morale of the nation.

C. Silvester Horne (1865–1914) died tragically young, burnt out by overworking. He was politically involved, and described himself in *Who's Who* as an "impenitent radical, and advocate of modern Puritanism". In the same work he described his recreations as "golfing, cycling and agitating". In fact he was Liberal M.P. for Ipswich from 1910 as well as author, pamphleteer, speaker and – what he cared most about – preacher. For some years he was the minister of Whitefield's Tabernacle.

Campbell Morgan (1863–1945), one of the greatest preachers of his age, was rejected as a candidate for the Methodist ministry. It was a sign of the times that in the year in which he applied there were 150 candidates for the Ministry and 105 of them were rejected. Campbell Morgan instead became ordained as a Congregational Minister, though he was no Sectarian, and preached in many Free Church pulpits in America as well as in England. His greatest and longest ministry – in two periods – was in Westminster Chapel. His sermons lasted between 50 minutes and an hour. They were expository. "The whole man", said a biographer, "appears to palpate with an incontrollable energy; he preached with every fibre of his being." He himself said of his preaching, "We are out to storm the citadel of the will, and capture it for Jesus Christ. Whether evangelizing or teaching does not matter. The appeal is the final thing, I have always felt, and never more so than now, that the work of preaching is not that of debating difficulties, or speculating, or considering philosophies, but that of proclaiming the Word of God." R. F. Horton (1855–1930) ministered for no less than fifty years (1880–1930) at Lyndhurst Road Congregational Church, Hampstead, a ministry as remarkable for its devotion as for its length.

R. J. Campbell (1867–1956) began his distinguished ministry as a Congregationalist. He was minister of the City Temple from 1903 to 1915, but left it to join the Church of England. He was scholar and author as well as preacher, and gave these talents successively to the Free Churches and the establishment. W. E. Orchard (1877–1955) spread his gifts even more widely. He started as a Presbyterian, but became minister of the King's Weigh House, a Congregational pulpit, and in 1932 became a Roman Catholic. He was a gifted preacher, a scholar, and a man of great charm. His proudest possessions were silver buckles from John Wesley's shoes. He was a humble man also, content to abandon his preaching gift when his last Church called him to what would have seemed lesser service to a lesser man.

Among Congregational scholars, C. H. Dodd (1884–1974) was among the most distinguished. A very considerable New Testament scholar, he held a professorial chair at Cambridge, and was the man responsible for the first new translation of the Bible to be made officially by churches working together since the translation of James I. P. T. Forsyth (1848–1921), of an earlier generation, became Principal of Hackney Theological College in 1901 and from there sent out a series of first-class works which made him the greatest Free Church theologian of his age.

A great Congregational preacher of a later generation was Martyn Lloyd-Jones (1899–1981). Assistant to Campbell Morgan, he himself became minister of Westminster Chapel and, in the tradition of his predecessor, filled the church with crowds to hear his expository sermons, his illustrations almost exclusively from the Bible. His style lacked all flourish. He made no concessions to popular appeal. It was the matter of his sermons, not the delivery, which gripped his hearers, and it was young people quite as much as old ones who flocked to hear him. Nathaniel Micklem (1888–1976) was a scholar. He was also one of the men whose views and influence helped in the foundation of the United Reformed Church long before it became a reality. He was created C. H. in 1974.

Roughly of the same period was Leslie Cooke (1908–1967), the use of whose talents demonstrates how men use them in different ways according to the needs of their day. He served Christ and his Church during the terrible bombing of Coventry in the Second World War by a passionate concern for suffering humanity, and after the war he gave his strength to the administration of help for those in need. As Associate General Secretary of the World Council of Churches and the Director of Inter-Church Aid and Refugee and World Service from 1955, he was able to help in mitigating sufferings after disasters across the world. Bernard L. Manning (1892–1941) was a layman, a scholar who spent his whole life in Cambridge. A staunch Congregationalist, he was also ecumenically minded. His influence was great, not only among undergraduates, but far beyond. Among his books was an excellent study of two hymn-writers, *The Hymns of Wesley and Watts*.

The most distinguished among the Baptists during the early years of the century have already been named. These were John Clifford (1836–1923) and J. M. Shakespeare (1857–1928). Clifford's remarkable life (he worked in a lace factory when ten and survived to become one of the greatest powers of Nonconformity and be given the C. H. in his mid-eighties) sprawled across two very different centuries. Shakespeare's sad decline in no way takes away from his great public record or the courage of his stand for union, when he was so sure of the rightness of his way. As great as either was F. B. Meyer (1847–1929) though he was a very different type of man. He was not a Church Statesman. He was primarily an evangelist. He was, for those days, remarkable for his travels, and spent time in Germany, Canada, North and Central America, the Near and the Far East, South Africa and Australia. He had been much influenced by the American evangelist Dwight L. Moody, and he determined to preach the gospel across the world. A prolific writer, he wrote some seventy volumes. With immense industry he toiled across the world. He was totally frank (he cited his own temptations in sermons) and utterly sincere, and congregations warmed to him. He was also committed to social and philanthropic work, and to the social gospel. He served two churches in Leicester but from 1892 was based in London, at Regent's Park Chapel from 1882 to 1892 and the Congregational Christ Church, Westminster Bridge Road, from 1892 to 1907 and from 1915 to 1921. It is under the Lincoln tower of Christ Church that the remains of the great Rowland Hill lie, transferred from his own Surrey Chapel in 1881.

T. R. Glover (1869–1943), another Baptist, was a distinguished classical scholar who lectured in Cambridge from 1911 to 1939. A fellow of St. John's College and Public Orator, he preached in all Evangelical Churches, and reached a much wider audience than his students through his published works. Ernest A. Payne (1902–1981) was a Church statesman of international reputation. He was General Secretary of the Baptist Union and President of the World Council of Churches. He was scholar and preacher too. The distinction of the C. H. was conferred on him in 1968.

The Presbyterian numbers were still small in England, great in Scotland. Among the most distinguished in England was William Paton (1886–1943), who spent most of his life organizing missionary work. He was a world traveller in that connection. His contribution to the foundation of the British Council of Churches was considerable. His stature among all churchmen may be judged from the fact that his memorial service was held in St. Paul's Cathedral, and Archbishop Temple gave an address. Presbyterian growth abroad, however, was great, and for this work the Church produced men of the quality of Thomas Barclay (1849–1935), who ministered in Formosa for sixty years, founded schools and training institutions, and translated the Bible.

Eminent among Methodists was J. Scott Lidgett (1854–1953). He took over the effective leadership of Methodism in succession to H. Price Hughes. He was scholar and theologian and Church statesman, but above all he was an apostle of Social Christianity. He was co-founder of the Bermondsey Settlement in London, and Warden of it from 1891 to 1949. From here he made an immense impact on practical Christianity among the underprivileged. He was leader of the Progressive Party of the L.C.C., an alderman of the City of London for six years, a member of a wide variety of Governorships, a member of a royal commission, a senator of London University, and was created a C. H. in 1933. He was one of the men most responsible for the Union of Methodism in 1932. The most vital concerns of his Christianity were education and social welfare.

Another distinguished Methodist of the earlier part of the century was F. Luke Wiseman (1858–1944), another scholar and statesman, and a considerable musician and composer as well. As an administrator he directed the Home Missions department of the Methodist Church (evangelism at home and for servicemen posted abroad) from 1913 to 1939.

Methodist scholars abounded. One of the greatest of his genera-tion was A. S. Peake (1865–1929), a layman, whose *Commentary* still holds an important place on ministerial shelves. Among Methodist preachers, Dinsdale Young (1861–1938) filled the Central Hall, Westminster, from 1914 to 1938. His style was slow, repetitive, compulsive. He was no great scholar and his approach to the Bible was fundamentalist, but he was a remarkable preacher, and his magnetic power forced attention. It was impossible to forget what he had said. W. R. Maltby (1866–1951) had a par-ticular preaching gift with young people. His work among students earned William Temple's deserved praise. Curiously, Maltby had a small, squeaky voice, but after a few sentences, such was the impact of what he had to say, the voice was forgotten and the message became all.

In the middle years of the century a distinguished trio of Methodist ministers preached in London. These were W. E. Sangster (1900–1960), Donald Soper (b.1903) and Leslie Weatherhead (1893–1976). Sangster, scholar and author, was primarily a preacher, but extended his preaching into more than thirty books and hundreds of articles. Like Dinsdale Young, he filled the Central Hall, Westminster, so that the crowds could not get in, and he did this for sixteen years. His work in the air-raid shelters of Westminster (he lived in one himself throughout the war) was long remembered. Soper (now Lord Soper) is another preacher, but he is best known for his astonishing gift of outdoor speaking, especially at Tower Hill, and for his very strong convictions on pacifism and Christian Socialism. As a life peer, Lord Soper now has the ears of government. Weatherhead, although a Methodist, was for many years minister of the City Temple, a Congregational church. His preaching – he had a small, beautiful voice of hypnotic power – drew multitudes, and his books sold in tens of thousands. He was also a pioneer of popular psychology, and helped a generation to understand the Christian approach to what was then the most mysterious of sciences.

The power of the Free Churches has ebbed considerably during the century. The four main branches now have some 6,000 trained ministers, but legions of committed laymen to supplement preaching needs. A modern apologist, asked why he was a Free Churchman, replied, "Because we believe that she (the Church of England) fails adequately to interpret and realize for the people of England the religion of Christ . . . Our specific form of churchmanship is at least as old as the historic Anglican settlement . . . It goes back to Geneva – to say nothing of the New Testament . . ." Dissent is "a mixture composed of three main ingredients: the historic deposit of the holy, apostolic, evangelical, catholic faith, the new apprehension of that faith which came to Western Europe in the sixteenth century, and certain ecclesiastical arrangements made in England in the sixteenth and seventeenth centuries."

Much of this, especially to those with an impatience about historical divisions, seems irrelevant to the needs of a country where less than 5 per cent attend any Church at all. What Free Churchmen (Methodists perhaps less than the other branches) used to share was the belief that religion was a matter between the individual soul and God, and that a Church cannot be governed by any state authority. A Church should be a 'gathered' community, a Christian fellowship of men and women, a regenerate company of believers.

Beyond this matter of principle, Free Church emphases remain in many ways like those of their Puritan forebears, but with less intensity, less single-mindedness of purpose. These are a stress on the authority of the Scriptures, the need for a personal experience of the saving power of Christ, a conviction of 'the priesthood of all believers', a certainty that the practice of religion is the first and only principle of life and should permeate the whole.

The freedom of the Free Churches is arguable. Certainly they are not subject to state authority, but they have become in a sense the prisoners of their own history, institutionalized after their own particular pattern. Congregationalism has ceased to be a distinct church and the conception of the 'gathered' Church is much weaker. The price of unity was the loss of individualism. It is also true, however, that there are a not inconsiderable number of Churches, all of an evangelical pattern, with the loosest possible connection to any larger Church organization – or even none at all. Yet their numbers also have fallen. As numbers have decreased and more centralization has been a conscious aim which has failed to halt the losses, as lack of confidence has grown, the Free Churches have become more and more uncertain about their own future, or futures, for it is not clear whether the differences among the Free Churches are greater than their collective difference from the establishment.

It may be that what some of the Free Churches are seeking is a new form of Puritanism more suited to the age. The sense of God's majesty, the sense of sin, the vital necessity of personal salvation, their bounding confidence in God's power and his purpose for them – these things exist only as pale reflections of their former selves. It is sure that at least some of them are seeking an absorption, for a greater strength, in a larger church community. Their problems are great. Now small in numbers and power, even collectively, no longer the conscience of the country, no longer a cultural centre, no longer pre-eminent in education, their differences seem irrelevant to a secular society. If the future of the Free Churches is no concern of these pages, their current attitude towards it certainly is. Is the decline more than temporary? Are we living in a period similar to the dark days of the early eighteenth century, before the Evangelical Revival burst over the land? Is a time of spiritual revival only round the corner? Or have the Free Churches fulfilled their mission? These are the questions Free Churchmen ask.

"The introverted Church," wrote one author, pondering the future of the Free Churches, "is one which puts its own survival before its mission, its own identity above its task, its internal concerns before its apostolate, its rituals before its ministry . . .

The more introverted the Church, the more it becomes subject to priestcraft." Have the Free Churches become introverted? Is the Church of England less so?

What serious choices face the Free Churches? Unless there is a revival of interest in spiritual matters, if they remain separated they may become even smaller, ever less influential, ever more introverted. They can, as three Churches have recently done, join other Free Churches, though it is difficult to see how some of them (Quakers, for instance) could ever join with others, since their points of difference defy compromise. The Free Churches might, if the matter is thoroughly prepared, join the Church of England, though the same problems would be critical, and the Church of England shows itself remarkably reluctant to merge with others, or even receive back into their fold a Church which was once part of them. The Free Churches might, since some of them have world affiliations which run into millions, seek closer association with those bodies rather than the established Church. Each of these possibilities is currently being explored. The very nature of the Free Churches means diversity of approach. There is no one way. The important thing is that the way is chosen by God, not by man. It was John Robinson of Leyden who said, "I am verily persuaded the Lord has more truth to break forth out of his holy Word." Free Churchmen are praying for direction.

Glossary

Absolution	Remission of sins by ecclesiastical authority.
Adoptionism	The belief that Jesus is the Son of God by adoption only.
Adventism	Belief in the second coming of Christ as Judge, and a stress on that belief.
Agitators	Delegates who acted on behalf of the common soldiers in the Parliamentary Army, 1647–1649.
Anabaptist	Name of a German sect which arose in 1521 and taught adult as opposed to infant baptism. The term was later indiscriminately used for any sect with these views.
Anglican	A member of the reformed Church of England.
Anglo-Catholic	A member of the Church of England who maintains its 'catholic' as opposed to its 'protestant' character.
Antinomian	One who maintains that the moral law is not binding on Christians, who live under the law of grace.
Apocalyptic	Concerning prophetic revelations of the future.
Apostasy	Abandonment of one's religious faith, usually for another faith.
Apostolic Church of Jesus Christ	One of a group of Churches formed in the twentieth century, with Pentecostalist views.
Arminian	A follower of the Dutch theologian Arminius, an opponent of Calvin, who maintains man's freedom of action against Calvin's theory of predestination.

195

Assemblies of God	One of a group of Churches, formed in the twentieth century, with Pentecostalist views.
Baptist	One who believes that baptism should only be administered to believers, and by immersion. Specifically, a member of the Baptist Church.
Benefice	A church living granted to a clergyman of the Church of England.
Bible Christian Society	A sect founded in 1815, an offshoot of Methodism. Later it became part of the Methodist Church.
British Israelism	A theory that the lost tribes of Israel became the British nation.
Broad Church	A body in the Church of England which leans neither to the 'catholic' nor 'protestant' extremes.
Buchmanite	A follower of Frank Buchman (1878–1961) who founded the Oxford Group, later called the 'Moral Rearmament' movement.
Calvinist	A follower of the doctrines of John Calvin, whose 'five points' were particular election, particular redemption, moral inability in a fallen state, irresistible grace, and final perseverance.
Catholic	Belonging to the Church of Rome, or, with reference to Protestants, having views similar to the Church of Rome.
Catholic Apostolic Church	A Church founded in 1832 by Edward Irving, who was concerned with prophecy, speaking with tongues and healing by faith.
Christadelphians	A sect founded in 1848 in America by John Thomas.
Christian Science	A quasi-religion founded in America in the nineteenth century by Mrs. Eddy, who believed that evil and disease could be overcome by spiritual truth.
Church Army	An Anglican organization of lay workers founded in 1882 on the model of the Salvation Army.
Church of England	The Church established by law in England in the reign of Henry VIII.
Church of God of Prophecy	One of a group of Churches formed in the twentieth century, with Pentecostalist views.
Church of Jesus Christ of Latter-Day Saints	The official title of the Church better known as the 'Mormons'. It is a large Church founded in America in the nineteenth century by Joseph Smith and Brigham Young.

Church of Unification	Better known as the 'Moonies', a sect of American origin, which many deny being Christian.
Churches of Christ	A sect with eighteenth-century roots formally organized in 1842. It practised believers' baptism. A reformed section of this Church joined the United Reformed Church in 1981.
Clapham Sect	A group of Evangelical clergy and laymen of the Church of England who became well-known for social and charitable work in the nineteenth century.
Closed Baptists	The branch of the Baptist Church which is exclusive in its outlook and doubtful of intercourse with other Christian bodies.
Clubmen	A vague term referring to bands of untrained and light-armed men, usually of extreme Protestant views, who joined for their own protection during and after the period of the Civil War.
Colportage	The giving or selling of religious books, especially Bibles, as an act of charity.
Congregationalism	A form of Church government which leaves all its concerns to the local congregation of believers. Specifically, the Congregational Church.
Conservative Evangelical	One who, in reaction against the evolutionary theories and biblical criticism of the nineteenth century, asserts the verbal inerrancy of Scripture.
Consubstantiation	The doctrine of the real presence of the body and blood of Christ in the bread and wine of the eucharist, though the bread and wine are not changed in substance.
Conventicle	A religious assembly, usually of an illegal kind, such as those of Nonconformists during Stuart reigns.
Countess of Huntingdon's Connexion	A sect founded by the Countess of Huntingdon and based on the doctrines of the Church of England in 1779.
Covenant	An agreement between God and men.
Darbyites	Followers of J. N. Darby, who was largely responsible for the foundation of the 'Plymouth Brethren' about 1828.
Deism	Belief in the existence of God, but rejection of his revelation.

Denominationalism	Concern over particular Church allegiance as opposed to a more general Christian allegiance.
Diggers	Radicals of the Commonwealth period whose brief influence began in 1649. They believed in social equality and common ownership of property.
Disciples of Christ	See 'Churches of Christ'.
Disestablishment	Belief that the Church should be free from control by the State.
Dissenter	A Christian who dissents from the authority of the Church of England. See also 'Free Church'.
Dissenting Academies	Small colleges opened by Nonconformist ministers to train young men for the ministry after the 1662 Act of Uniformity. After the 1689 Toleration Act they increased in number and influence.
Dissenting Deputies	A body elected by Nonconformists from 1732 to protect their interests and if necessary take political action.
Dutch Reformed Church	The major Protestant church in the Netherlands. It was founded in the sixteenth century.
Ecumenical	Representing the whole Christian world; believing in a universal Church.
Elect	Chosen by God, especially as in Calvinist theology.
Elim Pentecostal Church	One of a group of churches, formed in the twentieth century, with Pentecostal views.
Erastianism	Belief that the State is supreme in ecclesiastical affairs.
Episcopacy	Government of the Church by bishops.
Episcopalian	An adherent of episcopacy: a member of such a Church.
Establishment	The Church of England as by law established.
Eucharist	The sacrament of the Lord's Supper.
Evangelical	A protestant: a member of the Evangelical Revival of the eighteenth century: a follower of their principles.
Excommunicate	Exclude from the Church.
Exegetical	Concerning the interpretation of the Scriptures.
Expository	Explanatory, especially of the Scriptures.
Fifth Monarch Men	An apocalyptic sect which had some small influence during the Protectorate and was stamped out in 1661.

Free Church	A Christian Church established in England but not under the authority of the Church of England. See also 'Dissenter', 'Nonconformist'.
Free Church of England	A Church founded in 1863 on the doctrines of the Church of England but separated from it.
Fundamentalism	A belief in the literal inerrancy of the Scriptures. (see also 'Conservative Evangelical'.)
General Baptists	The branch of the Baptist Church, Arminian in theology, 'General' in contradistinction to 'Particular'.
Glassites	Followers of John Glas, who co-founded a high Calvinist sect with his father-in-law, Robert Sandeman, in the eighteenth century.
Greek Orthodox Church	Also called the 'Eastern Orthodox Church', it is a federation of self-governing churches, some of them of ancient origin.
Heresy	Theological opinion at variance with orthodoxy.
High Church	A body of opinion in the Church of England which maintains its 'catholic' as opposed to its 'protestant' character.
Huguenot	A French Protestant of the sixteenth and seventeenth century, especially one fleeing from persecution in France.
Incumbent	The possessor of a Church of England living. A parish priest.
Independency	See 'Congregationalism'.
Indulgence	Remission of punishment due for sin.
Irvingite	A follower of the Church founded by Edward Irving in 1832.
Jehovah's Witnesses	A sect founded in America by C. T. Russell in the nineteenth century, and concerned with the fulfilment of prophecy.
Justification	Action of God whereby man is freed from the penalty of sin.
Kilhamites	Followers of Alexander Kilham who founded the Methodist New Connection in 1797 after his expulsion from the Methodist Church.
Leveller	A party, political more than religious, which existed under the Commonwealth and made a variety of radical proposals for a more democratic parliament.
Lollards	Followers of John Wyclif, poor preachers sent by him to instruct the poor about Jesus Christ. They were formed late in the fourteenth century.

Low Church	The part of the Church of England which follows the Protestant as opposed to the Catholic (or high) tradition.
Lutheran	A follower of the doctrines of Martin Luther (1483–1546).
Mennonite	A descendant of the Anabaptists of the sixteenth century, a follower of the teaching of Menno Simons (1496–1561).
Methodist	A member or adherent of the Church founded by the followers of John Wesley.
Methodist New Connexion	A splinter movement of Methodism after Wesley's death founded by Alexander Kilham, who fought against the possibility of his Church's absorption in the Church of England.
Millenarianism	Belief that Christ will return to earth and reign for a thousand years.
Moravians	Founded about 1724, Moravian Brethren were essentially Protestant Evangelists and missionaries. They had a considerable influence on John Wesley and therefore on Methodism.
Mormons	See 'Church of Jesus Christ of Latter-Day Saints'.
Muggletonians	Followers of Ludowicke Muggleton (1609–1698) who founded a minor sect based on his visions.
New Testament Church of God	One of a group of churches formed in the twentieth century with Pentecostalist views.
Nicene Creed	It was promulgated in 325. Confusingly, the same term is used for the altered versions of the original.
Nonconformist	A Christian who dissents from the authority of the Church of England. See also 'Free Church'.
Open Baptists	See 'general' Baptists. The term 'open' has reference to the communion table, open to believers as opposed to 'closed' to non-members.
Orthodox Church	The 'right' Church, according to whoever uses the term. Sometimes used of the 'Greek' or 'Eastern' Church.
Orthodoxy	Correct belief, according to the users of the term.
Oxford Group	The movement founded by Frank Buchman (1878–1961), originally an evangelistic mission largely to the professional and upper classes. It widened its appeal in 1938 when it became the 'Moral Rearmament' movement.

Oxford Movement The High Church movement of the nineteenth century led by John Keble (1792–1866), R. H. Froude (1803–1836) and J. H. Newman (1801–1890).

Pantheism The belief that there is only one reality, God, that the whole universe is God.

Papist A usually abusive term for a Roman Catholic, a follower of the Pope.

Particular Baptists Members of the branch of the Baptist Church which practised closed membership and closed communion. They flourished in the eighteenth century. Most of them in 1891 merged with the general Baptists. A remnant remain, variously called 'Strict and Particular' or 'Closed', with a Calvinist theology.

Pentecostalists Fundamentalist Protestant sects that emphasize the gifts of the Holy Spirit including speaking with tongues. Some hold healing services.

Plymouth Brethren A church founded about 1825 by J. N. Darby. 'Open' or 'Closed' Brethren indicates the degree of tolerance shown to other Christians by the two branches of the Church.

Predestination The idea that God has predetermined an individual's ultimate destination as heaven or hell.

Prelacy The rôle of a prelate.

Prelate An ecclesiastic of high rank, such as Archbishop or Bishop.

Presbyter An elder in the Christian Church in early times: an elder in the Presbyterian Church.

Presbyterian A member of the Church holding the Presbyterian view of Church government.

Primitive Methodist Church A Church formed by secession from Wesley's followers soon after Wesley's death. The leaders were Hugh Bourne (1772–1852) and William Clowes (1780–1851).

Protestant A member of any branch of the Christian Church which repudiates papal authority.

Purgatory In Roman Catholic theology, a place between heaven and hell where souls wait.

Puritan A Protestant who regarded Elizabeth's Church settlement as incomplete and in need of further 'purification' from Roman Catholic influence. The successors of these reformers.

Quakers Term of ridicule once applied to the 'Society of Friends'. See 'Society of Friends'.

Ranters	A group of Protestant extremists of the Civil War period. They were antinomians and pantheists. The term was also used later of Primitive Methodists.
Roman Catholic Church	The Church owing its earthly allegiance to the Pope.
Russellites	Followers of C. T. Russell (1852–1916), who founded Jehovah's Witnesses, a sect concerned with prophecy, especially the date of the second coming.
Salvation Army	The Church founded by William Booth (1829–1912) in 1865. Its mission has always been to the poorest.
Sanctification	God's work of making his people holy.
Sandemanians	See 'Glassites.'
Schism	Dissension or division in the Church.
Scientology	A movement founded in the middle of the present century by L. R. Hubbard (b.1911) which claims to teach 'spiritual recovery and the increase of individual ability'. It is neither a religion nor religious.
Sect, Sectary	A religious order, usually a small Protestant one, or the members of that order.
Seekers	An early seventeenth-century sect. Adherents rejected normal Church worship, and waited for God to establish his Church. They were most numerous during the period of the Protectorate. Bartholomew Legate (c.1575–1612), one of their preachers, died at the stake.
Separatist	A name sometimes used as equivalent to 'Brownist' – a follower of the doctrines of Robert Browne (c.1550–c.1633) – but also used, more generally, of one who rejected the established Church.
Seventh Day Adventist	A follower of the doctrines of William Miller (d.1849) who prophesied the end of the world inaccurately. The fulfilment of prophecy is still the chief preoccupation of this denomination.
Seventh Day Baptist	A member of a small sect founded by John James, who was executed in 1661. He preached the second coming of Christ.
Shaker	A member of a now very small communistic sect in America, famous for its unusual forms in worship and the extreme simplicity of its community life.

Society of Friends	The name George Fox (1624–1691) chose for his followers. Most have always referred to them as 'Quakers'.
Synod	A church assembly. In Presbyterian Churches it is a court higher than the presbytery.
Tractarian	A follower of the Oxford Movement, which was inaugurated by a series of theological tracts.
Transubstantiation	The doctrine of the eucharist taught by the Roman Catholic Church. By the consecration of the bread and wine Christ is 'truly, really and substantially contained in the Sacrament . . .'
Unitarian	A member of a once large, now very small, Free Church, which follows Jesus as exemplar but does not believe in his divinity, and which most therefore regard as not Christian.
United Methodist Church	One of the three main Methodist Churches which united in 1932, itself a union of three churches which had seceded from the main branch.
United Methodist Free Church	A splinter group from the main Methodist body which joined the United Methodist Church in 1907.
United Reformed Church	The merging of the Congregational Church in England and Wales with the Presbyterian Church of England in 1972. One branch of Churches of Christ joined in 1981.
Wesleyan Methodism	The main branch of the Church founded by Wesley's followers after his death.

Further Reading

This is not a bibliography, but a suggested list of books which may interest those who wish to study the Free Churches further.

GENERAL

A long, but extremely readable and scholarly background to the whole history of the Christian Church is, *History of Christianity*, K. S. Latourette, 1954.

Free Church history is very much a history of personalities. Almost every name in this book has an entry in the *Dictionary of National Biography* (DNB). In most cases the entry is full, fair and accurate; rarely, the entry, in the light of more recent scholarship, needs rewriting. Each entry has a bibliography at its conclusion.

Most libraries contain two dictionaries of the Christian Church:

Oxford Dictionary of the Christian Church, ed. F. L. Cross, 1974.
New International Dictionary of the Christian Church, ed. J. D. Douglas, 1974.

These works contain brief entries on most Free Churches and sects, and on some of the personalities involved. The first of these, and much the better, ends each entry with a bibliography.

THE FREE CHURCHES

The Free Churches as a whole have not attracted many authors. The few listed here vary considerably. C. S. Horne's book is an admirable child of its age, itself a piece of Free Church history.

Davies, G. M. *The English Free Churches.* 1952.
Horne, C. S. *A Popular History of the Free Churches.* 1926.
Payne, E. A. *The Free Church Tradition in the Life of England.* 1944.
Routley, E. *English Religious Dissent.* 1960.
Slack, K. *The British Churches Today.* 1961.

Individually, the major Free Churches have their own historians. The larger the Church, the more self-critical these works are. Suggested books on the four main branches are listed below:

Congregational Church

Dale, R. W. *History of English Congregationalism.* 1907.
Grant, J. W. *Free Churchmanship in England, 1870–1940, with Special Reference to Congregationalism.* 1955.
Jenkins, D. *Congregationalism: A Restatement.* 1954.
Jones, R. T. *Congregationalism in England, 1662–1962.* 1962.
Nuttall, G. F. *Congregationalism.* 1951.
Routley, E. *The Story of Congregationalism.* 1961.

Baptist Church

If one omits authoritative tomes of the last century, a few shorter modern works remain.

Payne, E. A. *A Fellowship of Believers. Baptist Thought and Practice Yesterday and Today.* 1952.
Robinson, H. W. *The Life and Faith of the Baptists.* 1946.
Torbet, R. G. *A History of the Baptists.* 1966.
Underwood, A. C. *A History of the Baptists.* 1947.

Presbyterian Church

There are a number of weighty volumes on the Presbyterian Church of Scotland, very few specifically on the Presbyterian Church in England.

Drysdale, A. H. *History of the Presbyterians in England.* 1889.
Griffiths, O. M. *Religion and Learning. A Study in English Presbyterian Thought from . . . (1662) to the . . . Unitarian Movement.* 1935.

Methodist Church

The Methodist Church recently commissioned its official history. This is: (ed.) Davies, R. E. and Rupp, G. E. *A History of the Methodist Church in Great Britain.* 3 vols. 1965, 1978, 1982.

Only two other general books deserve special mention, the first of these is a short, very readable history.

Davies, R. E. *Methodism*. 1976.
Rupp, G. E. *Methodism in Relation to the Protestant Tradition*. 1952.

Finally, all libraries contain a wealth of recent popular works on individual reigns. To savour the background of a period, and to learn the mind of the monarch in ages when a ruler's influence was critical, by approval or rejection, is invaluable background reading. Such books, very well written, include:

Bowle, John. *Charles the First*. 1975.
Ashley, Maurice. *Charles II. The Man and the Statesman*. 1971.

Another series, the text much shorter and illustration greater, can still offer a valuable background. Examples are:

Ridley, J. *The Life and Times of Mary Tudor*. 1973.
Watson, D. R. *The Life and Times of Charles I*. 1972.
Earle, Peter. *The Life and Times of James II*. 1972.

FURTHER READING FOR INDIVIDUAL CHAPTERS

Chapter I

The following books cover the period of Wyclif and the Lollards:

Carrick, J. C. *Wycliffe and the Lollards*. 1977.
Deanesly, Margaret. *The Lollard Bible*. 1920.
Gairdner, James. *Lollardy and the Reformation in England*. 4 vols. 1965.
Hudson, Anne (ed.). *Selections from English Wycliffite Writings*. 1981.
McFarlane, K. B. *John Wycliffe and the Beginnings of English Nonconformity*. 1952.
Thompson, J. A. F. *The Later Lollards 1414–1520*. 1965.

Puritanism

This subject, on which there has been much recent scholarship, is the essential background to Chapters II to IV and to a lesser extent to Chapter V also.

Collinson, P. *The Elizabethan Puritan Movement*. 1967.
Dickens, A. G. *The English Reformation*. 1967.
Haller, W. *The Rise of Puritanism*. 1938.
Haller, W. *Liberty and Reformation in the Puritan Revolution*. 1955.
Hill, Christopher. *Puritanism and Revolution*. 1958.
Hill, Christopher. *Society and Puritanism in Pre-Revolutionary England*. 1969.
Knappen, M. M. *Tudor Puritanism*. 1970.

Lamont, William. *Godly Rule: Politics and Religion 1603–60.* 1969.
McGrath, Patrick. *Papists and Puritans under Elizabeth I.* 1967.
Nuttall, G. F. *The Puritan Spirit.* 1967.
Porter. H. C. (ed.). *Puritanism in Tudor England.* 1970.
Routley, Erik. *English Religious Dissent.* 1960.
Seaver, P. S. *The Puritan Lectureships.* 1970.
Watkins, Owen C. *The Puritan Experience.* 1972.

Chapter II

The most recent research into the lives of the first Congregationalists (before that term was used), is largely in 'Transactions of the Congregational Historical Society.' 'Elizabethan Nonconformist Texts' reprint and annotate contemporary books, journals and documents. Burrage's two books, however, have kept their place. The Mar-Prelate mystery may never, perhaps, be solved, but it will always intrigue. Fox's work, popular for centuries, is worth citing.

Burrage, C. *The True Story of Robert Browne.* 1906.
Burrage, C. *The Early English Dissenters.* 1912.
Foxe, J. *Actes and Monumentes (The Book of Martyrs).* 1563.
McGinn, D. J. *John Penry and the Mar-Prelate Controversy.* 1966.

Chapter III

Histories of the Baptist Church amply cover their beginnings, and the 'Baptist Historical Society' reports recent scholarship. Only two particularly important books are therefore cited.

Burgess, W. H. *John Smith, the Se-Baptist, Thomas Helwys and the first Baptist Church in England.* 1911.
Burgess, W. H. *John Robinson, Pastor of the Pilgrim Fathers,* 1920.

Chapter IV

Most of the religious turmoil of the age is discussed in the books on Puritanism listed above. Two biographies of Cromwell are suggested. The first is full and fair and most readable. The second is an excellent piece of scholarship slanted towards the religious problems of the times. Both George Fox's Journal and a recent biography are also listed.

Fraser, Antonia. *Cromwell, Our Chief of Men.* 1973.
Hill, Christopher. *God's Englishman. Oliver Cromwell and the English Revolution.* 1970.
Nickolls, J. L. (ed.) *Journal of George Fox.* 1952.
Wilders, H. E. *Voice of the Lord. A Biography of George Fox.* 1965.

Chapter V

Congregationalist, Baptist and Presbyterian historians cover this period for their respective Churches. The Society of Friends is particularly well documented for these years. See:

Braithwaite, W. C. *Second Period of Quakerism*. 1919.

One general scholarly study is a helpful background to the period:

Western, J. R. *Monarchy and Revolution; the English State in the 1680s*. 1972.

Another work is recommended for its insight into the support by Dissenters of Monmouth's rebellion, this is:

Trench, C. C. *The Western Rising*. 1969.

The fate of the ejected clergy is considered in:

Matthews, A. C. *Calamy Revised*. 1933.

and the definitive work on the Dissenting Academies is:

McLachlan, H. *English Education under the Test Acts, 1662–1820*. 1931.

The nastiest side of the Protestant underworld is revealed in:

Kenyon, J. *The Popish Plot*. 1972.

Chapter VI

The best background work on the eighteenth-century Church remains:

Abbey, C. T. and Overton, J. H. *The English Church in the Eighteenth Century*. 1887.

In the early part of the century the Church of the age is strangely revealed in:

Holmes, G. *The Trial of Doctor Sacheverell*. 1973.

There is a vast literature on the Evangelical Revival. The following are commended. Luke Tyerman was an excellent biographer. His pages have more feel for his subjects than later biographers'. The third cited here is the life of the saintly Fletcher of Madeley. Clarke's work is on the Evangelical movement. Manning's work is a study of the two greatest hymn-writers of the age.

Clarke, W. H. L. *Eighteenth Century Piety*. 1944.
Elliott-Binns, L. E. *The Early Evangelicals. A Religious and Social Study*. 1953.

Manning, B. L. *The Hymns of Wesley and Watts.* 1942.
Tyerman, L. *Life of John Wesley.* 1870.
Tyerman, L. *Life of George Whitefield.* 1877.
Tyerman, L. *Wesley's Designated Successor.* 1882.

Two books on the Dissenting Deputies (the first has the Quakers for its other study):

Crowther-Hunt, N. C. *Two Early Political Associations.* 1961.
Manning, B. L. *The Protestant Dissenting Deputies.* 1952.

Chapter VII

The controversy that Darwin's theories provoked is treated in:

Himmelfort, G. *Darwin and the Darwinian Revolution.* 1959.

A short account of the Christian Socialists is:

Vidler, A. R. *F. D. Maurice and Company.* 1966.

Some contemporary literature is to be found in:

Chadwick, W. O. (ed.) *The Mind of the Oxford Movement.* 1960.

The following three books are on politics and the Nonconformist Churches:

Cowherd, R. G. *The Politics of English Dissent.* 1959.
Machin, G. I. T. *Politics and the Churches in Great Britain.* 1977.
Wearmouth, R. W. *Methodism and the Working Class Movements in England 1800–1850.* 1937.

The Missionary expansion of the century is given in their own Church histories. Payne's short work is more general:

Payne, E. C. *The Church Awakes.* 1942.

The Congregational Church has a book specific to this period:

Peel, A. *History of the Congregational Union of England and Wales, 1831–1931.* 1931.

The life of William Booth and the story of the Salvation Army is well told in:

Collier, R. *The General Next to God.* 1965.

Dr. Barnardo's story is in:

Wagner, Gillian. *Barnardo.* 1979.

Chapter VIII

The major themes of the twentieth century are the closer combining of
branches of the individual churches, the ecumenical spirit of the age, the
union of some Free Churches, the emergence of new ones, and the
question, in the light of their falling numbers, of the future of the Free
Churches.

Three books are recommended on the ecumenical spirit and
ecumenical progress. These are:

McNeill, J. T. *Unitive Protestantism*. 1964.
Neill, S. C. *The Church and Christian Union*. 1968.
Payne, E. A. *The Churches and Christian Unity*. 1962.

Two more concern the work of the British Council of Churches and
the World Council of Churches. The latter now has more than 300
Churches in membership, and this handbook gives their origins:

Payne, E. A. *Thirty Years of the British Council of Churches 1942–72*.
1970.
Ans, J. van der B. (ed.) *Handbook of the Member Churches of the World
Council of Churches*. 1982.

Two more books tell of the unsuccessful attempt of the Church of
England and the Methodist Church to become one; of the success
which the United Reformed Church conceals in its name. These are:

Davies, R. E. *Methodists and Unity*. 1962.
Slack, K. *The United Reformed Church*. 1978.

The Pentecostalist movement is briefly but fairly described in
Ottosson's book, while the West Indian branch is described in Colley's:

Ottosson, K. *The Pentecostal Churches*. 1977.
Colley, M. J. C. *God's People. West Indian Pentecostalist Sects in England*.
1965.

Finally, a highly controversial book of 1952 looked into the future.

Driver, C. *A Future for the Free Churches?* 1952.

As far as personalities are concerned, one moves progressively as one
reaches the present day from the Supplements of the DNB, to *Who was
Who* to *Who's Who* and after that one studies religious newspapers and
periodicals.

Index of Names

Abbot, George, 53, 57
Abney, Sir Thomas, 120
Addison, Joseph, 118
Ainsworth, Henry, 38, 49
Anne, Queen, 3, 114–15, 118, 121
Annesley, Captain, 107
Arch, Joseph, 147
Arminius, Jacobus, 20, 195
Askew, Anne, 17
Atterbury, Francis, 117
Aygge, Robert, 10
Aylmer, John, 35, 36

Bancroft, Richard, 46, 53, 55
Barclay, Thomas, 190
Barnardo, Thomas, 166
Barnes, Robert, 16, 17
Barrowe, Henry, 32, 33, 34, 37, 38, 43, 180
Bastwick, John, 61, 63
Bauthumley, Jacob, 69
Baxter, Richard, 69, 71, 72, 79, 87, 93, 96, 103
Beard, Thomas, 66
Benson, E. W., 152
Berridge, John, 124, 125, 133, 134, 135

Biddle, John, 76
Bilney, Thomas, 15
Binney, Thomas, 150
Boleyn, Anne, 16
Bolingbroke, Henry St. John, Viscount, 118
Booth, Bramwell, 160
Booth, Catherine, 159–60
Booth, William, 21, 159–61, 173, 202
Bothwell, James, 19, 40
Bourne, Hugh, 143–4, 201
Bownde, Nicholas, 44
Boyes, Mrs. Thomasine, 38
Bradbury, Thomas, 117, 118, 121
Bray, Billy, 144
Brewster, William, 48, 49, 52, 53
Bright, John, 155–6, 168
Broadhurst, Henry, 147
Brontë, Charlotte, 146
Browne, Robert, 2, 27, 28, 29, 30, 31, 32, 38, 43, 45, 53, 67, 180, 202
Buchman, F. N. D., 184, 196, 200
Buckingham, George Villiers, Duke of, 47, 56, 57, 97
Bunting, Jabez, 143, 144, 149, 154
Bunyan, John, 91–2
Burt, Thomas, 147
Burton, Henry, 61, 63